WIRA OF WARSAW

Dear Baroness Cox

Thank you for such an inspiring speech at the St. Benedict's Prize Giving. My daughter, Emma was very proud to receive her awards from yourself.

This is the true life story of Emma's grandmother, Wira, who also worked at the MAFP store for many years. I thought you might be interested to read it. Please note Emma's image on the cover.

George Szlachetko

Szlachetko

(Emma)

WIRA
OF
WARSAW

Memoirs of a girl soldier

George Szlachetko

Emedal

First published in Great Britain in 2015 by
Emedal Publishing

ISBN: 978-0-9933406-0-4

A CIP catalogue record for this book is available from
the British Library.

Cover design by Emma Szlachetko

Printed and bound in Great Britain by Clays Ltd, St Ives plc

Pamiętamy

—––

We remember

CONTENTS

CONTENTS

ILLUSTRATIONS

MAPS

Original map of Warsaw with changing territory held throughout the Uprising. (*From the collection of the Polish Underground Movement (1939–45) Study Trust – London*)

Original map of Warsaw with illustration showing German positions and direction of attacks. (*Map from the collection of the Polish Underground Movement (1939–45) Study Trust – London, illustration by Richard Green*)

Original map of Warsaw with illustration showing Wira's key locations during the Uprising. (*Map from the collection of the Polish Underground Movement (1939–45) Study Trust – London, illustration by Richard Green*)

PROLOGUE

My mother, Danuta Szlachetko (née Banaszek), was born in 1929 into a world that was about to be destroyed. The grand city of Warsaw, Poland's capital, found itself at the centre of perhaps the greatest clash of opposing ideologies in the history of the West. Fascist Germany stood on the western borders and the Bolshevik Soviet Union dominated by Russia to the east. The first bombs fell when Danuta was ten years old, followed swiftly by a brutal five-year German occupation. By the end of the occupation about half of the city's population had been ruthlessly murdered. During this protracted bloodbath the Russians stood by waiting for the Polish resistance to be crushed, before subjecting the whole country to a further 46 years of domination by a foreign power.

This is the true story of my mother's life. It starts with a girl growing into her teenage years under the German occupation. She was too young to comprehend the broader politics but old enough to know that her country and city were being suffocated out of existence. She could not stand idly by; she made the decision to join the underground resistance movement. The whole city would pay a terrible price for its indomitable spirit of resistance. The movement culminated in the Warsaw Uprising of 1944, surely the greatest and most tragic act of resistance of any occupied country during World War II. During a 63 day period from 1st August 1944, blood flowed through the streets and buildings of Warsaw as the city expired.

Taken into captivity as one of the first female Prisoners of War in history, Danuta could only reflect upon both her own personal losses and the brutality of mankind while contemplating what might become of her. She was liberated from a German prison camp by her own army. Yet there was no going back to her life before the war; Poland was no longer free and the Soviet-imposed national government was openly hostile to those who had risked everything to save Poland.

My mother's friendship with a Polish army officer eventually led them both to begin a new life in Britain together. This book sheds light on why and how the original post-war generation of Polish immigrants came to Britain, badly scarred by what already seemed like a lifetime of sad experiences, beaten but not broken. They arrived with nothing, vilified by Soviet prop-aganda through certain sectors of the British press. They toiled to rebuild their lives, forming communities and surrogate families. Initially wary of this influx of foreigners, the British people grew to accept and even respect these hard-working, law-abiding Poles. Their children would become fully integrated members of British society while never forgetting their ancestry.

I decided to write this book in the first person because it is based entirely on my mother's words from hundreds of hours of interviews with her. There have been many historical books written about the Warsaw Uprising but this is a personal story. My mother could not be aware of many historical events at the time. This is an attempt to write an account entirely based on my mother's experiences, thoughts and emotions. I have focused on truth and accuracy without embellishment.

There are inevitable gaps in my mother's memory 70 years on, and where necessary I have attempted to piece events together in the best way I could with her help. I have also added some historical context, derived from personal research, where I felt it would interest the reader. Overall, however, I am amazed by the clarity of my mother's recollections; some events and emotions remain as fresh in her memory as if they happened yesterday.

This is a story not of victimhood but of the invincible human spirit of a generation of Polish heroes, as seen through the eyes of one woman. It is intended as a tribute to my mother, a woman of incredible integrity, courage, strength and love.

What would I have done in her place?

George Szlachetko Ealing, London. October 2015

Chapter 1

A SHORT CHILDHOOD

We used a child's spade to dig the holes. "Is that deep enough yet?" I giggled. My sister leant forward to arrange the delicate roots in the ground, her hair falling across her face as she concentrated on giving it the best start in life. I did the same. We patted the earth down and admired our twin saplings, both lost in our contemplation of the future. Then, like true sisters, we argued over whose oak tree would grow bigger and stronger. Fate would decide this for us. Over the years mine grew tall but crooked, while Henia's tree withered and died.

I, Danuta, was born on 16th July 1929 in Warsaw, Poland's beautiful capital city. It was a time of great pride as Poles were relishing their recently reacquired freedom after more than a century of foreign rule. This freedom turned out to be all too brief. Little could I know during my short childhood that within a matter of years half of the 1.4 million population of my beloved city would be dead, many cruelly murdered.

I lived with my mother, Maria Banaszek, and my older sister Henia. Jasia had been the first born but had died in infancy from scarlet fever. My parents separated when I was about six years old but despite this I had a blissful early childhood.

We lived in a rented ground-floor apartment in a stately rectangular block, which surrounded three spacious courtyards interlinked by high arches. Hundreds of people lived in this building and the courtyards were always vibrant with activity. A gateway opened onto the fashionable street of Nowy Świat (New World) at number 57.

Nowy Świat lies in the heart of Warsaw on the historic Royal Way. A mile to the north is the Royal Castle in the Old Town. At a similar distance to the south lies Warsaw's largest and grandest park, Łazienki.

Here, by the entrance, stands the Belweder Palace, a former presidential residence, and within the park the Palace on the Isle sits majestically on its own lake.

Among the expensive fashion boutiques on Nowy Świat were glamorous cafés. I have always had a sweet tooth and I loved walking past the famous café Blikle where the most wonderful cakes were displayed. Along the way I would pass by street vendors selling tasty-looking tubes of pastry filled with cream: I dreamed of being able to buy one. I had a friend whose relative worked in a nearby patisserie on Jerozolimska Boulevard and sometimes she gave us some leftover cakes, which was a rare treat.

The national soup was called *barszcz* – rich red and sour, made from beetroot – but my favourite was potato soup, which Henia and I learned to make at a very young age. I also enjoyed *pierogi*, pasta-like dough parcels usually filled with meat, cheese or cabbage. We often gathered our own berries and prepared berry soup with noodles, which was delicious. Trips to the forest to hunt for mushrooms were always great fun and a very Polish tradition. We would sauté the mushrooms in butter with cream, a gorgeous dish. Hunting for mushrooms is not easy and it requires a talent that I sadly do not possess.

Warsaw was called the 'Paris of the East'. Imposing buildings with ornate facades represented virtually all European architectural styles. I loved the long, wide boulevards which ran through the city, always busy with traffic. From my room I could hear in the distance the heavy hooves of horses drawing their carriages called *dorozki*. *Ryksza* drivers furiously rang their bells to clear the way ahead for the three-seater cabins they were pushing on their bikes. There were few cars in those days. The trams fascinated me; I would often lie awake at night listening to the 'ding ding' sound coming from them as they arrived at a nearby stop before moving off again. I loved hearing that sound in the still of night.

I attended primary school on Krucza Street, which was about a ten minute walk from my home. In those days there were no concerns about safety and young children walked to school by themselves. After school I often went to a social club connected to the school where we did our homework and various organised activities.

My life was full of simple pleasures. At Christmas we would make toys and Christmas decorations such as baubles out of paper; most toys were made by hand. At Easter we would decorate hollowed eggs in pretty colours and take them to the church for blessing, a much-loved Polish-Catholic tradition. I recall the excitement of choosing our food from the market; we would buy a traditional live carp for Christmas from the nearby Żelazna Brama (Metal Gate) market. At other special times we would buy a duck, goose or chicken. The stall-keeper would wring the bird's neck while the children looked away.

I was very close to my mother and sister and they were dear to me. My mother was the rock of our family and her way of dealing with life had a great impact on me. She was a strong and determined lady who always knew her mind. Above all, my mother valued honesty and hard work. She was kind and loving with the ability to listen. She brought us up to respect and help others. However, my mother could also be tough and, although we were close, her strict nature meant I was somewhat afraid of her.

Henia was almost four years older than me. We were quite different in many ways and we did not look similar. Henia loved children and people and she showed a lot of care towards our mother, more than I did. She had a calm nature and was both understanding and dependable. She was more serious and introverted than me; a good student and able to make interesting conversation. She was sensible, whereas I was a bit silly. We quarreled regularly about unimportant things but she was protective of me and completely trustworthy. Henia was a truly lovely person; we had a wonderful relationship and I loved her very much.

My father left home when I was six years old, I believe by mutual consent with my mother. I think they had first met through their shared farming backgrounds. Later my father joined the army. I have only one vivid memory of him before he left home. He was trying to punish Henia for being naughty, and put her across his knee so that he could smack her; but just as he brought his hand down Henia bent her leg back and he hit the sole of her shoe instead, hurting himself. In pain he dropped her onto the floor. It was a funny moment and I wanted to laugh but I dared not as my father was so angry. Nevertheless, after this incident I never saw him try to smack Henia again.

Perhaps the clearest memory I have, although a slender one, is of a few happy weeks my father spent with us in the country after my parents had separated. Naturally I always wanted my parents to be together, but at least they lived harmoniously in separation; they were never divorced. I believe my father was a good man, although perhaps of a different character from my mother.

Like most Poles my family was religious and we regularly attended our local Catholic church, the Church of the Holy Cross. It was an important part of our lives and we were involved with many of its thriving clubs and societies. One such society was the Marian Father's Sodality, which was run by my religious education teacher at school and family friend, Father Jan Paszyna. Henia and I spent a lot of time at Sodality gatherings in the church hall and on frequent excursions with them.

My mother, whose maiden name was Lipinska, came from a large family from Sieraków, a small country village about eight kilometres outside Warsaw, where they owned a farm. She had three brothers and four sisters. Franek was the youngest of her siblings, only a few years older than me, so Henia and I treated him more like a brother than an uncle. My grandfather died some time before I was born. On his deathbed he divided the farm equally among his children. Four stayed on the land in Sieraków, the others sold their shares and moved away. Janek, the oldest, bought an apartment in Warsaw's Old Town with his wife Alinka. Franek later joined them, along with my widowed grandmother. Traditionally in Polish families people deferred to their elders; this was certainly the case between Alinka and my grandmother, who was particularly fond of her daughter-in-law. Meanwhile our aunt, Janka, married a policeman and became Janka Dybowska. In those days policemen were admired, respected and well paid. Janka's husband received a post with a large apartment in the mainly Jewish town of Kałuszyn about 60 kilometres east of Warsaw. Janka used most of her inheritance furnishing the apartment and providing for their life there. I recall how dashing her husband looked in his uniform. A few years later Janka would come back into our lives under sad circumstances.

My mother sold her share of the inherited land in Sieraków and bought a smaller piece of land about three kilometres away in Laski, a small country community about six kilometres outside Warsaw. The land bordered a famous institute for the blind. With the help of friends Mother had a house built on the land, and, being resourceful, she also did a lot of the work herself. She decorated a heating stove with ceramic tiles, painted the house and busied herself making a country home for us. The house had four apartments and my family used one of these for a two-month holiday every summer. Of the other apartments, one was rented to a family friend. She was a widow and we treated her as an auntie. The other two apartments were rented to families for holidays or to visitors to the blind institute. I have many happy childhood memories of Laski, such as swimming in the pond behind our house and playing with the children from other families. When I was 12 I met my first childhood boyfriend, Januszek, there. On Sundays we would attend mass at a small, rustic chapel built out of tree trunks on the grounds of the institute. There were frequent religious processions there, including a beautiful one at Easter when the girls would throw flowers.

Our land in Laski measured just under three square kilometres. My mother planted a hundred fruit trees as well as vegetables, giving us a plentiful supply of homegrown food. There was an abundance of apples, pears, plums, morello cherries, currants, raspberries and strawberries, and two walnut trees that produced the finest nuts. One day Henia and I decided to plant one oak tree each near the house and we looked forward to seeing whose would grow bigger and stronger…

I loved walking from Laski to visit our family in Sieraków. The three-kilometre path took us through the beautiful Kampinos Forest which was on our doorstep. I recall the smell of the trees and the leaves, the softness of the moss beneath our feet and the singing of birds. Uncle Józek and his wife Genia would warmly welcome us with freshly made black country rye bread, homemade butter and buttermilk, which I adored. My most memorable times at Sieraków were the overnight stays, which normally took place when there was a bigger family gathering: cousins, uncles, aunts and local children joined in. In the evening we would build a campfire in the meadow, roast potatoes on the fire and drink more buttermilk. Then we would jump over the fire amid great laughter; often one of the boys didn't jump high enough and his trousers caught fire, or a girl would burn her skirt. That smell of the grass in the meadow, the flames from the campfire and the happy atmosphere created by the children are memories that have stayed with me for my whole life.

The forest could also be a frightening place. Henia and I were returning from Sieraków late one afternoon when we took a wrong turn and got lost. Every tree and clearing looked the same. We seemed to be wandering for ages and as the sun went down it became pitch black. Every branch seemed like it was about to grab me and each noise took on a sinister tone. Henia tried to comfort me as I burst into tears. Eventually we heard a dog barking. Henia led us towards the barking and to our great relief we came out of the forest at Izabelin. We were well off track but at least we knew our way home from there.

My mother was close to her brother Józef and his wife Genia. I could tell that Genia was extremely fond of my mother and she frequently came to her for advice and to hear the latest news and gossip about life in Warsaw. Whenever they visited us in Laski they would bring food from the farm and Mother would often give them fruit from our garden.

Overall my early life was an ordinary childhood, peaceful and happy. But things were changing. I could hear the adults talking about strange things, saying that the Germans could not be trusted and that war was surely coming. As a nine-year-old I had no idea what this all meant and I could not comprehend the seriousness of our situation. My mother seemed concerned and decided that we should store some food. We prepared a large quantity of preserves and juices using the fruits and vegetables from our garden. After digging some deep holes we buried the precious jars in a number of places close to the house in case we should need it in the future. Little did any of us know how terrible and soon that future would be, ending my childhood and everything I had ever known almost overnight.

THE BOMBS START FALLING

Soon after my tenth birthday, on 1st September 1939, war began. Germany attacked Poland and their troops headed for Warsaw. Bombs started falling and by 7th September Warsaw was besieged as the Polish forces fought for survival. I recall hearing megaphone announcements by our President Starzyński calling for the population to stick together and fight to the end. Hunger soon set in as supplies were cut off. One day Henia and I were passing along the Royal Way when we saw a large queue of people at a soup kitchen outside our Church of the Holy Cross. We decided to join the queue. When we returned home and told our mother about this she became angry with us, saying that we didn't need such help yet, that others needed the soup more than us and that we were not to accept such charity again. I think there was an element of pride in my mother's objection but we did not dare to argue.

About two weeks later the mood in the city worsened as news reached us that the Soviet Red Army had invaded Poland from the east. I heard the sense of shock in my mother's voice as she spoke of it. Hitler and Stalin had made a secret agreement to divide Poland between themselves. Stalin had torn up the Soviet–Polish Non-Aggression Pact of 1932 and we had been 'stabbed in the back'. All seemed lost; Poland was being crushed.

Then on 25th September, 18 days after the siege of Warsaw had begun, came a ceaseless aerial attack. Bombs were hurled down on us for the whole day and night without a break. It was too dangerous to stay in our apartment and our building didn't have a proper basement so we left to look for better shelter. Outside was chaos. Fires burned all around, buildings tumbled and people ran in panic in all directions. We searched for somewhere to hide as the bombs rained down. I recall being too scared to look up. Somehow we joined up with my mother's oldest brother Janek, his wife Alinka and their baby daughter. Later that day, after it had turned dark, we were still trying to find a place to rest. Alinka was carrying her baby, little Elżbieta, in a traditional baby carrier, which was a type of small duvet folded over and tied on both sides with ribbons. It looked like a pillowcase. In the panic the ribbons kept untying and Elżbieta fell out onto the ground more than once! We had to keep picking her up and fortunately she was unhurt. Having left our homes in panic we had no food. We came across a shop which people had broken into and somebody passed us a large tin of pickled gherkins. The satisfying taste of those gherkins still remains in my memory. Somehow we managed to all stay together, eventually finding a place to shelter under one of the big gates that typically stood at the entrance to Warsaw buildings. We tried to sleep there for a while as the bombs continued to fall.

Over the next few days things went quieter, turning to complete silence. We waited, not knowing what to expect. Then finally, as we stood in the ruins watching, the German army arrived. They marched triumphantly, six abreast, in their pristine grey-green uniforms. They sang victoriously as they strutted along the boulevards of Warsaw. We wept. We were the frightened mice in the house and they were the well-groomed, hungry cats coming to a feast.

The siege of Warsaw had lasted 20 days during which time the city had become the last Polish island in a German sea. Eventually, after heavy losses on both sides, our defenders capitulated. Our position had become untenable and civilian casualties were high. We no longer had the strength to resist.

Perhaps hoping to win us over, the Germans were cordial and polite at first; but everyone knew this would not last. It quickly became clear to the occupying army that the Poles would never passively accept subjugation and 'Germanisation'. So began a brutal occupation lasting more than five years, during which the Germans would try everything they could to obliterate Poland's national identity.

After the bombing we went back to our home in Nowy Świat to find our building had been completely destroyed. If we had stayed there during the bombing we would have been killed. We spent the next few days sleeping in various underground cellars and scavenging for food. Living among the ruins in the dirt without food was not sustainable so after a few days my mother decided that we would go to Laski. Janek and his wife Alinka chose to stay in Warsaw along with my grandmother and Franek. We had no further contact with my father from there on; I presumed he also stayed in Warsaw but it would be years before I found out what happened to him.

When we reached Laski we found the land dug up into trenches. We immediately realised that the area had been a front line of defence for the Polish army and that everything had been taken from our house, including the furniture. To our great relief, we found that our buried store of food had remained undiscovered despite a trench having been dug just a few metres away. This luck would help us survive that severe winter of 1939–40, during which half of our fruit trees would perish.

With no furniture we initially lived and slept on the floor in our house. Over time my mother used her resourcefulness to scavenge items for furniture. Wooden crates became our table and chairs, and later my Uncle Józek helped us piece together a bed.

After a few months my mother's sister Auntie Janka joined us in Laski with her two children and mother-in-law. Kałuszyn, where they had lived before the war, had experienced particularly heavy fighting between the Polish and German forces, leaving the town almost entirely destroyed. Janka's apartment and belongings had been burnt to the ground, leaving the family with nowhere to live. Kałuszyn stood near the meeting point of German and Soviet forces, who at that time were allies in attacking Poland. Having lost all contact with her husband, Janka then heard that he had been taken prisoner by the Soviets. It would be another 50 years before we finally had confirmation of his fate, when his name, Feliks Dybowski, appeared in 1991 among a list of Poles executed in the Katyn massacres.

Towards the end of the summer of 1946, Henia and I started attending the local school along with Janka's children Krysia and Jurek. The school was three kilometres away and we walked there and back every day. Krysia was a few years younger than I was and had a somewhat naughty nature so the local children gave her the nickname *diabeł Dybowskiej*, meaning 'little devil Dybowska'. Janka and her family stayed with us for a few months before she rented a nearby shop and the family moved into it. Later, when the shop got into difficulties, they moved back into our house, where Janka would stay for the rest of her life.

We sometimes visited the family on the farm in Sieraków as we followed our well-trodden path through the Kampinos Forest. I was blissfully unaware that during our time in Laski this forest was gaining a grim history. In the first two years of the occupation the Germans secretly executed over 2,000 of Warsaw's professors, teachers, priests, politicians and other members of the professional classes whom they feared might become leaders of the resistance movement. The execution site was at Palmiry on the edge of the forest. Bodies were piled in unmarked ditches, roughly covered with earth and hastily-planted pine trees, only a few kilometres from our family home.

Over time the forest would offer refuge to groups of Polish partisans hiding from the Germans. They emerged to launch various attacks or to get medical supplies before disappearing again. The partisans were mainly members of the Polish resistance army and many of them spent much of the war living in the wild. Many would play an important role in the Warsaw Uprising. The nuns at the blind institute would assist them with food and medical treatment, normally under the cover of night. These partisans were hunted throughout the war, first by the Germans and later by the Soviets.

Chapter 2

OCCUPIED WARSAW

We had been at Laski for almost two years and our time there was generally unhindered by the Germans. Although we were managing to survive, the level of education was limited and my mother began to think of the future. As Hitler reneged on the pact with Stalin and attacked the Soviet Union, it seemed that the German focus was shifting eastwards. My mother appeared hopeful that we could resume some semblance of our former lives and in the summer of 1941, as I approached my twelfth birthday, she decided that we should return to Warsaw.

More than ten percent of Warsaw's buildings had been destroyed in the 1939 attack. Most of our building at 57 Nowy Świat, including our apartment, was now a pile of rubble. Having housed hundreds of people before the war, the building was now almost deserted. The back section had also been badly damaged but was still standing and some rooms on the lower ground floor could be made vaguely habitable. My mother managed to contact the building owners or managers and got permission for us to make the most of what was possible. We therefore moved into a one-room apartment on the lower ground floor to the side of the third courtyard and began to make it our home. We all lived and slept in that one room. In addition we had a small kitchen and a toilet but there was no bathroom. All electricity in the building had been cut off so we had to use candles for light at night. Due to the bomb damage our courtyard could now be accessed directly from Świętokrzyska Street over what used to be part of the building, as well as in the normal way from Nowy Świat.

Besides ourselves the only other people living in the building were the Kaminski family with their four young children. Mr Kaminski acted as a caretaker, looking after what remained of the building for the owners. We hadn't known the Kaminskis before the war but we would get to know them quite well over time. We would remain the only two families living in the entire building throughout the occupation.

Entering our section of the building through a large gate, we would go down some stairs to our apartment past an open lift shaft. At night we had to feel our way against the wall, in the pitch darkness, as the handrails on the stairs had been blown off. One evening, while our mother was away, Henia and I were either squabbling or laughing as we approached the open lift shaft. I must have somehow nudged Henia and she fell into the shaft, down one whole level onto a pile of rubble. I shouted down at Henia but there was no response, just silence, and it was too dark to see anything. I was in a panic, fearing she was dead. I scrambled my way to Mr Kaminski's apartment for help. By the time we got back we could hear some moaning as Henia had recovered consciousness. Mr Kaminski managed to climb down and help her out; she was badly bruised and dazed but fortunately not seriously hurt. I blamed myself and was absolutely petrified of what my mother would say when she got back but Henia protected me and made sure I did not get the blame.

I rejoined my former school on Krucza Street for my final year of primary education. I have few memories of my primary school other than that I was happy there and met Danusia Chmielewska, who became a close friend. Danusia lived near us on Chmielnia Street. Her parents liked me a lot and her mother was particularly keen for us to be friends as Danusia was an only child. This became particularly important soon afterwards when Danusia's father died. I spent a lot of time at Danusia's apartment and her mother would often feed me as much as she could spare.

I do remember playing truant from school a number of times with a few other girls. We wandered down Agrykola Road towards the nearby Łazienki Park and played around outside the botanical gardens. It didn't take long for the school to notice our absence and they demanded an explanation. Scrabbling around for excuses I pleaded that I had been unwell, but to no avail: I was given a note asking for my mother to confirm the reason for my absence. I was petrified of what my mother would say and so I managed to delay for a while by making up more excuses. In the end there was no way out as the school would not let go of the matter. I begged a friend to come with me when I handed the note to my mother hoping it might help – I can't remember if it was Danusia or another girl. The plan did not work. My mother was polite in front of my friend but after she had gone she spoke to me firmly and also rebuked me for not having the courage to face her alone. There was no shouting or beating in our house; I was told that I had my own mind, that I should know how to behave better and that if this ever happened again there would be no question of leniency. Once my mother had spoken, her word was not to be disobeyed, and I paid heavily for my truancy with many hours of extra study as punishment.

Even though I was just 12 years of age I couldn't fail to notice the restrictions of life under German occupation as food was extremely scarce. Curfews had been imposed to keep Poles off the streets after dark, commencing at about 9 or 10pm in the summer and at about 7pm in the winter. Entrances to public areas and public transport displayed signs saying *Nur für Deutsche* – only for Germans – and we weren't allowed in certain tram or train carriages. Parts of the city where only Germans could live and where they had their administrative offices were also designated 'Nur fur Deutsche', such as the area around the infamous Szucha Street where the Gestapo had their headquarters. German soldiers stopped local people in the streets at will. I always felt nervous just walking on the street and my mother made sure that Henia and I kept away from the more crowded areas. I also learned quickly about the Jewish Ghetto.

In 1939 Poland contained the biggest Jewish population in Europe – 3.2 million, approximately ten percent of the population of Poland. This vastly exceeded the Jewish population in Germany, which in 1933, before the Nazis came to power, was around 500,000 (0.75 percent of the population). Warsaw had a particularly large Jewish population, which at 381,000 was 30 percent of the capital city's population.

When I was about four years old we had lived in a Jewish area of Warsaw, although I have no recollection which area it was or what it was called. I have only one vague memory of seeing a Jewish religious festival and sneaking a look into one of the temporary huts or *kutski* that had been erected in the courtyard for prayer. After we moved to Nowy Świat I had little contact with Jews as few seemed to live in that area. In the last years before the war I occasionally overheard talk about incidents of Jews being beaten by Poles which had been reported in the press. At the time I had no understanding of why these beatings were happening but my impression was that they were taking place in poorer, less sophisticated parts of the country. As a nine-year-old I believed that people in Warsaw generally got along well with each other. I was never taught to differentiate between Poles and Jews at school or at home. At the same time my lack of contact with Jewish people would suggest that our two communities were not very well integrated. This is borne out by the 1931 census in which only 12 percent of Poland's Jewish population listed Polish as their first language. The rest listed mainly Yiddish with a smaller number listing Hebrew.

Soon after the German occupation began in 1940, all Jews in Warsaw were ordered to relocate into an area of central Warsaw which had the predominantly Jewish area of Muranów at its heart. The Polish population had been removed from here and this became known as the Jewish Ghetto. In November 1940 the ghetto was closed to the outside world and surrounded by a high wall. This was the situation upon our return to Warsaw in the summer of 1941. Along the way I heard that Jews were also being brought into the ghetto from outside Warsaw.

At first I thought little about the Jewish Ghetto and the idea of going to look at a wall never occurred to me. The ghetto was not discussed with teachers and I recall my mother only mentioning some news about it to me once or twice. I suspect that she had discussions with Henia about such matters but that she regarded me as too young and childish. At school the children talked about the ghetto on occasions and passed around snippets of information. I occasionally heard stories of the terrible treatment of the Jews there and about their great hunger. Some school friends would recount stories about Jewish children sneaking out of the ghetto in search of food to take back, and people trying to pass food to these children or into the ghetto. Occasionally I would hear unspecific stories about Jews being hidden outside the ghetto. Even in those younger days when we talked about such things, it was with a sense of respect and sympathy for the Jews and with some fear for ourselves.

MY MOTHER THE SMUGGLER

Before the war it was unusual for mothers to work, but as so many men were interned as POWs, fighting overseas or missing in action, the women had to become providers. Although some shops had produce for sale, we had no money. Occasionally we were able to get some fruit and vegetables from our land in Laski. My mother would let us eat the smaller fruit and we sold the rest but otherwise we had very little to eat. Soon, like many other people at the time, my mother turned to the risky business of smuggling. Every couple of weeks she would leave early in the morning for the countryside and return late at night, normally well past midnight and the curfew hour. Money was borrowed from friends and shopkeepers. From these trips she would often bring back eggs, butter and cream, various meats including sausages and occasionally a chicken and some pork fat. This pork fat, which we called *słonina*, was a particular Polish favourite. We would fry onions in the fat or use it as a spread on bread – much tastier and cheaper than butter. My mother tended to go to the same family farmstead each time: they knew roughly when she would be coming and would have the produce ready to be collected. After a short break at the farmstead, where she would be given tea and something to eat, the goods were wrapped up into a bundle in a blanket. The parcel was tied onto her back and she would make the long journey back to Warsaw hoping to avoid being caught by the Germans.

If my mother's journey was successful we would sell most of the goods to a friendly shopkeeper a little way off Ordynacka Street and the rest to friends, only keeping a little for ourselves. I was often asked to deliver the food to the shop; Henia seemed to me to be asked much less often and this became a constant source of squabbles between my sister and me. I was convinced that Henia fared better than I did, particularly when she got a new coat. My mother had engaged a cousin of ours who was a tailor to make a coat for Henia and I got her old one. Of course my mother explained that there was nobody above Henia to pass clothes down to her but this didn't stop me feeling jealous and second best.

I used to think that the smuggling trips were easy and, with youthful naivety, asked my mother if I could join her on one of these excursions into the countryside. Surprisingly my mother agreed. Perhaps she thought we could carry a little more with two of us or maybe she just wanted me to understand the real risks involved. We left early in the morning and the train ride from Warsaw Central Station took about four hours. We headed eastwards out of Warsaw, stopping at numerous stations along the way. After arriving in the country we had to walk for another hour or so to reach the farmstead. Many others seemed to be doing the same as us. Having loaded up and taken a short break for some food we walked back to the station. Our train home was totally packed, with barely room to stand. As the train headed back to Warsaw I watched, petrified, as German soldiers searched through some of the carriages on our train. Fortunately they didn't come into ours. We still had a long way to go and every stop was a further reason to be afraid. Finally our train pulled into Warsaw well past midnight. The German-imposed curfew had already started at around 10pm, though the station guards seemed less concerned about the curfew than the German street patrols which terrorised us every night. The kilometre walk back to Nowy Świat from Central Station was incredibly tense for me. We dodged through back alleys and doorways to avoid being spotted and finally made it home with great relief. Mother must have seen how traumatised I was by the whole experience as she did not take me again and I never asked. From then on I knew how difficult it was for her!

The Germans must have known this kind of activity was taking place and although it was certainly not permitted, such smuggling was generally tolerated. This was the only way that Warsaw could feed itself. However this tolerance was unpredictable and unreliable, and there were many periods of harassment and repression. The Germans would often conduct unan-nounced searches at train stations. At the first sign of a search people would warn each other and stay back or find another way onto the train. It was probably easier for the occupying army to catch smugglers on the streets in Warsaw where there were more Germans around; it was harder to hide on the streets and everybody on the trains was heading into the city anyway. In effect, the Germans could do whatever they wanted: they could stop and search anyone, dish out punishment or just help themselves to whatever they wanted from us.

Mother did get caught a few times. I remember one particular time she returned home distraught and in tears after the Germans had confiscated all her goods but at least they had let her go. After a while she dusted herself off and started again from the beginning with new loans from friends and shop-keepers. One couple were particularly helpful to us. They owned a shop and as they had been unable to have children they took Henia and me to their hearts and often gave us spare scraps of food. I would see them later in the Uprising for the last time. My mother continued smuggling food right up to the start of the Uprising despite the threat of increasingly harsh punishments by the Germans, including arrest, deportation and worse.

AN UNDERGROUND EDUCATION

Before the war the typical structure for schooling in Poland was primary school from 7 to 12 years of age, four years at grammar school up to 16, and then lyceum for another two years up to 18. After that some students might progress to university. Now, however, it was German policy that education for the Poles be restricted to basics. Schools were no longer allowed to teach academic subjects such as mathematics, sciences or history. The Germans intended to reduce the Polish to a nation of ignorant slave workers. In order to have a chance of being allowed to remain open, schools were required to remodel themselves to offer only the most basic teaching and vocational training in manual labour.

In the summer of 1942 I finished primary school and was enrolled into a grammar school on Bagatela Street which before the war had been aimed at preparing girls for a career in the education service. Like many mothers, mine had wanted me to become a doctor, but times were different now. Henia was already attending a lyceum on Królewska Street, a school formerly geared towards international commerce. During the summer holidays, about a month before the start of term, the Germans closed down more schools. This included the one I was about to attend and left me without a place.

This was an anxious time for my mother and me. My mother tried everywhere to find a school place for me but at such short notice, and with so many other children searching for places, this was seemingly impossible. Out of desperation my mother turned to Father Jan Paszyna at the Marian Sodality. Like most other Polish organisations, the Sodality had been banned by the Germans and had gone underground.

The Catholic Church had played a significant religious, cultural and political role in Poland for nearly a thousand years. The Germans viewed the Church as a symbol of national identity and sought to eliminate religious institutions during the early years of occupation. Throughout the country, churches were shut down and the clergy arrested and deported to concentration camps. By the end of the war nearly one fifth of all Polish priests and nuns had been murdered, most of those in the first two years of the occupation.

In addition to teaching at my primary school, Father Jan taught at a private grammar school called Haliny Gepnerówny. He agreed to appeal to the headmistress there on my behalf. To avoid closure the school had reorientated itself as a millinery school. The trade of hat-making was sufficiently innocuous to escape adverse attention. However, Mother worried that, even if I could get a place at the school we couldn't afford the fees. Determined as ever, she resolved to find a way. The headmistress confirmed to Father Jan that the school was full for that year but offered us some hope. She said that, if I agreed to home study for the coming year and passed the year-end exams, she would let me have any place that became available for the following year. Given our circumstances and as a further favour to Father Jan Paszyna, the headmistress agreed to reduce the fees in my case. Meanwhile, to help me with my home studies, the headmistress recommended a tutor. This was her brightest pupil, Krysia Biernacka, who was in the final year of grammar school. Krysia was happy to tutor me; she lived very close on Czackiego Street with her mother and circumstances were difficult for them, so they needed the money.

Every day after school Krysia would come to my home to review my homework and set me more for the following day. We covered all the main and now illicit academic subjects. I liked Krysia very much and admired her. She was almost four years older than me and full of knowledge, and I felt comfortable in her presence. Krysia was pretty, vivacious and she always looked so glamorous. I recall she often wore beautiful long culottes, which were very fashionable at the time. As our apartment had only one room, my mother and Henia did their best to stay out of the way while Krysia was tutoring me.

Learning about Polish history was a particularly emotive part of my development as a young girl. I was moved by the numerous heroic struggles and uprisings by Poles against foreign invaders. The January Uprising of 1863 against the Russian Empire was a particular source of pride and inspiration. Many Poles lost their lives during this Uprising and many more were deported to prisons in Russia. Some managed to escape abroad in the final throes of the Uprising, mainly to France and Britain. I heard how, after the Uprising, survivors were revered. They would wear their uniforms with pride and people would take their hats off to them in the street. I felt very proud of their sacrifices. It was easy for me to see a strong link to my past and to the situation that Poland now faced, and this played a part in shaping my thinking and identity.

I had turned 13 years old when Krysia started tutoring me. I knew my mother was struggling to pay for my education so I was prepared to work hard to pass the year-end exam. That year with Krysia would be the beginning of my awakening as a young adult.

As Krysia and I got to know and trust each other she started talking more openly to me about her life and about what was happening to Poland under German occupation. She told me that in the early days of the occupation her older brother had been arrested by the Gestapo and interrogated for 14 days. He was transported to the Pawiak prison and then to Oświęcim, which the Germans called Auschwitz, where he died a month or so later. Filled with grief, Krysia's father succumbed to a heart attack and died. Krysia's twin brother had then left home to join the Polish resistance, never to return.

The year progressed. I think it was around January 1943 when my mother and sister were out and we were alone that Krysia revealed to me that she was a member of the Polish underground scout movement called the Szare Szeregi (the Grey Ranks). She said that the Grey Ranks were

affiliated to the resistance army, known as the Armia Krajowa (the AK), and
that both were involved in the Conspiracy against the German occupiers.
She told me her pseudonym was 'Kali'. I was terrifically excited as I had
learned in earlier history lessons about Polish scouts fighting in the 1920
war against the Bolsheviks and more recently about their role in the 1939
defence of Poland. I was particularly thrilled by the history of boy scouts
bravely stopping invading Soviet tanks with petrol bombs at the Battle of
Grodno in Eastern Poland.

Throughout that year I learned about the history of my country, how we
were being systematically annihilated and how young Poles were fighting
back.

Once a strong and proud country, Poland was one of the largest and
most populous states in Europe in the sixteenth and seventeenth centuries.
Following a series of invasions and partitions by the Russian Empire, the
Kingdom of Prussia and the Austrian Habsburg Monarchy, Poland lost
her independence in 1795 and ceased to exist as a country for 123 years
until 1918. During the various occupations, Polish identity was maintained
through cultural education. Throughout this period there were intermittent armed Polish uprisings, notably the November Revolt of 1830 and the
January Uprising of 1863. After the First World War, when the partitioning
powers were defeated, the opportunity to regain independence was seized,
bringing about the birth of the Second Polish Republic. This was confirmed
in 1919 at the Treaty of Versailles and consolidated by the Polish defeat of
the Red Army at the Battle of Warsaw in 1920, which halted the advance of
Communism into Europe.

The twenty years before World War II were happy times for those Poles
who remembered what life was like during the years under partition and
foreign domination. Massive strides were made in rebuilding Poland's
independence under the multinational and pluralist Sanacja government of
Marshal Piłsudski.

When World War II started, all branches of the Polish State went
underground and became the Polish Underground State. The Underground
Army was formed, eventually becoming the Armia Krajowa (Army of the
Country or Home Army). This army is generally referred to as the AK. The

AK became part of the political and legal framework of the Polish Underground State with allegiance to the constitutional Polish coalition government-in-exile. The latter was formed in France after Poland was invaded and moved to London when France capitulated.

The AK was tasked with fighting the enemy on home soil through clandestine methods. It grew to become one of Europe's biggest resistance movements. By mid 1944, estimated sworn membership of the AK around the country was over 350,000 with significant additional numbers unofficially involved in underground activities. Women constituted approximately ten percent of AK personnel.

Without hesitation the scout movement joined the Conspiracy against the occupiers and went underground as a parallel, clandestine organisation to the AK. The male underground scout movement took the pseudonym Szare Szeregi (Grey Ranks) on account of their pre-war uniforms. The Grey Ranks were effectively paramilitaries. The organisation comprised three sections. The youngest section for 12 to 14-year-old boys was called Zawiszy. Its objective was to train boys for auxiliary service for an eventual armed uprising. The next age group – 15 to 17-year-old boys – belonged to the Combat Schools, which were to be engaged in small sabotage. Finally the third section, for boys aged 17 and above, was the Assault Groups, trained to conduct major sabotage and armed struggle. A small number of girls were attached to the latter two sections. By May 1944 there were 8,359 members of the Grey Ranks.

The Girl Scouts organisation operated separately from the Grey Ranks and adopted the pseudonym Koniczyna (Clover Society). The primary role of the Clover Society was to train its members in liaison and medical aid as nurses, and to support the male military activities. By 1944 the Clover Society had about 5,000 members.

I was learning how Poles were being uprooted all around the country. Germany had annexed much of western Poland and ethnic Germans were being resettled in our place. Meanwhile in the eastern Soviet-occupied regions, Poles had been deported in large swathes to Siberia. What was left of Poland had effectively been reduced to a German administrative district which the Germans called Generalgouvernement (General Government).

This district constituted little over a quarter of Poland's pre-war territory. It was increasingly clear that the Germans intended that Poland should cease to exist and our land should simply be absorbed, becoming part of Germany's Lebensraum (living space).

Krysia would tell me stories about German atrocities and how the underground was fighting back. She said that Warsaw's youth were stirring, that they wanted to fight and that this was a matter of honour.

I was also hearing more about the plight of the Jews. Over the following months with Krysia I began to understand more about what was happening. I paid more attention to conversations among adults about the terrible conditions and disease that existed in the ghetto. I heard that the Jewish children who had crawled through holes in the wall to find food on the outside were often caught by the Germans and shot on the spot. Sometimes I would ask my mother about the ghetto and she would explain a little. Usually she would end up begging Henia and me to be careful where we went and what we did. A few times she told us about Poles who had been caught hiding Jews in their houses and how their entire families were executed by the Germans as punishment.

In fact, helping Jews in Poland carried greater risks than in other occupied countries. Only in Poland was it officially decreed that any kind of help for Jews was punishable by death for both the helper and their entire family. Such aid included merely feeding Jews, let alone sheltering and hiding them.

Information started to circulate that Jews were now being deported from the ghetto. Krysia and I discussed this at length and she reflected the views of some of her colleagues in the Conspiracy. She told me that, given what the Germans were doing to Poland as a whole, it didn't make sense that they would simply herd the Jews into a ghetto simply to leave them there, and that the Germans clearly had further plans for the Jews. This then led to the inevitable conclusion that whatever was to be the fate of the Jews would also be our fate next. I gradually came to accept this conclusion although I had no idea at the time what was actually unfolding.

Any animosity between the Poles and the Jews that may have existed before the war was not at all evident to me during the occupation. Any differences that there might have been seemed to me to have been forgotten and all I saw was that Warsaw Poles felt for their fellow citizens in the ghetto. From my perspective there was no 'them and us', as whatever was happening would ultimately affect us all.

Towards the end of 1943 I started hearing from Krysia that the Jews were being taken to concentration camps. The existence of camps such as Auschwitz was well known to us by now. Auschwitz had been used since 1940 to hold Polish political prisoners. These prisoners were simply any who resisted or might resist German occupation. From 1941 it was also widely known that Poles were being murdered at Auschwitz; Krysia had already lost her brother there. Much grim speculation about the fate of the Jews began circulating and talk gathered that they were being taken to death camps.

The Jewish and Polish underground movements were in close contact and information about what was happening to the Jews soon started to filter out beyond Poland to the outside world. In August 1942, after the deportations had begun, a Polish courier from the AK, Jan Kozielewski (pseudonym 'Jan Karski') was twice smuggled into the Jewish Ghetto by the Jewish underground in order to gather information. The AK also followed the trains packed with Jews leaving the ghetto to Treblinka concentration camp about 100 kilometres north-east of Warsaw, and also to Bełżec and Sobibór concentration camps. This led to the terrifying conclusion that the Jews were being exterminated at these camps.

Karski travelled under cover to Britain with his report and other observations stored on a microfiche. After reporting to the Polish government-in-exile, Karski met with British Foreign Secretary Anthony Eden. On the basis of Karski's information the Polish government-in-exile produced one of the earliest and most accurate accounts of the treatment of the Jews in the form of a booklet entitled 'The mass extermination of Jews in German-occupied Poland', addressed to the United Nations in December 1942.

From Britain, Karski went to the US where he met President Franklin D. Roosevelt. Karski also told many important members of the American political and media establishment what he had seen and heard. On hearing

Karski's report about the horrors befalling the Jews in Poland, Felix Frank-
furter, a Jewish-American member of the US Supreme Court and advisor to
President Roosevelt, responded: "I am unable to believe you". This typified
the general reaction Karski received in the West.

The Polish government's account of the treatment of Jews in Europe was
supplemented a few months later by information from Polish AK member
Witold Pilecki. In 1940 Pilecki volunteered to be imprisoned in Auschwitz
in order to gather information and to form a camp resistance organisation. After his escape in April 1943, Pilecki wrote a detailed report about
the brutal camp conditions he experienced there, the inhumane treatment
of Soviet POWs, and the start of the mass murder of Jews at Auschwitz-
Birkenau. This was the first record of the Jewish Holocaust that included
details about gas chambers and the magnitude of the daily murders. Information from Pilecki's organisation was passed to the British by the Polish
government-in-exile but not acted upon.

Over time, I would learn about Żegota. After the start of the deportations in Warsaw it was decided that a large-scale, well-supported and well-
funded organisation to help Jews was urgently needed. In October 1942 the
Polish underground announced the formation of the Polish Council for the
Aid of Jews, codenamed Żegota. It was created by ethnic Polish members of
the underground and operated jointly by the Polish Underground State and
the Jewish underground under the auspices of the Polish government-in-
exile. The organisation quickly developed a large network and embarked on
rescuing Jews, be they in the ghetto or hiding on the outside. In addition
to providing food, medical care and money, Żegota forged a huge number
of documents for Jews to avoid capture on the outside. In all of occupied
Europe, Poland was the only country where an organisation existed specifically to help Jews.

In March 1943 we heard about a major armed operation conducted
on the streets of Warsaw by the Polish resistance which became known as
Operation Arsenal. This was an operation to free Grey Ranks troop leader
and AK activist Jan Bytner (pseudonym 'Rudy') and 24 other prisoners. It
was conducted by a Grey Ranks unit. The successful attack took place as the
prisoners were being transported from interrogation at the Gestapo head-

quarters at Szucha Street to the Pawiak prison. I was immediately overtaken by a sense of duty and a desire to belong to this underground movement. Everybody knew there would be reprisals for such acts of resistance but I had been born into a country and people for whom honour and patriotism were deeply ingrained. I was beginning to realise that personal danger was a price we had to pay to save our country.

On the day following the Rudy escape operation 140 civilians were executed in retribution by the Germans and many more arrests followed. Rudy died a few days later from wounds sustained from being tortured before the breakout action. His friend 'Alek' died the same day from wounds sustained while taking part in the breakout. The two SS men responsible for Rudy's torture in jail were identified as Schulz and Langer and were assassinated two months later by the Grey Ranks.

Soon after, a Grey Ranks member, Alexander Kaminski, wrote a non-fiction book about underground activity by the Grey Ranks culminating in Operation Arsenal. The book was entitled *Kamienie na Szaniec* (Stones for the Rampart), and became an iconic part of underground propaganda. I would later help conceal numerous copies of this book ahead of distribution as part of my underground activities.

By now I was determined to join the Conspiracy: for me, it was an absolutely necessary step. I liked everything Krysia had outlined to me about the resistance, she was my friend in the Conspiracy. I knew that something had to be done and I desperately wanted to serve my country and to free Poland from this oppression. One question kept repeating itself in my mind: "How can someone else come to our home and tell us what to do?" It was intolerable for me that we had to cower everytime we walked along our own streets and that we were constantly at the whim of any German. For some, it was easier to keep their heads down, accept the situation and hope things would eventually change. Others were held back due to a cultural obligation for one of the children to look after the mother. Some people simply never had the opportunity to join the underground Conspiracy. For many, however, passive submission was not an option once they were given the opportunity to fight back. Like the majority of Warsaw's young people at the time, I belonged to this category. I was aware of the

potential dangers to which I would be exposing myself but participation in
the Conspiracy was something I felt compelled to do. Despite the danger I
didn't imagine anything bad would happen to me.

THE GHETTO BURNS

1943, the fourth year of occupation, had arrived. It would be a brutal year.
I recall April 1943 vividly and with great sadness. Easter was approaching, one of my favourite times of year. It was 19th April and I was painting
bright patterns on hollowed eggs to be blessed in church. I loved this Easter
tradition. Suddenly a family friend arrived at our apartment shouting
that the Jewish Ghetto was on fire. We decided to go as a family to see for
ourselves what was happening; it would be the first time I saw the ghetto. As
we hurried behind groups of other people I soon became aware of smoke
reaching into the sky. After about 20 minutes we reached a spot about 300
metres from a wall which stood about three metres high; this was the outer
ghetto wall. Armed guards prevented anybody from getting closer and I
would have been too scared to get nearer anyway. Behind the smoke I could
hear intermittent gunfire and I sensed that something crucial was taking
place behind the wall.

We stood among quite a large crowd of people. I could hear people
exchanging information. Somebody said that when the Germans had
deported many of the Jews from the ghetto, a desperate young group had
stayed behind determined to fight until the end. As I stood there watching
and listening to what the crowd were saying I felt an overriding emotion
of great pity for those left in the ghetto. I wondered whether they could
possibly save themselves...

It came to my mind that on a number of occasions Krysia and I had
discussed that we should start an uprising. I wondered how it might look,
whether it would be the same as what I could see in front of me in the
ghetto. As I stood there I felt an even greater hatred for the Germans and
for what they were doing to us all. In secret, I prayed for those fighting in
the ghetto and for the rest of the day my thoughts were with them. The sight

and sound of the fighting and the burning of the ghetto lasted for three days, maybe four, before silence descended.

In some ways I wasn't surprised that the Jews were fighting back; I already knew about the Conspiracy and that the AK were preparing to fight. I also knew that the AK were in contact with the Jewish underground and were doing what they could to help and so it seemed that both were essentially part of the same Conspiracy. It also dawned on me with considerable sadness that if the Jews were fighting to prevent deportation against such overwhelming odds then the rumours about death camps must indeed be true.

The fighting in the Jewish Ghetto became known as the Ghetto Uprising. This was the final heroic act of resistance by a few hundred poorly armed fighters as the Germans began to deport the remaining 55,000 Jews from the ghetto. The fighters chose to die rather than passively accept their fate. They fought with the small quantity of weapons smuggled into the ghetto, some from the AK. Simultaneously the AK launched a number of pre-agreed diversionary attacks against the Germans to help create escape routes.

The last surviving leader of the Jewish Combat Organisation, Marek Edelman, wrote a personal account of life in the ghetto and the Jewish Uprising. He states that the Germans suffered around 300 casualties. Very few of the Jewish fighters survived, although Edelman did manage to escape and join the Polish resistance movement. Thirteen thousand Jewish civilians were killed during the Uprising as the Germans adopted an urban warfare policy of burning building after building. After the fighting was over, the remaining Jews were deported and the ghetto finally fell deadly silent.

In desperation the Jewish Bund Party leader and member of the Polish government-in-exile Szmul Zygielbojm committed suicide in London in May 1943. His death was a protest at the world's inaction in response to the extermination of Jews. In his suicide letter Zygielbojm wrote: 'I cannot continue to live and to be silent while the remnants of Polish Jewry, whose representative I am, are being killed. By my death I wish to give expression to my most profound protest against the inaction in which the world watches and permits the destruction of the Jewish people.'

Following the Ghetto Uprising the Germans scoured the vacant buildings of the ghetto for anything of value which remained. In later years I would hear that after the Germans had cleared the ghetto some Poles would go *na szaber* (looting), taking what little remained in the empty houses. It was clear that the Jews were not coming back; nevertheless in subsequent years stories about this looting have caused resentment among sections of the Jewish community.

The Ghetto Uprising has become an important symbol of Jewish defiance for generations of Jewish people to come. As for me, the deportations of the Jews and their likely fate further confirmed to me where all this was leading for the rest of us remaining in Warsaw. I was already fully committed to joining the resistance before the Jewish Uprising in April 1943 but I would say it played a part in strengthening my resolve. I decided that if the Jews could fight then so could we. It would be many years before I became aware of the full magnitude of the murder of European Jews by the Nazis.

Chapter 3

THE GREY RANKS

I had worked hard all year and early that summer I successfully passed the year-end school exam. I spent a lot of time contemplating joining the Conspiracy and what it might mean for me and my family. Krysia was open and honest with me and she did not try to push me to join. She informed me about the dangers involved. She told me I could be arrested, tortured or killed. The most difficult part was knowing that if I were caught my family would suffer. It was not a decision I took lightly despite my initial excitement. I told Krysia that I wanted to join and that I was wholeheartedly committed. Krysia said she would make the arrangements.

In September 1943 I started my second year of grammar education at Haliny Gepnerówny Private Millinery School. Named after its founder, Halina Gepnerówna, it was located at 8 Stanisław Moniuszko Street. I had just turned 14 years of age. From my first day it was clear that my new school was a hotbed of anti-German activity. Pupils were furtively talking in small groups and I heard more about Polish resistance to the occupation. Despite the restrictions on education a full curriculum was secretly taught at great risk and behind closed doors. Often the Germans would make surprise inspections of the school. We always had somebody keeping watch and as soon as the Germans were spotted, the look-out would signal. The teacher would tell us to quickly hide our books in specified places and wheel out mannequins used for hat-making. This drill was well-rehearsed and succeeded in presenting a seamless impression of a lesson in progress. The German soldiers would walk into our class, look around and ask the teacher a few questions, before proceeding to another class. It was frightening to watch them searching through cupboards and drawers but fortunately they never found any incriminating evidence. Despite the Germans' intrusions I enjoyed my school. We had about 20 girls to a class; I had many friends there who also belonged to my underground Catholic Sodality and the atmosphere was good. I also actually enjoyed learning how to make hats!

Early that autumn, German bulletins were displayed announcing that an illegal underground printing press had been discovered and that those caught there had been punished. The Germans clearly wanted to set a public example and to this day the image is etched with great sadness in my mind. Each of the boys responsible had been hanged from a balcony overlooking the street and left there for the people of Warsaw to see. There were nine of them, maybe more, hanging lifelessly in what seemed like a tight, diagonal row from the same fairly long balcony. I presume the lengths of ropes were different, hence their bodies were at different heights. They seemed to be hanging in order of size, the smallest and youngest of them first and lowest. As I walked past his body his feet reached down to my chest, he could not have been more than 16 years old. Seeing these young men hanging had a tremendous impact on me. I cried the whole time and I still cry when I think about it today. It also made me extremely angry and desperate to play a part in fighting back – as I'm sure it did for many others.

In November 1943 Krysia arranged a meeting for me at a private house with some senior girls in the Grey Ranks. One of the girls introduced herself to me only as 'Miki', which was her pseudonym. I think she was about 20 years old. In total there were about five other girls including Krysia at the meeting. I spoke about myself and explained why I wanted to be involved in the underground. During the meeting Miki and the other girls told me about their activities of minor sabotage and the personal risks involved. Overall I had the sense that this was an interview; it was partly about getting to know one another but also to establish my willingness and commitment. At the end of the meeting Miki asked me if I still wanted to join, to which I resolutely replied that I did. After the meeting I walked home full of pride and excitement.

The next two months were spent preparing me for action and assessing my mental condition for underground work. During this time I started attending regular education lessons with other girls in how to conduct conspiracy. These educational sessions continued throughout my entire involvement with the Conspiracy. Often we would meet in a private apartment in Warsaw; I am sure Miki's home on Górska Street was often used. Other times we would travel out of Warsaw and meet under the cover of woods. These out-of-town meetings took place at weekends so that our families didn't find out. I normally told my mother I was just going to a friend's house. We would travel by train in pairs for about 30 minutes to the outskirts of Warsaw. After leaving the train we headed into the woods and met up at a designated location. There would normally be about ten of us, including two older girls who did the teaching. The sessions lasted about two hours, during which we were taught how to distribute and display propaganda, basic firearm skills such as dismantling and reassembling pistols, city orientation and administering medical treatment. We were also taught how to behave if captured by the Germans in a compromising situation in order to reduce the risk to the rest of the organisation. The sessions also had some physical exercises and regular scouting activities including performances and singing scout songs. All this training was very much oriented towards preparing for underground activity culminating in an armed uprising. The meetings in the woods always finished with the scout song *Here comes the night*.

I am sure our wandering through the countryside on these excursions must have looked a little suspicious even as we tried to give the impression that we were just out for an innocent walk. People would see us and no doubt suspect that there was more to our gathering than meets the eye, but fortunately everybody kept such thoughts to themselves. In general the civilian population were aware of the underground movement and very supportive. People were always prepared to help and let each other know when there was danger but we also had to remain constantly aware of spies among the population.

Of course, training in the woods was very different from the real missions, so to assess my mental suitability I was given minor delivery tasks around Warsaw. Miki would hand me a note and an address where it was to be delivered. With every new recruit the girls were putting their lives at risk and they had to be sure that each one could cope with the stress involved. I presume I passed this period of assessment.

In January 1944 my formal initiation into the Grey Ranks took place in a private house. Presiding over the initiation was the head of the Executive Group who was introduced to me only by her pseudonym, Ewa. Miki was there and a number of other girls aged mainly between 14 and 17. I did not know any of these girls until that moment. In the middle of the room on a table lay a scout's cross. I made the regular peacetime scout's pledge and also the additional wartime promise to serve the scout movement with all my ability, to safeguard the secrets of the organisation, to obey orders and to not hesitate to sacrifice my life if necessary. I was then presented with my cross, which I received with honour. Next I was told to choose a pseudonym and the girls helped me to come up with the name 'Wira', pronounced Vera in English. I can't recall how this name came about. The group congratulated me and welcomed me into their ranks as one of their own. From then on I was known only as Wira.

From the very beginning I understood our role to be to maintain the nation's morale, undermine the enemy and prepare for the inevitable uprising against the occupiers. Each one of us dreamed about the day we would rise up, for we knew that that day must come.

I quickly learned that secrecy was of the essence in the Conspiracy. There was no contact upwards; one did not know who was above one's immediate superior. We did not know each other's real names and we never asked. Everybody was referred to only by their pseudonym. This was so that we could not give others away in case of capture and interrogation. These pseudonyms have lasted many years. Even today those who remain often still use them even though we have long known each other's real names. Having sworn to secrecy I could not even tell my mother or sister about my involvement with the Conspiracy. I am sure there were many other girls in my school who belonged to the underground but apart from Krysia I did not know who they were or how many: one never asked and it was never discussed.

The Grey Ranks had codenames for the various units. A troop was codenamed a 'Family'. The Family I was now part of was the all-female

Grupa Wykonawcza (Executive Group). A Family consisted of a number of squads, codenamed 'Bees'. The Executive Group had about ten to twelve Bees consisting of three to five girls each. My Bee unit was called the Squirrels. Headed by Miki, it consisted of only myself and 'Iga'. The national headquarters of the Grey Ranks was codenamed *Pasieka* ('Apiary') which is, of course, a collection of beehives. The internal secrecy within our organisation meant that even though the Germans were fully aware of our activities, they had little success in penetrating the organisation throughout the occupation.

The all-female Executive Group had been set up in 1940 and differed from the Clover Society of female scouts in that it emanated from the male Grey Ranks. The Grey Ranks leadership felt that direct female help was needed for certain activities so Ewa formed and headed up the female Executive Group, supported by her sister in law 'Horpyna'. We were attached to the male Family called Władysława Jagiełło 54 (after an early fifteenth-century Polish king) which was based at the Apiary and headed up by Ewa's husband. As far as I know we were one of only two all female Families within the Grey Ranks.

Over the next year our primary activity was minor sabotage. This included distributing and displaying our propaganda while destroying that of the Germans. The objectives were to promote AK unity and morale, undermine German confidence and, above all, make sure that the Germans knew the underground was continuously active and increasingly well organised.

We frequently painted patriotic and anti-German slogans on walls around the city. Sometimes we painted '*Niemcy Kaput*' or '*Deutschland Kaput*' ('Germany is broken'). The most popular and famous sign we painted, however, was the *kotwica* (anchor). The *kotwica* became the 'Poland is fighting' symbol as it has a 'P' for Poland superimposed over a 'W' for *walczy* (is fighting). As a graphic, the letters looked like an anchor. The *kotwica* first came into use in 1942 when the Bureau of Information and Propaganda (BIP), within Department VI of the AK, held a competition to create a symbol for the Conspiracy. The winner was a Grey Ranks instructress and student of history at Warsaw university, Anna Smolenska.

One of the reasons her *kotwica* was chosen was that it could be daubed easily and quickly, which was essential. Later that year, 23-year-old Anna was arrested, along with most of her family, and taken to Auschwitz, where they all died. The *kotwica* became one of the most potent symbols of the Polish underground movement and is still frequently seen today.

At other times we distributed printed propaganda leaflets and publications – a role officially termed *kolporter* (distribution). I believe these were printed and supplied by the BIP. They included counterfeit issues of German newspapers, which were intended to undermine German confidence by highlighting their defeats on the Eastern Front. Some of the publications were presented as the work of fictitious German political groups who were opposing Hitler, with the aim of fomenting discontent among ordinary German soldiers with the Nazi regime. We also distributed and displayed updated information about the struggle for freedom to boost the morale of our civilians. We destroyed symbols of the occupier and tore down German flags and propaganda designed to pacify our population.

I found displaying posters more stressful than distribution, ripping down German propaganda and insignias, or even painting graffiti on walls. Sticking up posters took the longest time and therefore exposed us to greater risk of capture.

My main area of operation was from Warsaw Old Town in the north down to City Centre South, and from the central railway station in the west to the Poniatowski Bridge, which crossed the Wisła (Vistula river) in the east. This was the area I knew best. I would travel on missions either by myself or with another girl – never more than two of us as that might attract attention. One of us would stand on guard at a nearby corner while the other performed the action. Sometimes we had to take a tram to our destination, always making sure we were as far back as possible from the first carriage, which was reserved for Germans only. Civilians, as ever, played an active role in helping the likes of us avoid capture. Everyone knew about the underground so when people saw Germans conducting searches they would immediately start warning one another. Often the tram driver would a warning glance towards the back. If the situation started to get dangerous we would try to leave the tram as it slowed down and disappear.

We carried the propaganda in standard handheld bags or briefcases, or sometimes hidden on our bodies. Our training helped us conceal illicit materials so that we would not be detected. Paint, for example, would be carried in small amounts in flat, waterproof containers. Paint brushes had to be small and easy to conceal. We had small penknives for ripping down enemy posters. We were also taught how to quickly dispose of materials if we were in a tight spot, and how to react if we were actually caught.

The missions would normally take a day or two to prepare for and about half a day, or occasionally a whole day, to execute. On average I undertook two missions a week; any more would have been too much for my nerves to bear. My instructions would come directly from Miki; she would give me any materials I required or direct me to a location where they were to be collected. If we ran out of time we would keep the papers with us overnight and complete the mission the following day. This had the added complication of needing to be done without my mother finding out.

As ever, luck was a vital element. I recall on one occasion I was sent to paint the 'Poland is fighting' sign on a nearby wall in Nowy Świat with a friend. I had a small tin with black paint and a small brush. It was a quiet afternoon. My friend stood guard as I started to paint. The civilians who walked past pretended not to notice anything but I could tell they walked a little faster past me. I could only hope that there were no spies among them. I had managed to paint the 'W' and was about to add the 'P' when I heard my friend whistle. Three German soldiers had appeared from Świętokrzyska Street and stood on the nearby corner with Nowy Świat where the Europa cinema used to be. I darted into a gateway, trying to get out of sight. In the gateway there was a small staircase which I stood in and waited with bated breath. I was sure that I had been spotted. The Germans stood on the corner for a while and, to my immense relief, left in the other direction.

On another mission, my colleague heard the shout of *Achtung*! (Halt!) from behind and turned around to see a German soldier walking towards her. Her briefcase contained compromising materials: it was a fraught situation. Afterwards she told me that she was sure her time was up and that she had resigned herself to her fate. Miraculously the German simply looked at her and then let her go. I'm not sure whether it was the calmness stemming from her training or her resigned acceptance of her fate that prompted the German to let her go. Whichever one it was, it probably saved her life.

The main German military presence on the streets was the regular army soldiers of the Wehrmacht in their grey uniforms. In general we were less afraid of the Wehrmacht even though they had complete power over us and could stop us at will. Many were involved in atrocities throughout the occupation but – without excusing what they did – most were simply obeying orders and were not ideologically driven. Most of the time the Wehrmacht didn't bother to stop you without a reason. Our main threat came from the SS, particularly from the secret police, the Gestapo. The Gestapo had much smarter grey-green uniforms that were slightly darker than those of the Wehrmacht and distinguished further by the distinctive red swastika armband. They were much less visible on the streets but whenever I saw the Gestapo it would send a chill down my spine. Once the Gestapo were involved in any situation it usually meant the worst.

A key target of our propaganda was to foster insecurity among those who had signed the Deutsche Volksliste (the German People's List) and were therefore either working for or sympathetic to the German occupier. In theory those eligible to sign up to the Volksliste were Polish citizens of German ethnicity and ancestry with varying degrees of attachment to the German cause. This did not apply in all cases as some Poles chose to sign up in order to improve their lot. In general we referred to all those on the Volksliste as *Volksdeutsche* and regarded them as traitors. By signing up, they were afforded certain material benefits such as access to German-only shops. In exchange they were required to spy on the local population. I understand that they were also subject to German military conscription. Statistics I have read subsequently suggest there were around 15,000 *Volksdeutsche* in Warsaw. It was easy to spot a German soldier in uniform but as civilians the *Volksdeutsche* were invisible and hence we feared them the most. Their collaboration ranged from merely reporting unusual activity to informing about specific members of the underground, Jews in hiding and those helping them. Many people lost their lives due to betrayal by *Volksdeutsche*. The AK tried to counter their threat with various tactics, which ranged from minor undermining activities such as those I engaged in, to the ultimate punishment in specific cases.

A few Polish girls fraternised with the Germans. These were also regarded as *Volksdeutsche* regardless of whether they had signed up to the Volksliste. They were often dealt minor punishments like having their heads shaved. They could easily cover up by wearing headscarves, which were part of normal attire in those days. One of my friends from primary school who lived off Ujazdowskie Boulevard near the German administrative district told me that her older sister was in a relationship with a German soldier. She even sounded somewhat boastful about the benefits this brought her family, including access to places reserved for Germans only. I recall seeing her sister once, she was a fine-looking girl. I decided not to report her sister to the underground out of loyalty to my friend. Even if my friend was gaining from the situation it wasn't her fault and it was also possible that her sister was working for the AK as a spy. Nevertheless hearing about this girl's fraternising changed the way I regarded my old friend from that moment onwards. I would see her for the last time during the Uprising.

Sometimes I was told to paint a slogan on a shop front urging people to boycott the shop because it was being frequented by Germans. There was some injustice in this: a barber, for example, would have no option but to cut a German's hair if so commanded. Nevertheless people would boycott these businesses as civilians were also hostile to anybody deemed to have interaction with the occupier. For our part, we had our orders.

One day I was ordered to stick a poster on a wall next to a barber shop which was frequented by Germans. The poster read '*Niemcy kaput, niech zyje Polska*' ('Germany is broken, long live Poland'). I took the poster out of my bag and moved quickly towards the wall. Just at that moment the shop door opened and out came a man in German uniform. The man looked around then saw me standing there like a stone, frozen with fear. He spoke to me in perfect Polish and said, "Run away, girl, and best you take greater care in future because next time it could be much worse for you." Looking back, I am absolutely sure that he was one of our own dressed in German uniform who had been spying on the Germans in the barber shop, listening out for loose talk. Nevertheless I was a nervous wreck and it took a few days to regain my courage.

On a couple of occasions I was also instructed to deliver money to the family of an AK girl who had been arrested or killed, to help them get by. In such cases a request would be made by one of the seniors to the AK treasury and money would be passed down. I think this money came from the Polish government-in-exile in London. Miki would then give me the money with instructions to make contact with the family and arrange a suitable drop-off time. The system was well established so that the families knew some financial help would come at some point. The families of deceased girls would receive a bit more. My role in these cases was only to deliver the money; I did not need to know the family or anything about the girl's background.

From my very first mission until the last I was constantly afraid all the time. If I were caught I would be interrogated and I doubted whether I could hold out under the pressure of interrogation. I may have been only a young girl with limited knowledge about the underground but I knew enough to put others at risk. Once the Gestapo got a lead they would pursue it as far as possible and people would normally die as a result. I also knew that I was putting my own family at great risk: if I had been caught they would also have been taken to Gestapo headquarters for interrogation. Even if the Gestapo decided that I had little to tell, if I were caught with propaganda I would not return home. Most likely I would have been passed through the Pawiak prison and onto a concentration camp somewhere. Despite the many risks, like all of Warsaw's youth I was driven by a sense of duty, defiance and what was right. We all so desperately wanted to be rid of this brutal oppressor. It has never been in my character to be told what to do; I thought, "Why should I have to accept others coming to my country and doing as they please to us, especially these criminals?"

Instinct became crucial to survival. I recall hearing about two of our boys who would often play their piano at home. While they were out on errands some German soldiers arrived at their home looking for them. The boys' mother said they were not at home and so the Germans waited for them.

As the boys approached home they could hear somebody playing the piano and, as their mother could not play, they knew immediately something was wrong. One of the waiting Germans had decided to take the opportunity to practise on the piano. Sensing danger, the boys turned away and escaped.

Whenever Germans visited one of our locations it would be deemed 'burnt' and not used again for underground activities. Our many AK underground printing presses which printed information and propaganda were constantly under threat of detection. If there was a suspicion that a location had been compromised, the people and machinery would be swiftly moved to another hideout. This was not always successful and many brave conspirators lost their lives as a result.

The need for absolute secrecy meant that we operated in small units with only very limited contact with girls from different Bees. Occasionally I took part in joint missions or met other girls on educational trips to the woods but overall I had frequent contact with only a very small number of people. I knew that other girls in my school were involved in the Conspiracy but apart from Krysia I did not know which ones and such matters were never discussed.

I had joined the Grey Ranks at a savage time. By the end of 1943 the population of Warsaw was reeling in utter shock and perpetual terror from the brutality of the occupation. The tide of war had changed following the German defeat at Stalingrad in February 1943, making the Germans feel increasingly insecure. The AK heightened this insecurity by increasing its activities. The final deportations from the Jewish Ghetto had taken place in May and the Germans then escalated their viciousness and brutality against the rest of Warsaw. To add to our misery that year, the Germans had uncovered mass graves at Katyn in Russia. The graves were full of Polish officers, each of whom had been shot in the back of the head. The Germans claimed these murders dated back to 1940, before their attack against Russia, and therefore they attached the blame to the Soviets. Throughout 1943 we also heard of atrocities by ethnic Ukrainians against Poles in German-occupied Eastern Poland, although the scale of these crimes would not emerge until much later. The feeling that Poland as a nation was being annihilated grew ever stronger.

One constant exercise of German terror which became part of everyday life for the population of Warsaw was called *łapanki*. The word means the action of catching, and this random mass round-up of civilians had begun taking place in Poland as early as 1942. The Germans would appear in numbers without warning and encircle a street, square, courtyard, tram or railway carriage. The trapped civilians would then be packed standing onto tarpaulin-covered trucks, around 50 people in each. We called these trucks *budas* (dog kennels).

In the early days these *łapanki* were directed against those likely to offer organised resistance to the Germans, either as members of the underground or the intelligentsia, and at Jews who had managed to remain outside the ghetto. The fate of these groups was normally to be transported to concentration camps and imprisoned or simply murdered. Gradually the escalating need for manual labour to support Germany's war effort meant that large numbers of Poles were simply taken into forced labour in Germany. Unlike in other occupied countries, the Germans accepted that the uncooperative Poles could not be coerced into voluntary work. The few who did volunteer included AK spies. This increasing need for workers led to a massive increase in the frequency of *łapanki*. Victims would be taken from Warsaw wearing only the clothes on their backs and their families were left to guess why their loved ones had not come home. As underground resistance grew during the year, these *łapanki* were increasingly used to terrorise the civilian population as retribution for their defiance.

Throughout the war nearly two million Poles were deported to Germany for forced labour in this way. Between 1942 and 1944 in Warsaw alone, *łapanki* claimed 400 victims on average every day. On 19th September 1942, nearly 3,000 were taken in a single day.

In the earlier years of occupation I had not been too aware of *łapanki*. Nowy Świat was a fairly narrow road and did not have many open spaces; this had been a slightly more upmarket part of town before the war and not a place where crowds formed. Many parts of Nowy Świat had also been badly damaged during the bombing in 1939. My mother made sure that Henia and I didn't wander too far afield and she would tell us to be always on guard as the Germans were taking people from the streets. Having spent the 1942–43 academic school year at home, I was even more sheltered in my area. Occasionally I had heard people talking about others being rounded up but it hadn't seemed very close to home at the time.

Having joined my school in 1943 and joined the Grey Ranks not long after, I started travelling further from home. I was soon aware I was more exposed and at risk. On two occasions in early 1944 I finally experienced *łapanki* first hand and came close to being caught myself. Early one afternoon I was in a large courtyard surrounded by residential buildings. There was only one access driveway for vehicles into this open area, which otherwise was closed to traffic. Suddenly a German truck appeared at speed with around five soldiers sitting in the back. People around me started running and shouting. I was near the far end of the courtyard when I saw the truck and the commotion. I saw some people beckoning to me as they ran into a partial gap between two buildings so I followed them. As the gap reached a dead-end we surged through a door into the building and hurried along the ground floor. Thankfully there was another exit on the other side of the building which we used to get outside. From there we disappeared in various directions. About two months later I was walking along when people started shouting "*Buda, buda* coming". This early warning gave me and the others around me just enough time to escape again. On both occasions I was utterly terrified.

The increase in German hostility and the growing sense that we were all being annihilated caused a rapid rise in the young flocking to join the AK. Membership grew rapidly but the inevitable consequence was a vicious circle of brutality, resistance and retribution.

In order to counter the ever-growing *łapanki*, two special units consisting of older boys from the Grey Ranks were formed in the early autumn of 1943. One unit was called Agat – derived from Anti-Gestapo. The name was subsequently changed to Pegasus and finally renamed Parasol (Umbrella) in 1944. Parasol specialised in assassinating German officials who were deemed particularly barbaric. Lists were drawn up of German leaders and those responsible for organising *łapanki* and torture. Underground AK courts then tried these Germans as well as known collaborators and criminals who blackmailed Jews and any Poles who were protecting them. If a death sentence was declared for crimes against Polish citizens, Parasol would then carry out these sentences. My friend Krysia, 'Kali', went on from the Executive Group to join Parasol.

The other special unit was named the Zośka Battalion after the leader of the Rudy breakout attempt in early 1943 and was formed from the Grey Ranks unit that had orchestrated that attack. Zośka specialised in breaking prisoners out of captivity, including attacks against convoys transporting prisoners from interrogation at the Gestapo offices on Szucha Street to the Pawiak prison.

During my time with the Grey Ranks, information would increasingly pass down to me through the AK grapevine. I would frequently hear about successful resistance operations, attacks on German transportation links, assassinations and attempts to free AK members from captivity. Such information about notable successes helped maintain morale within the AK and reminded everybody, not least the Germans, that Poland was fighting back.

The Germans responded with ever greater terror. This escalation was clear for all to see, though I wasn't particularly aware that it coincided with the arrival in Warsaw of Franz Kutschera. SS-Brigadeführer Franz Kutschera was appointed head of the SS and Police in the District of Warsaw in September 1943 in response to escalating AK resistance. He had already distinguished himself by the fanatical suppression of resistance in Belarus. His arrival in Warsaw heralded the beginning of the next phase of terror in Warsaw.

In an attempt to quell unrest and to turn the civilian population against the AK, łapanki were dramatically increased and the terror tactic of mass street executions was introduced under Kutschera's leadership. Executions of Poles had commenced immediately from the start of the occupation but with a few exceptions these were mostly out of sight. Kutschera's new policy was to make such executions public as a regular event. Groups of maybe 20 people at a time, some taken indiscriminately in łapanki, were brought out onto the streets of Warsaw, where they were shot. After the first few executions the victims were always gagged to stop them shouting patriotic chants. After the executions Jewish prisoners left behind in Warsaw for clean-up operations were forced to load the bodies onto trucks, hose the blood away and cover the street with sand. The places of execution were then initially cleared of onlookers but soon afterwards people would gather and say a prayer, light candles and perhaps lay some flowers. Soon after the Germans would display the names of those executed on pillar boxes which stood on pavements and were used for displaying information. It was stated that the executions were punishment for acts of resistance by the AK.

Wherever I travelled around Warsaw I saw flowers and candles on the pavements denoting recent execution sites. I would stop momentarily and make the sign of the cross, though I didn't linger as I could never be sure it was safe. There were a few execution sites close to my home, two in particular were just a few doors down from our entrance at 57 Nowy Świat. Outside number 49, 20 people were killed on 12th November 1943. On 2nd December between 34 and 50 people were shot outside number 64.

These *łapanki* and executions became virtually a daily event and caused great panic among the civilian population. German street patrols increased substantially and not just streets but whole areas were cordoned off during *łapanki*. Nobody was safe. Yet although there was a clear increase in terror against the population, to me this did not seem very different from the way in which we had already been forced to live.

In January 1944, Ala and Filipek from our Executive Group were arrested together. I had met Filipek a number of times in the street while on operations; I had only heard about Ala. Ala was caught in possession of underground publications that were due to be distributed among her Bee colleagues. Filipek only had a distribution list on her, which fortunately she was able to swallow before being searched. These arrests put the Group in jeopardy; extra precautions were taken and some of the girls went into hiding. News reached us through the network that after interrogation at Gestapo headquarters in Szucha Street, the girls were taken to the Pawiak prison. Ala had been badly tortured, Filipek a little less. While at Szucha Street, before interrogation, the girls took an opportunity to agree their story. They claimed that they didn't know each other and only happened to be in the same place by complete coincidence. They were then able to maintain this story during interrogation which probably saved Filipek from more severe torture, particularly as she had no incriminating evidence on her. Ala was not so lucky.

I did not have to be on the AK grapevine to hear about the most famous assassination of all. For the many atrocities he committed against the people of Warsaw, Kutschera was sentenced to death by an underground AK court. An audacious plan to assassinate him was put in place and successfully implemented on 1st February 1944 when Kutschera's car was intercepted shortly after leaving his residence on the way to the SS head-quarters.

Many years later I would meet a man named Andrzej Uszycki in London. Andrzej explained to me how, as a teenager, he was tasked with timing German car movements in and out of Szucha Street and along Ujazdowskie Boulevard. His vehicle timings were used in the planning and implemen-tation of the Kutschera assassination, carried out by his AK platoon, Rafał, which was part of the Konrad Battalion.

News of Kutschera's assassination spread round the city very quickly but, along with the initial joy, there was also the fear of the inevitable retribution. The day following Kutschera's assassination 100 Polish civilians were publicly executed. More executions followed over the next two weeks. Two days after Kutschera's assassination the streets of Warsaw were cleared for his funeral procession, which was conducted in silence. That same day Ala was taken from the Pawiak prison and executed in the ruins of the ghetto, one of 13 Polish women killed that day. She was 19 years old. The following month Filipek was transferred from the Pawiak to Ravensbrück concentration camp for women.

Soon after Kutschera's assassination in early 1944, news reached us that my priest and family friend Father Jan Paszyna had been arrested and was being held at the Pawiak prison. I suspect that like many other priests, he was involved in helping the underground. Father Paszyna was still a teacher at my school so, perhaps naively, a few of us organised a collection for him, to which some of the girls contributed food and clothes. We packed up the items and set off with a couple of friends to the Pawiak. In reality this was a hopeless attempt to help. We weren't allowed to see Father Paszyna and all we could do was leave the parcel with the guards in the main office.

I have no idea if he ever received our package but I doubt that he did. Fortunately this was the only time I was in the Pawiak prison. Given the fate of most victims that passed through that place I always assumed the worst for Father Jan Paszyna. I wouldn't find out what actually happened to him until many years later.

The notorious Pawiak (Peacock) Gestapo prison stood on the grounds of the former Jewish Ghetto. Throughout the occupation approximately 100,000 people had been imprisoned in the Pawiak. A large proportion of these were women; most were members of the AK, political prisoners or simply those taken captive in random street round-ups. Approximately 37,000 of the inmates were murdered and 60,000 sent to concentration camps.

I heard in later years how the underground established a communication link with the prisoners in the Pawiak which enabled information to be passed outside. This link was mainly through scribbled messages which were called *gripsy* and written by prisoners. The notes passed along a chain of Polish prison guards and were smuggled out by Polish nurses and other prison workers despite the close scrutiny of German guards. Quite often this process was successful but if someone was caught the Germans would administer severe punishment to large numbers of prisoners. This was meant as a deterrent but had little success stopping the practice.

My mother had been unaware of my involvement in the Conspiracy but in April this changed. I was asked by another Bee squad to help hide a large amount of propaganda material packed into cardboard boxes and it was suggested that the ruined building in which I lived would be ideal; the upper floors had been badly damaged and nobody went up there. I agreed to this and so a few of us girls, perhaps three of us, sneaked up to the top floor – I think it was the fifth – carrying a box each. I didn't look into my box but one of my co-conspirators, Iga, said that her box was full of copies of the now famous book, *Kamienie na Szaniec*. We pushed the boxes into cavities which we thought were good hiding places and covered them with rubble so that they couldn't be seen. But our movements had been observed. Mr Kaminsky had noticed us sneaking upstairs. After we left he climbed up to see what we had been up to and found our stash.

I came home later that day to find my mother sitting at the table and crying. I had never seen her cry. The occupation had worn her down gradually and she had lost some of her strength and self-assurance. But I had never seen her quite so helpless as now. Her appearance of authority was completely gone and she looked a broken, distraught woman. I was terrified that something had happened and asked why she was crying. "My child, what are you doing?" she said. She then explained that Mr Kaminsky had called round to tell her about his find. He told her that I was hiding banned material and that I was undoubtedly involved in the underground. She said that Kaminski had left her with an ultimatum, that either I remove the boxes or he would report me to the Germans. There was no point in denial or pretence and so I confessed. It was an emotional moment. My mother did not raise her voice throughout but something had changed forever. I had the impression that she was caught in an internal conflict, that she knew something had to be done about the occupation but that she did not want her daughter and the family to be at greater risk. She urged me to consider carefully what the consequences of my actions might be. But I also sensed an air of resignation, that she knew she could no longer influence or determine my actions. I think she already knew that I would not leave the Conspiracy.

The next day I gathered a few of the girls and we moved the boxes to another location. They did not complain, they understood the situation and accepted it as part of the life we were leading. I told my mother that the boxes were gone and we did not speak any more about it. From that moment onwards she watched me like a hawk, all the time until the Uprising. I had to be more devious in my activities but nothing could stop me from performing my duty. The next time I saw Mr Kaminski he made a point of explaining that he had to protect his wife and four children, that he had no choice. I understood this and there was no argument. I don't know if he would have actually followed through with his threat. Henia had not been present during the discussion with my mother but I'm sure she was told and understood. She knew that the young were agitating. But from that day onwards my family lost something: the little sense of security that we had had.

My mother's decline in spirit was sad to see but easy to understand. The regular smuggling trips which she continued to make were a great strain on her nerves. Trying to provide food for us and pay for my education must have been a constant source of worry to her. But her decline was typical of the population at large. 1943 had been a year of hell and by 1944 all of Warsaw was traumatised by the horrors of occupation. People seemed to me to be increasingly depressed and at breaking point.

It seemed it was only a matter of time until we would all be murdered. Even if the Germans were forced to retreat from Warsaw, I thought they would massacre us before leaving. We had to take action rather than passively waiting for our end; for many of us there was no other choice but to fight. The young who rushed to join the underground army as I had done were not ideologically driven. We all wanted a free and independent Poland but primarily we just wanted to survive. In this sense there was no difference between the AK and the civilian population. In addition, the civilians were not somehow different to us AK members in Warsaw, they were our families, our relatives and friends. The Germans may have tried to turn the civilians of Warsaw against the AK with terror tactics but this could never have worked. Finally it was simply not in our nature as Poles to submit passively, so everybody in the city supported the resistance.

When you look at the causes of the Warsaw Uprising, it is crucial to understand Warsaw's mindset at the time rather than focusing on whether the military strategy or timing was right. The Germans had pushed us Poles beyond the point of no return and we were desperate to overthrow the occupier. Open conflict was inevitable.

In his book *Rising '44*, published in 2004, historian Norman Davies writes; 'evidence that emerged after the war from Nuremberg [trials] confirmed the worst suspicions of the Poles, up to 85 percent of Poles deemed unsuitable for Germanisation were destined for liquidation or for expulsion to Siberia.' This view is based on the Nazi Generalplan Ost (Master Plan for the East), which came to light at Nuremberg. Details of other plans also emerged, such as The Pabst Plan, which envisioned destroying virtually the whole of Warsaw and building in its place a provincial German model town. The new town would house 130,000 ethnic

Germans on the west side of the Vistula river and 80,000 Polish slave labourers on the east side. The remaining 1.2 million Poles were to be removed or liquidated.

After the war information also came to light about 50,000 to 200,000 'suitable' Polish children who had been forcibly taken from their parents to be sent to families in Germany for Germanisation. Those who failed subsequent 'suitability' inspections were murdered; many of the others never returned home.

Wira in 1935 aged six.

Wira's mother, Maria Banaszek.

Wira in 1938 aged nine.

Henia in 1941 aged 15.

Father Jan Paszyna and Henia, 1942.

59 Nowy Świat after the 1939 bombing. Wira's home was next door at number 57.

View along Świętokrzyska Street towards the Prudential building in 1939. The bombing created access to Wira's building, part way down on the left.

Early days of the occupation, showing German soldiers opposite Wira's home on Nowy Świat. The Church of the Holy Cross tower is in the distance.

German troops marching along Wilcza Street in City Centre South during the occupation.

Some of the 1,700 Polish victims blindfolded before being executed at Palmiry on the edge of Kampinos Forest, near Laski, between 1939 and 1941.

Paying the price for resistance in Warsaw, inmates from the Pawiak prison executed in February 1944 during Franz Kutschera's vicious regime.

Kotwica (anchor) – AK symbol meaning 'Poland is fighting' painted by the resistance.

'Germany is broken' graffiti painted by the resistance during the occupation.

Colleagues from the Grey Ranks Executive Group, from left to right: 'Grażka', 'Ala' who was executed on the day of Franz Kutschera's funeral, and Krysia Biernacka, 'Kali', who recruited Wira.

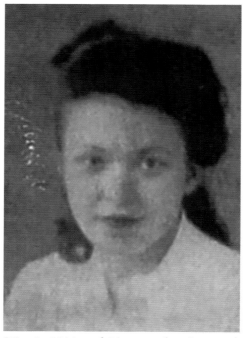

Wira in 1944 aged 14, soon after she joined the resistance.

The all-female Grey Ranks Executive Group Wira is in the centre wearing a white shirt. Next to Wira is her 'Squirrels' colleague 'Iga'. Above them is their unit leader 'Miki'.

Chapter 4

THE WARSAW UPRISING

From about May 1944 I knew the Uprising was approaching. The whole atmosphere in the city had changed. There seemed to be fewer Germans patrolling the streets and those there were stuck together in groups and seemed less confident. I had the impression that they were cowering a little as if they knew something was about to happen. The war was going badly for the Germans and they no longer seemed invincible. In July my mother returned from a trip to Laski and told us that she had seen two dead Germans lying in the street on the outskirts of Warsaw. It seemed to her that the usual commotion leading to reprisals was not taking place and that the balance of power was shifting; ordinary Poles were becoming bolder while the Germans were losing their stranglehold. I was being given ever more leaflets saying *Niemcy Kaput* (Germany is broken) to display around the streets of Warsaw.

In the run-up to the Uprising the war was unfolding on many fronts in many ways – some of which I heard about, some of which I didn't and some I couldn't fully comprehend. Information was sketchy and I was too young to understand the bigger political and military issues. In May I knew that our Polish army was fighting abroad at Monte Cassino, which gave me some comfort. I didn't know until much later how important their role was in the final victory at that impregnable monastery fortress. I knew that the 1st Independent Polish Parachute Brigade in Scotland was waiting to help us liberate Poland. I knew that the Allies had opened the Western Front in June although I did not know how far away they were or how it was going. I did not know about the assassination attempt on Hitler in July, although clearly others did as it added to speculation about the imminent collapse of the Third Reich. I was equally oblivious to large numbers of trains passing

through Warsaw carrying hordes of wounded German soldiers back from
the Eastern Front.

I knew little of the Tehran Conference held at the end of 1943 when
our allies sacrificed our independence to the Soviets. One day this act of
betrayal would explain many of my questions about the imminent fate of
Poland and the Uprising. I heard that in July the Soviets had set up the
Lublin Committee but I understood little of its significance. This Lublin
Committee was a provisional puppet Polish government set up in Soviet-
occupied Polish territory in direct opposition to the Polish government-in-exile in London. In July everybody knew the Soviets were very
close to Warsaw. It was also well known that advancing Soviet troops in
Eastern Poland were initially joining forces with AK partisans to fight
the Germans and subsequently arresting them. Suspicions about the
Soviet Union's responsibility for the mass graves at Katyn were high. It
was certainly impossible to forget the 'stab in the back' in 1939 when the
Soviets had invaded Poland from the east only 17 days after the Germans
had invaded from the West, carving Poland in half. It was made clear by
our leadership that we should receive the Soviets only as guests in our city
rather than as our liberators.

Towards the end of July 1944 we heard of many Soviet calls for the Poles
in Warsaw to rise up against the occupiers, promising that the Red Army
was coming to our aid. We didn't have access to a radio so I didn't hear the
renowned appeal from Soviet-controlled radio:

> Citizens of Warsaw, to arms! The whole population should
> support as one man the National Council and the under-
> ground army. Attack the Germans, prevent the plan of
> destroying public buildings. Help the Red Army in its efforts
> to cross the Vistula!

The Soviet calls to arms were supplemented by leaflets dropped from
the sky. I saw these leaflets and glanced through them but, like most Poles,
I had absolutely no trust in the Soviets after everything they had done and
continued to do. Our AK leadership had to decide how to respond to these

calls to arms but I always suspected we could not count on Soviet help and this view was to prove sadly correct.

On 27th July the Germans called for 100,000 Polish men between the ages of 17 and 65 to report for work at several gathering places in Warsaw the following day. They were to dig trenches and to construct fortifications against a Soviet attack. Virtually nobody turned up for this work. By this point nobody cared about German orders; the Uprising was imminent and people no longer seemed afraid of possible retribution. If the Germans had tried to impose some sort of collective punishment for this snub then it would have been opposed. Perhaps this might have brought the Uprising forward by a few days but otherwise such an order would have been an impotent gesture and the Germans knew this.

The mood in the city darkened dramatically. The air was thick with apprehension and there were few Germans on the streets. It was just a matter of time before the Uprising broke out. It had been a hot summer and that last weekend of July was no different. Despite their fears, people made the most of the weather by strolling through the parks and enjoying picnics. That Sunday 30th July, the churches were packed as usual.

The following day, in anticipation of the inevitable Uprising, a friend of mine and I decided to bury our scouts' crosses. We chose a place near the corner of Wiejska and Prusa Streets, just beyond Three Crosses Square. This area was near a lot of official buildings such as embassies, many of which had been commandeered by the Germans for the administration of Warsaw. Because of this we thought the area would be inaccessible and therefore might avoid much of the destruction which was about to come. We hid the crosses under rubble in a ruined building and marked the spot, hoping and intending to return in a few days to collect them.

BAYONETS

Tuesday 1st August arrived. I went out early in the morning to see if there was any news. I met with one of the girls from the Executive Group and was given orders to report by 5pm that day to 28 Świętokrzyska Street in City Centre North, which I later discovered was to be a second Grey Ranks headquarters. I was not surprised to receive these orders; it was not necessary to ask their occasion as it was obvious to me. I was overjoyed as I had been longing for this day with all the courage and naivety of my youth. The Warsaw Uprising was about to begin.

When I returned home my mother announced that she had decided that we should go to Laski for a few days, probably sensing that something was about to happen. This decision forced my hand and I desperately tried to talk her into allowing me to visit a friend first. She eventually agreed on the condition that Henia escorted me. I was sure that by now Henia knew about my involvement in the Conspiracy. As we turned the corner outside our building I stopped and said to her, "Henia, you know I won't go to Laski; I have to go to Danusia's apartment first and then we are going to the Uprising together." Henia's unsurprised reaction confirmed to me that she did already know about my involvement. I continued, "Take care of Mother!" Henia responded simply, "Of course I will, I won't leave Mother on her own." We walked together a little further to the main street where I said, "We'll see each other later." "Keep well," said Henia before we kissed and hugged each other goodbye. It still hurts that I never said goodbye to my mother. Later that day my mother and Henia would make their way to Laski without me.

I had just turned 15 years old. I was naive and had little concept of how things might turn out. I had been told that the fighting would only last a few days and as it was a very hot month I wore only summer sandals and a summer dress. My dress was made of cotton, light-coloured with a floral pattern. My hair was plaited. Full of youthful optimism, I believed we would prevail. I had no idea about warfare or about our military strength but it seemed to me that all of Warsaw was involved or behind us. I trusted in our leadership and I believed that we were invincible. I felt prepared for anything that might come.

I was sure that our Western Allies and Polish forces stationed overseas would come to our support. I hoped that the Red Army would soon cross the Vistula river and help us fight the common enemy in Warsaw, although I didn't have too much faith in this. We were all fighting the same enemy and surely it made sense for the Soviets to take advantage of a Polish uprising to drive the Germans out of Warsaw, thus easing the route for their advance towards Berlin? Above all, surely America and Britain would apply as much pressure as necessary on Stalin to do something to support us? It seemed inconceivable that the Soviets would not help us in some way. But I knew without a doubt that, after the years of brutal occupation and underground resistance, the Uprising simply had to happen, and I was filled with great joy, optimism and determination.

The beginning of the Warsaw Uprising was set for 'W' hour, which was 5pm on 1st August 1944. 'W' stood for *wolność* (freedom), and to this day this moment is officially recognised as the onset of hostilities.

It was early afternoon as I made my way to Danusia's apartment on Chmielna Street. I had tried previously to recruit Danusia into the Grey Ranks but as her father had recently died and she was an only child she felt obliged to stay safe on account of her mother. But, like many other civilians, as the Uprising drew near Danusia wanted to be involved. Soon after I reached her apartment we heard the first sounds of gunfire. Fighting had broken out prematurely at the technical college nearby, just round the back of Chmielna Street. Apparently the Germans had spotted some of the students gathering with hidden weapons. To get to Świętokrzyska meant running right past the college and Danusia seemed uncertain about attempting this. I agreed to wait for a while until there was a better opportunity to move and because I sensed Danusia was wavering. I wanted to give her as much time as she needed in the hope that she would come with me. A few hours passed and it started to get dark, at which point Danusia suggested we spend the night at her house and leave in the morning. Her mother prepared a meal. Afterwards when we were alone, before we lay down to sleep, Danusia gave me the news which I had been hoping not to hear. "Listen," she said, "I can't go with you tomorrow, I can't leave my mother on her own." I wasn't surprised by her decision but I was disappointed. I felt that with Danusia by my side it would be much easier to deal with the fear of what lay ahead, and I lay awake for a while that night, listening to some more gunfire and feeling alone and uncertain. Early the next morning I left the house by myself and headed towards my post, following the sound of heavy fighting which had already begun that day.

My base at Świętokrzyska 28 was about 500 metres from Chmielna and my route took me along Szpitalna Street, which led onto the long and narrow Napoleon Square. At the north end of the square, running perpendicular, was Świętokrzyska Street. Number 28 Świętokrzyska was but a short distance away on the other side of the road, by the north-west corner, overlooking the square. On the east side of the square nearer to me stood the main Post Office, heavily defended by the well-entrenched Germans. To my left, opposite the Post Office, stood residential buildings, some of which had been devastated by earlier bombing.

Heavy fighting was already raging when I reached the square and bullets were flying from all directions, particularly from the Post Office. With the pavement on my left impassable due to debris, I realised that I would now have to run quite a distance through the middle of the square along the front of the Post Office to reach my base.

It is hard to describe my first experience of war other than to say that it was overwhelmingly petrifying. I had contemplated what it might be like in the security of my own mind but the reality was beyond any of my imaginings. Even the bombing of 1939 had not prepared me for this. Back then I was just a little girl and although I had been scared, I had the comfort of having my family and others around me. I had thought that at least Danusia would be by my side, but here I was, early in the morning, alone and about to enter a cauldron. A heart-stopping and stomach-wrenching noise of battle filled the air with menace. Would this be my last moment of life? The feeling was indescribable.

I had just entered the square when there was a tremendous explosion to my left and I saw an image that has haunted me all my life. A bomb had just hit a large building, causing it to collapse, and there amid the fresh ruins, about one floor up from the ground, lay an old lady partly covered with rubble. The lady's clothes had been completely blown off. She lay with arms outstretched, hair standing on end, her body wounded all over, barely alive. I will never forget that look of complete wildness in her eyes.

There was no time to stop and I continued running for about 100 metres through the square as fast as I could, looking straight ahead. I kept my head down as low as possible in an attempt to avoid the bullets coming from my right. I made it to the north end of the square past Warsaw's tallest building, the Prudential, which our boys had taken in battle the previous day. Crossing over Świętokrzyska, I arrived at my designated meeting point at number 28. The Uprising already held much of Świętokrzyska from Napoleon Square all the way to Marszałkowska Street to the west. To the east was a battle zone leading towards Nowy Świat, still held by the Germans. As I ran across, bullets were flying from the direction of my old home.

By the time I got to number 28, many of the girls were already there. Some had arrived the day before and others were still arriving. Some didn't make it at all. Despite the heavy fighting raging outside, I was immediately struck by the spirit of great joy and optimism among our gathering. There were smiles and laughter and everybody was busy preparing the base for various functions.

From our building we had a good view across Napoleon Square and of the main Post Office which stood about 150 metres away on the left. I could see the battle for the Post Office as it began early that afternoon – it was like watching a film. A group of about fifteen AK men and at least two women from the Kiliński Battalion emerged wearing the red-and-white armbands of the Uprising. They made their long way from Świętokrzyska towards the big metal gate that guarded the small courtyard in front of the Post Office building. The group moved slowly, all hunched to avoid the fusillade coming from the German defenders in the Post Office. Once the boys from Kiliński reached the gate, a fierce gun battle took place. They tried to force the gate open with only a low wall for protection from German bullets. Our boys were poorly armed; only a few had rifles, some had pistols and I think they had a few homemade grenades which we called *filipinki*. We were all amazed at and filled with admiration for their pure courage and determination. The Germans defended themselves fiercely as our fighters threw everything they had at them while trying to force open the gate. Suddenly after about an hour I heard a roaring "Hoorah!" as the gate swung open and our soldiers surged across the courtyard into the building. Our euphoria on seeing this was immense: it seemed as if nothing could stop them. After that, the battle was over very quickly. The Post Office was captured; the

Germans were relieved of their weapons and taken prisoner. I know that the Kiliński Battalion recovered 300 rifles, numerous pistols, grenades, ammunition, food and fuel from the Post Office.

FIELD POST OFFICE

Everybody in our building worked tirelessly for the Uprising as our boys and some of our older girls fought on the front line, which was always just outside or around the corner. At first cooking facilities were quickly organised in order to feed the fighters in our area. We also began putting into place initial arrangements for a field postal service. This was necessary to allow civilians and AK combatants to maintain contact with their families and loved ones in Warsaw and was organised by the Grey Ranks.

In due course there would be 40 letter boxes placed around Warsaw and seven sorting offices, the main one being in Napoleon Square. Boys aged between 12 and 14 belonging to the youngest section of the Grey Ranks, called Zawisza, would collect and bring in the letters, which would be sorted onto shelves according to region and street. The boys would then endeavour to deliver the letters to the intended recipients. There was never any shortage of these determined and eager young Zawiszas for the task. After the first week, postmarks were created – the first of which, I have since discovered, was carved from a potato cut in half. Eventually there would be ten different postmarks made from more robust materials. Later, in early September, the postal service would come under direct command of the AK and the name would be changed from the Grey Ranks Post to the AK Field Post. Five official AK stamps came into use with different colours, each denoting one of the liberated regions of Warsaw. On average throughout the Uprising, 5,000 letters were delivered per day; the record was 10,000 on 13th August. In total about 200,000 letters were delivered during the 63 days of the Uprising. I later learned that many letters failed to reach their destination due to buildings having been bombed, the recipients no longer being traceable or the letter boys not being able to complete their journeys. Years later, many unopened letters sent during the Uprising were still being recovered from the ruins of Warsaw.

I have subsequently seen a photograph of myself taken in the early days of the Uprising in the initial sorting office at Świętokrzyska with some of the girls and 'Kuropatwa' who commanded our postal service. I think that to start with there were about six of us in that sorting office before the operation moved to the main Post Office building in Napoleon Square and expanded significantly.

FREE AT LAST

Many of the early battles in my area went our way and we captured more and more buildings. The taking of the Post Office had been significant for our sector as it provided a certain degree of control over Napoleon Square. The Germans still held various buildings in our vicinity, such as the nearby college, but already it seemed certain that we would soon have control on the ground of our small part of Warsaw. By the end of the third day we controlled much of the City Centre North, though there would always be areas which were not completely ours and where it was necessary to take be vigilant.

The atmosphere was joyful and patriotic, though I would not describe it as euphoric as we were under no illusions about the Uprising being over. Again, perhaps naively, I felt that we were invincible. A Polish flag was drapped from the Prudential building and another now fluttered from the main Post Office. We were tasting our first little bit of freedom in five years!

Elsewhere within the first few days of the Uprising we had also gained control of most of the City Centre South, the districts of Żoliborz, the Old Town and the former Jewish Ghetto, Powiśle, Czerniaków, Mokotów and the sub-district of Sadyba. Our attempts to take control of Praga on the eastern side of the Vistula proved impractical; first, because the district was separated from the rest of the AK fighting forces by the river, and secondly, because overwhelming numbers of German troops were gathered there in anticipation of an attack by the Red Army. We failed to capture the bridges over the Vistula river and Okęcie airport. as well as other heavily defended strategic positions throughout the city, which would prove significant.

My knowledge of the respective strengths of the AK and the German forces in Warsaw would grow during the Uprising. I knew that our numbers were large but also that most of us had only limited training, we were clearly poorly armed and many of us were practically still children. I often saw a group of about ten AK boys going off to fight. Three might be carrying rifles, two perhaps a pistol each and maybe a few grenades. The rest would be empty-handed, armed only with their courage and the hope of capturing arms from the enemy. The number of soldiers and armaments have now been documented. At the beginning of the Uprising there were around 47,000 members of the AK in Warsaw, including around 5,000 women. Out of this total, however, only 23,000 were combat-ready and, crucially, fewer than 3,000 were armed. Meanwhile, with reinforcements, the German forces pitted against us in Warsaw soon grew to a total of 30,000 heavily armed soldiers. Some may have been poorly trained but many were battle-hardened and well-entrenched. In support the Germans had tanks and some of the heaviest artillery available in their army, as well as a small number of Stuka dive bomber aircraft. Throughout the Uprising the Germans relied heavily on their overwhelming firepower.

Without further supplies of arms we had barely enough to sustain fighting on the scale of the Uprising for more than a few days. Our stock at the outset consisted of 1,000 rifles, 1,700 pistols, 300 automatic pistols, 60 sub-machine guns, 35 anti-tank guns and PIAT bazookas, 25,000 hand grenades and seven machine guns. For defensive operations we had about 12,000 Molotov cocktails (petrol bombs). We counted on airdrops of arms from our allies, further weapons production by AK workshops in Warsaw and capturing weapons from the enemy. In fact, during the Uprising, AK workshops produced an additional 300 automatic pistols, 150 flamethrowers, 40,000 grenades and a number of mortars and bazookas.

There was hope that AK fighters from outside Warsaw would penetrate the German encirclement of the city to help us. The Kampinos Group were AK partisans living and fighting in the Kampinos Forest, which bordered our country home at Laski in the north-west. Other AK groups were also expected to try to access Warsaw from the Chojnowskie and Kabaty woods in the south. Unfortunately none of the groups were able to make a significant breakthrough. I had also been told that the 1st Polish Independent Parachute Brigade would be flown from Britain to join our fight. I often imagined how wonderful it would be when the Brigade arrived to help us. Sadly that never happened.

MY PERSONAL TRAGEDY

After the first few days of the Uprising, German Stuka ground-attack planes appeared above us, enjoying the freedom of the skies as they strafed Warsaw, dive-bombing low and shooting at anything that moved. They seemed like bloodthirsty bats encircling their prey and sent a chill down my spine. I could hear these Stukas diving overhead and tried to keep well out of their sight. These aerial attacks became a fact of daily life and were a constant threat from then on.

I had been constantly thinking about my mother and sister; I was desperate to know how they were and whether in fact they had gone to Laski as planned. By 5th August, with our immediate area of the City Centre North largely secured and with the heavy fighting in my area having subsided, I decided to seize the moment to run home to see if my family had actually left Warsaw. I ran along Świętokrzyska, not turning into Napoleon Square but heading towards Nowy Świat. This stretch was no man's land. Crouching all the way, I moved swiftly along Świętokrzyska for about 300 metres. I headed towards the German positions, then turned right into the side access and scurried across the courtyard towards my apartment. I later heard this was the route taken by my mother and sister a day earlier.

As I approached my apartment I was surprised to see my Auntie Janka: I'd thought she was in Laski. She was standing at our semi-basement window, which was only a little above ground height, looking out at me as I ran towards her. As I got close she opened the window and beckoned me to climb in through it. I looked around for my mother and sister but I couldn't see them. My world was about to fall apart.

My Auntie started to explain what had happened. My mother had indeed taken Henia to Laski that day but they returned with Janka the following day on what must have surely been the last opportunity to enter Warsaw before it was cut off. Janka's children had stayed in Laski with her mother-in-law. I will never know why my mother and sister returned to Warsaw; I presume it is because they did not want to leave me there alone. The following day, or the day after, my mother and Henia went searching for me, calling at the houses of some of my friends – but to no avail. Janka told me that she was watching from the apartment window when my mother and Henia returned home across the large open courtyard in front of our apartment block. Just then a German Stuka plane flew overhead and dived towards them. They were exposed as the rear gunner pressed the trigger on his machine gun. The first bullets hit my mother in the legs and she fell, unable to continue. Henia was hit in the hand, which was blown off, but she managed to run a little further. She was almost at our apartment when she was shot in the heart and fell dead.

Eventually, as evening descended, it was possible for Janka to come out of the apartment and get to my mother, but she too was dead. With Mr Kaminsky's help she managed to dig a shallow grave. They wrapped the bodies of my mother and sister in sheets and buried them with whatever they could, using sand and rubble from the destroyed buildings. They had died on the fourth day of the Uprising.

Of course I was absolutely devastated. In shock, I couldn't bring myself to go and look at my mother and sister. I was tired and dirty and so I agreed to stay the night with Janka. I recall Janka washing my hair that evening. Before settling down to sleep, she locked the outside door that opened onto the staircase leading down to our semi-basement apartment. We lay down next to each other for the night with me on the wall side of the bed. I felt myself falling asleep as I heard the sound of the outside door being unlocked. Next I listened in terror as footsteps came down the stairs and the door to our apartment opened. Then, whether in pure exhaustion or something else, I fell asleep. When I woke up it was morning; Janka was there and everything in the apartment seemed as it had been the night before. I told Janka what I had heard and asked if somebody had been in our apartment. Janka said she had heard the same sounds and that it had been my mother, that she had come to take me, saying that I was on my own and that it would be better if I went with her. Janka said she argued with my mother and promised she would look after me and that eventually my mother agreed and left. I have absolutely no doubt that I heard those footsteps coming into the apartment and I firmly believe that Janka was telling the truth about her spiritual conversation with my mother. Despite the many near misses I went on to experience, I believe that from that night my mother was always watching over me and that I was destined to live.

That day I returned to my post on Świętokrzyska. I hadn't even thought to change my clothes and summer sandals for something more appropriate for urban warfare as I was too traumatised. Janka stayed in the apartment as there was no way of getting back to her children at Laski now that the city was a war zone. I cried endlessly for the next few days and couldn't see the point of carrying on. For a few days I didn't care about anything; the grief was too great. I would have been happy to die in the Uprising. I had not imagined that my mother and Henia would be taken from me so abruptly.

I kept thinking about a time just three months earlier when I had persuaded Henia to go to the Old Town with me to see a fortune teller. I went first and the teller spent a long time talking to me about going on a long journey far away from my family and my country. When Henia's turn came, the fortune teller said very little, just the obvious things about Henia being a young lady and at school, as if she was hiding something. I had ignored her words at the time but looking back I thought what was and what wasn't said were a sign. I loved Henia so much and I have never stopped missing her badly.

The girls rallied round me, aware of my personal trauma. My former colleague Iga recently told my son that most of the girls would occasionally visit their homes to see their parents, wash and get fed before returning to their duties. Iga's parents lived outside Warsaw – too far away – but at least she knew Miki's parents well and was able to visit them instead. But everybody knew that I had nobody now and the girls made extra efforts to comfort me. They kept me going.

On 6th August our postal operation was moved the short distance from Świętokrzyska to the main Post Office in Napoleon Square. I was stunned with grief and of little use to anybody in those few days. Heavy fighting was taking place in other parts of Warsaw but our area of City Centre North was relatively calm. There was still plenty of shooting coming in our direction from the Germans, particularly at the Polish flag draped from the Prudential building. Yet it was possible to move around a little more freely, particularly in the square and along Świętokrzyska towards Marzsalkowska. I decided to run across the street with a friend to the Prudential to see what was going on there. The ground floor of the Prudential had become a transit and gathering point for the Uprisers. It was essentially a base brimming with activity, with boys and girls mingling. After a while we headed along Świętokrzyska towards Marszałkowska to take a look. When we got to Marszałkowska, we saw an unexpected sight a little way in the distance. There was a group of about 15 or 20 men wearing similar outfits with vertical blue stripes on them. It was the first time I had seen such uniforms but I immediately realised these were Jews, as I had heard that the Germans made their Jewish prisoners wear outfits with such patterns. The group was heading towards us but at some point they turned out of sight and I never saw them again.

When we got back to our area I was able to discover why these Jewish men had been there. After the liquidation of the Jewish Ghetto in 1943, the Germans had installed a concentration camp on the vacated grounds called Gesiówka (Goose Farm). The AK had known that Jewish prisoners were being kept there in order to 'clean up' the former ghetto. The prisoners were forced to perform various unpleasant tasks such as demolishing remaining ghetto buildings, burning corpses, seeking out bunkers where Jews might still be hiding, gathering clothing and searching for hidden valuables. Some of these Jews were also used to clean blood off the streets and dispose of the bodies of Poles murdered in street executions.

In the run-up to the Uprising the Germans had started murdering prisoners at the Pawiak prison as well as some of the Gesiówka Jews. It was feared that the remaining Jews would be eliminated immediately once the Uprising started, so the AK decided to launch a pre-emptive attack against the camp. This took place on 5th August and was undertaken by the Grey Ranks Zośka Battalion. Apparently many of our attackers wore German tunics taken from various raids. After 90 minutes of fierce fighting, the attack was successful and 348 Jewish prisoners were liberated. Eighty-nine of these Jews were Polish citizens; most of the others had been brought in from Greece, Romania, Holland and Hungary. According to subsequent reports, the prisoners had feared the worst at first when they saw these German uniforms and were then elated when it became clear that these were real Polish liberators. Many of the Jews were physically exhausted but some of those who still had enough strength asked to join the Uprising. I believe it was a group of these Jews that I saw as they were being led away to get changed or to join one of the AK units. For whatever reason, this momentary sighting has stayed in my memory.

The wearing of German tunics by AK soldiers became a regular sight during the Uprising due to their practicality. The tunics were camouflaged and lightweight, making them ideal for summer battle. We called these tunics *panterki*. In addition to *panterki* some of the boys started wearing German helmets for protection, although I believe this practice was later banned to avoid errors in identification.

From the beginning, all AK combatants wore distinctive red-and-white armbands, large numbers of which had been made in preparation for the Uprising. I received mine at Świętokrzyska and as I only had a summer dress with loose short sleeves I had to secure the armband in place with a safety pin. At first people wore the armbands on whichever arm they preferred before an order was issued that all armbands were to be worn on the right. I felt a great sense of pride wearing mine.

MASSACRES

From 6th August small numbers of civilians started arriving in City Centre North, bringing disturbing news from the districts of Wola and Ochota which adjoined the City Centre. As the most western of the liberated districts of Warsaw, Wola and Ochota bore the brunt of the first major ground attack by the Germans. The force of the assault meant our fighters were unable to hold out for long and they retreated mainly eastwards to join other units in the Old Town. These civilians who had managed to escape the German onslaught seemed to me to be in a state of utter mental breakdown. They talked of indiscriminate and merciless murdering, raping and looting. The reports described such inhumanity that they were hard to believe. In our minds, although the Germans were brutal, they had generally gone about things systematically and efficiently, not with extreme sadism. People reported seeing drunken young Russian volunteers committing some of these massacres. These Russians were generally refered to as *Własowcy* after the military commander and Russian collaborator, Andriej Własow. The news was worrying and upsetting; it made us angry but not afraid. I would say we felt a sense of security in the City Centre as we felt too well defended for such killing to spread to our area.

With time, more details emerged about this slaughter of civilians. Soon after the outbreak of the Uprising, Heinrich Himmler, head of the SS and Gestapo, had ordered that all of Warsaw's inhabitants were to be killed. No prisoners were to be taken and the city was to be levelled as an example to the rest of occupied Europe. At the time, the area of Warsaw was approximately 130 square kilometres and the remaining population about a million. Of the German units sent into Wola and Ochota, two were particularly infamous for war crimes. The Dirlewanger Brigade was headed by Oskar Dirlewanger and was a special penal unit within the Waffen-SS consisting of criminals convicted of major crimes. Dirlewanger himself was a convicted child molester and rapist. The other was Kaminski's Russian National Liberation Army (RONA), which had been formed from anti-Soviet Russian peasants and integrated into the German army.

On 5th August 1944, mass executions of civilians in Wola began. Accounts tell of civilians being lined up outside their homes and shot en masse while others were herded together and burned alive. Witnesses report seeing babies impaled on bayonets and waved out of windows like flags; women hung upside down from balconies in rows; hospital patients were shot in their beds or dragged outside, along with their doctors and nurses, to be shot. Women were gang raped before being murdered. The list of sickening acts still seems endless. Himmler had hoped that the sheer violence and terror of the onslaught would cause us to surrender quickly. However it quickly became clear that the bloodthirstiness and atrocities of the Dirlewanger and RONA brigades were getting in the way of the military objective. They had become too inhumane and crazed even for the Germans; hence the policy of the systematic murder of all civilians was changed to apply to men only, and was eventually halted altogether on 12th August. In those few days in Wola and Ochota, 50,000 civilians, mainly the elderly, women and children, had been slaughtered.

POWIŚLE

During the occupation the Grey Ranks had a separate command structure from the AK's, although the organisations worked together. Some of our Grey Ranks, such as the Parasol and Zośka units, also belonged to the AK. From the start of the Uprising the entirety of the Grey Ranks became officially integrated into and ultimately under the command of the AK. On 8th August I was issued with an AK pass card which now resides at the Warsaw Uprising Museum. The pass card is headed 'Command of the Armia Krajowa (AK)' and states:

> Citizen Danuta Banaszek "Wira" soldier of the AK under the
> command of the VI Branch of the Staff Office (of the AK)
> fulfils the commissioned function of liaison. All organs of the
> army are called upon to provide help to her.

The pass is stamped by the 'Command of the Armed Forces in the Country' VI Branch, dated 8th August 1944 and signed by 'Opel' (Antoni Nowak-Przygodzki), head of VI Branch – Bureau for Information and Propaganda (BIP). My pass card granted me the right of free movement around the city as it proved to our people that I was not a spy. Throughout the Uprising I carried this pass card with me at all times and displayed it when required.

Although some details are no longer clear in my mind, I believe that around this point I was attached to the newly formed WSS, which stands for 'Wojskowa Slużba Spoleczna' (Military Service for the Community). The WSS consisted primarily of female scouts and was tasked with taking care of the civilian population in any way possible during the Uprising.

Soon, along with five boys and one other girl from the Grey Ranks, I was sent eastwards to a Grey Ranks post on Tamka Street. The post was in the riverside district of Warsaw called Powiśle ('by the Vistula river'). Powiśle was coming under heavy attack from all sides and our positions were under intense pressure. I presume we were being sent there to help the civilians. The boys were all between 17 and 20 years old.

Our route took us through Napoleon Square and along Szpitalna, turning left onto Chmielna Street. As I ran past Danusia's building I wondered if she was sheltering with her mother in the cellar. We crossed Nowy Świat onto Foksal Street. It was safer crossing Nowy Świat here, as the approach from Świętokrzyska was still no man's land and more exposed to shooting from German forces a little way up along Krakowskie Przedmieście. Nevertheless it was still necessary to watch out for shooting, particularly from the BGK building on the right. Once across we we headed back up along Kopernika Street and turned right onto Tamka Street with the sound of gun battles becoming incessant.

Just past the School of Music we arrived at the Grey Ranks post. Once inside, for some reason my group separated and I ended up in a room with just one of the boys. We talked for a bit: I don't know what we were talking about but we were both laughing about something. Then the boy bent over and stuck his head into a wooden coal barrel lying nearby. "What are you doing?" I asked. The boy replied, "When the Germans start shooting again they can shoot me in my backside rather than in my head!" I laughed. Just then a massive bomb hit our building and everything went dark. By the time I regained consciousness it was the middle of the day and we were already heading back to City Centre North.

I remained in a state of confusion for the next few days. I was unable to hear anything for a while and I have very little memory at all of what happened after the bomb hit and for some time afterwards. I have no idea who dug me out of the rubble or how long we had been at the house. I think we must have been there overnight at least, if not longer. I presume we returned to City Centre North because it became hopeless to carry on. A few of us were clearly good for nothing at this point, and two of us had been killed. I don't know for sure if the boy in the barrel had survived, but I suspect not, as I don't recall seeing him again.

I have tried subsequently to fill the gaps in my memory; unfortunately it remains blank, and I have not been able to find anybody who could tell me more about what happened in the few days following the explosion.

The joy that had come with our first taste of freedom now seemed a distant memory. My initial optimism had been cruelly shattered by my personal loss and in some ways I had stopped caring about what the future held for me. The elation was also vanishing for the Uprisers and for the civilians of Warsaw. There was no sign of the 1st Independent Polish Parachute Brigade from Scotland; we now know they had been prevented from coming by the British, who wanted the Brigade on the Western Front. Meanwhile there was no sign of the Soviets on the other side of the Vistula river. It was becoming clear that the Uprising would not be over quickly. Our tragedy was continuing to unfold.

In order to maintain the offensive against the Germans we needed large-scale air supplies of arms from our allies. Due to the distances involved, these airdrops required landing and refuelling facilities. It was at this moment that Soviet intentions towards the Polish nation, already highly questionable, became absolutely clear to the whole world. The Soviets controlled over a hundred airfields within range of Warsaw but they refused allied planes any access to land. I only became aware of this hostile act the following month.

Without landing and refuelling facilities, allied supply flights had to be undertaken from distant bases in southern Italy: Bari, Brindisi and, later, Foggia. The 'Warsaw Airlifts' or 'Warsaw Air Bridge', as the operation came to be called, began officially on 12th August, although a few flights were undertaken earlier. The Polish Special Duties Flight operating within the British Royal Air Force carried out the initial flights. Later missions were in conjunction with British, Australian and New Zealand pilots of

the RAF and with the South African Air Force. The gruelling round trip
was 2,815 kilometres over enemy territory and took about 12 hours. The
carrying weights of the flights had to be light. Once over Warsaw the
drops had to be made at slow speeds and at low level and due to anti-
aircraft defences they had to be done at night. The flights were therefore
extremely hazardous and losses were very high – almost 17 percent of the
186 aircraft that took off from Italy. Some aircrews even reported being
fired at by Soviet planes and batteries near Warsaw when they strayed into
Soviet-controlled airspace.

Once over the Vistula there was no difficulty in finding Warsaw although
the reason for this was macabre. In the words of one SAAF pilot, "the
aircrews became aware of a dim glow on the horizon. As they approached
it would slowly become bigger until it developed into a bright inferno.
This was Warsaw burning." Another observation from years later was that,
"with huge fires burning in Warsaw, it was almost impossible to pick up the
target marker flares." As a result, although these airlifts from Italy managed
to drop over 200 tonnes of supplies throughout the Uprising, most were
behind enemy lines, with only about 45 percent estimated to have made it
into the hands of the Uprisers. These days the airlifts are viewed as having
been politically driven by Winston Churchill to help the Polish people but
with poor military rationale due to the suicidal nature of the flights. The
impact of these heroic flights was ultimately limited in the context of the
scale of the Uprising but it was still significant. In early September the AK
acknowledged receipt of 250 PIAT anti-tank weapons, a thousand Sten
sub-machine guns, 19,000 grenades and two million rounds of ammunition. A debt of honour is owed to these brave pilots.

To supplement the airdrops, the AK weapon factories were producing
as much as possible, while the AK was also adept at capturing arsenal from
the Germans through various raids. Huge numbers of the effective *filipinka*,
the homemade grenades, and petrol bombs were produced in the factories.
Soldiers were ordered to use ammunition sparingly; posters were displayed
urging 'One German, One bullet'. We had the urban cover of destroyed
buildings but it was all too little without outside support.

TROJAN HORSE

Around the middle of August, I was caught in another emotional upheaval when good news from the Old Town turned to tragedy. There were minor celebrations among us when we heard that our boys in the Old Town had captured a small tank intact. Not long after, I was in my base with the girls when a few boys arrived looking distressed. They described how the captured tankette had been brought through the barricade deep into our positions and how crowds of AK and civilians had flocked to it to have a look and enjoy the victory. Suddenly there was a terrible explosion killing hundreds of people and scattering limbs over a wide area. What remained of the surrounding buildings was drenched with blood and human remains. Hearing this hurt us all greatly – particularly given the scale of the catastrophe and the shock of it all after the initial good news. It was also distressing because everybody believed that this had been a Trojan horse trap and we couldn't understand why the Germans needed to resort to such tactics; they had enough military hardware not to need such trickery. I sensed this was another pivotal moment in our Uprising.

I have subsequently learned that the tankette was actually a Borgward IV remote-controlled heavy explosive carrier, one of the first used by the Germans during the Warsaw Uprising. Its purpose was to deliver heavy explosive material, weighing 500 kilograms, with a timed fuse set before departure. More than 300 Polish soldiers and civilians were killed in the explosion and another four or five hundred people wounded.

Around this time, mortar shelling of my area of the City Centre began; the Germans brought in a fearsome multiple rocket launcher, which they fired from the direction of the nearby Saski Park. The Nebelwerfer, nicknamed the 'Moaning Minnie' and 'Screaming Mimi' by the Allies, fired six rockets in succession. As these weapons were fired from forward positions, the sound of the launchers could be clearly heard and brought immediate terror. Upon launch each rocket made the most terrifying grinding or howling sound. The launcher was nicknamed 'Szafa' ('Wardrobe'). I believe this nickname came from the noise a heavy wardrobe might make when being dragged across floorboards. Others called it 'Krowa' ('Cow'), as the noise resembled that of the bellowing of a cow in pain. I have subsequently seen a famous AK warning poster showing a bellowing cow with the slogan, 'When the Cow Bellows, don't stand in the gateway'. There was nowhere to hide from these rockets and anybody caught in their deadly path had no chance. Once you heard the terrifying grinding noise there were only seconds before the rocket hit with devastating destructiveness and no telling where or when the next deadly missile might land. For even greater psychological effect, some of the rockets were also incendiaries, causing fires to break out where they fell. As more and more Nebelwerfers were introduced, the noise and pounding became almost constant. Nobody who experienced it could ever forget the Nebelwerfer; it was probably the most frightening of the German weaponry.

To supplement the onslaught the Germans also brought in the Karl-Gerät mortar – the largest self-propelled weapon in service, weighing 122 tonnes. It measured 11 metres in length, weighed 2,170 kg and was able to deliver 60-centimetre calibre shells from a range of 50 kilometres. Only seven of these heavy guns had been built. As well as tanks the Germans also introduced remote-controlled demolition vehicles that could smash through a barricade then explode. These included the Goliath, otherwise called the 'Beetle Tank', and a larger version named the Borgward IV. With all this terrifying weaponry at their disposal there seemed little doubt that the Germans intended the complete destruction of Warsaw.

Around this time I had my first direct encounter with a German tank. I recall standing on the second floor of a building overlooking Świętokrzyska Street as a tank rolled by just beneath me. One of the boys gave me a petrol bomb to hold; it was a simple bottle filled with petrol and partially wrapped in a rag. The boy lit the fuse which protruded from the neck of my bottle and I threw it down in the direction of the tank. I threw it as quickly as I could, realising that the fuse did not take long to burn. I have no idea whether my bomb hit the tank or not as others were thrown simultaneously but I recall seeing the tank on fire before retreating at speed. The experience left me exhilarated and overcome with triumph.

Tanks would increasingly roll through the streets firing their heavy guns and our soldiers resisted in any way they could. Overall our fighters had some success against them. The tanks tended to point their gun barrels forwards when travelling so it was possible to make quick assaults from the sides. When a petrol bomb hit its target the burning fuel would spread all over the tank and a fair number were destroyed in this way. I have since read that a major tank attack on the City Centre took place on 15th August. Our boys managed to repel the attack and destroy nine tanks. On a number of occasions I saw the German crew of a tank (of which there were normally four) as they escaped through the hatch and ran for safety with AK soldiers shooting at them. Occasionally our fighters managed to capture a tank intact and use it against the enemy, as in the case of the earlier attack on Goose Farm.

From the early days of the Uprising I had heard that in some cases, to prevent the AK attacking tanks, the Germans stooped to using civilians as human shields. The first reports of this had come from the Ochota and Wola districts of Warsaw, followed by more from the Old Town. Reports described how 20 people, mainly women but sometimes children, were tied together by a rope which was secured to the tank, then forced to walk at the front and the sides of the tank as it moved forward. This was horrific for us to hear. We were treating German prisoners well and the fact that the Germans were treating Polish civilians this way shocked us. I am thankful that I did not witness this myself.

IN THE CELLARS

On my return from Powiśle, still in a state of shock and disorientation, I had been assigned to WSS activities in the City Centre North and South. My WSS unit had been set up by Scoutmaster Jerzy Kozłowski, pseudonym 'Jurwiś'. With the ever-intensifying onslaught by the Germans, concerns were growing within the AK about the wellbeing and state of mind of the civilian population. The general role of the WSS was therefore to provide moral, physical and material support to civilians.

Virtually every building in Warsaw had a communal cellar where the majority of the citizens sheltered from the fighting and bombing above ground. There were maybe ten or twenty people living in each cellar. By now many had spent over two weeks living below ground, spending all day and night in these damp and dirty cellars, increasingly terrified of what might lie ahead. The cellars only provided limited shelter, as a direct hit from a German rocket would bring the whole building down upon those below. Everybody had heard reports of how, in other parts of Warsaw, the Germans had thrown grenades into crowded cellars and shot any survivors. This potentially made the cellars into living coffins and understandably contributed to the increasingly fragile mental state of civilians.

Over the next period my role was to travel among the civilians and provide support. If possible I would deliver food, water, blankets and medical supplies, help care for the sick and injured, and fetch doctors when needed. When food started running out I would beg people who still had supplies to share with those most in need. It was particularly important to help mothers cope with their little children. Sometimes I distributed AK press leaflets to keep civilians informed about events on the ground, to boost morale and to reassure them. It was important to maintain contact between civilians and the AK and we tried to encourage them to remain engaged with the Uprising. In this context I was also required to gather information about the situation and circumstances of the civilian population, including their security, living conditions and their general mood. I may have been only 15 years old but everyone knew from my armband that I was with the AK and that I was there to help. People counted on us and were happy to see us.

I travelled among the cellars through makeshift tunnels. Within the first few days of the Uprising, when it was already clear that the fighting would last longer than initially expected, cellar walls between buildings were knocked down to create underground walkways. As almost every building had a cellar, these underground routes became a vast network of tunnels. Signposts were scrawled by the AK and by civilians clearly indicating directions as it was easy to get lost. The passageways were generally left unobstructed so that combatants could move around quickly. Inhabitants were always eager to help with directions. This method of travel quickly became the safest way to move around the city and one could cover virtually the entire western side of the city underground. It was only necessary to emerge above ground when a building had been destroyed, or when crossing the wide boulevards between districts with only the recently constructed barricades for cover.

The barricades had been erected from the first days of the Uprising with the help of significant numbers of civilians. Anything that came to hand was used, including earth, sandbags, furniture, trees, rubble, paving stones and even vehicles like trams and cars.

Every morning I would get instructions on where to go that day. If I was required to leave City Centre North I would be given a password for the crossing: there was a new password each day. In addition to passwords some girls received daily written pass cards. The special permit card I had been given by Opel meant that I was already properly equipped. I would often travel with a friend whom I had recently met, also called Danusia, and we would look after each other. After a while we would split up and patrol the cellars separately. In that short period of my life, as we patrolled the cellars together, I became very close to Danusia. She was an incredibly brave person, always helpful and a good friend. We were of similar age although I would say she was more mature than me. Once, as we were running beneath a barricade, I stumbled and fell over. Without hesitation Danusia turned back and helped me to my feet despite the risk of being shot.

After each day of patrolling I would normally meet up again with Danusia and we would travel back to base together. Those days of patrolling the cellars were relentless and physically daunting; I always returned exhausted. On return we each had to submit a report to Jurwiś on our daily activities with our observations on what we had seen. This report had to be detailed and submitted in writing by 5pm. After handing it in I would join the other girls of the Grey Ranks at my base for the night.

For the greater part of my time in City Centre North after my return from Powiśle I was stationed in the basement of the Prudential building in the north-western corner of Napoleon Square. Due to its height, the Prudential had been an easy target and the upper floors had already been heavily damaged by artillery fire. The building had actually been in flames at one point but still the vast basement up to the first floor provided some degree of shelter for the numerous members of the Grey Ranks and AK in City Centre North who were then based there.

The ground floor of the Prudential was mainly reserved for regular military activity, while the basement, and to a limited extent the first floor, were for sleeping and social activities. The basement was spacious and I recall it as a vibrant place with constant activity. All sorts of meetings and get-togethers were constantly taking place in the basement. Every day priests conducted a number of masses, normally containing spirit- and morale-boosting sermons. Some masses were for fallen friends, others just for us, and everybody prayed. In the basement, courting couples could be seen cuddling in corners, unsure of how long they had left together.

Throughout the Uprising there were quite a few weddings, initially in the churches, but later, as these were destroyed or lost to us, wherever possible. I saw two or three take place in our basement in the Prudential. These were special moments; the happy couple would declare undying love and make arrangements where to meet later. But shortly after the ceremony the boy would go back to the battle front line – as often as not, never to return.

Every night at base I would exchange news and stories with other girls about the day's events, some happy, most increasingly sad. A piano was sometimes played in the background. Around the same time each night I would sit with other Grey Ranks in a circle on the ground around a few logs as an improvised campfire. In scout tradition, we would sing scout and Uprising songs, then a senior scout would tell a story and together we would share some joy and laughter. These 'campfires' were brief moments of normality and I would remember happier days sitting around a real fire in a field or surrounded by trees.

One of my favourites of the scout songs we sang was 'Jak dobrze nam zdobywać góry' ('How wonderful it is conquering mountains'). Probably the most famous Uprising song was 'Hej chlopcy bagnet na broń' ('Hey boys, fix bayonets') written by Krystyna Krahelska in 1943. Before the war, Krystyna Krahelska's face had provided a model for the famous mermaid statue overlooking the Vistula, which was based on Warsaw's coat of arms.

She was killed on the second day of the Uprising. The 'campfire' would normally finish with the scout song 'Idzie Noc' ('Night is Coming').

In these brief moments I experienced some momentary happiness and relaxation, forgetting what the following day might bring or what I had lost. After the campfire we settled down to sleep on the ground next to one another wherever there was space. The exhaustion swept over me and I was fast asleep in an instant.

The following morning I would say a little prayer and, after receiving my orders for the day, get back to patrolling the cellars. Sometimes on these patrols I would see people I knew from before the Uprising hiding down there. On two occasions I saw the helpful couple from the shop my mother had known so well; it was a sad moment when I informed them of the deaths of my mother and sister. The couple were hiding in the cellar of their own house and as it seemed quiet above they insisted that I go upstairs to their apartment, where they prepared some food for me, which was a great treat. They also gave me some biscuits and sweets to take with me. I was warmly invited to come back whenever I could. I only managed to benefit from their hospitality once more, after which I never saw them again.

On another occasion in the cellars I saw my former school friend whose sister had been fraternising with a German soldier before the Uprising. I was quite surprised to see her; for some reason I imagined she would have found somewhere safe, but here she was, far away from her home, hiding from the bombs with all the other Poles. I couldn't see her sister anywhere: I suspected she was with the rest of her family but I couldn't tell. As always I wore my red and white armband and it must have been clear that I was in the AK. Our eyes met, I could tell she wanted to acknowledge me. I don't know whether it was my surprise at seeing her or because I was in a hurry but in the spur of the moment I didn't say a word as I ran past. Deep down I think things had changed and that I now wanted her to know that she was a stranger to me and that we did not belong to the same category of person. My eyes must have shown disgust and she looked down sheepishly. I never saw her again.

One day, while above ground, I saw a group of German prisoners being marched through the street, having been taken captive by our fighters.

A large number of civilians had surfaced from their hiding places in the
cellars to watch and show their anger: many of them spat at the prisoners
and made gestures towards them as they moved with heads hung low,
looking cowed and timid.

Given the location of this sighting, I believe these German prisoners
were some of the 115 taken prisoner after the battle for the telephone
exchange building called 'PASTA'. AK soldiers won this battle on 20th
August. The victory was viewed as a major success in my area of the city due
to the strategic value of the building. Standing on Zielnia Street overlooking the junction of Świętokrzyska Street and Marszałkowska Boulevard,
PASTA served two important functions for the Germans. Primarily it was
a main telecommunications link between the German army in the east and
Berlin and, more locally, with German positions in Saski Park. The building
also overlooked the City Centre and so enabled German snipers to shoot at
Warsowians, whether soldiers or civilians.

The 150 Germans defending PASTA had been besieged for many days,
fending off AK attacks while German attempts to relieve their fellow
soldiers were beaten back. The fighting was intense, floor by floor and
room by room. Finally the Germans surrendered. One can now read some
desperate letters written by German soldiers during their defence of the
building as their situation deteriorated and their colleagues fell.

During the Uprising about 2,000 German soldiers were taken prisoner by
the AK. Strict orders had been issued by the AK leadership that all German
prisoners were to be treated well. When captured the Germans were made
to perform certain work for the Uprising but they were always treated in
accordance with the Geneva Convention. Conversely the Germans did
not regard us as legitimate armed forces and therefore did not observe the
Geneva Convention, executing any captured AK fighters. They continued
this policy even after Great Britain and the USA finally issued a statement
at the end of August recognising us as an integral part of the Polish Armed
Forces with combatant rights. Nevertheless this declaration by our allies
was a boost for us.

Street battles were taking place in various areas around the City Centre
and bombs continued to fall. On 28th August the Prudential building was

further badly damaged when it was hit by a two-tonne shell from a Karl-Gerät mortar. After this it was no longer possible to use the first floor of the building. Once Warsaw's tallest building and the second-tallest in Europe, the Prudential now looked like a shell of its former self, and the upper floors like a ghostly ruin. Recently I have read that in the course of the Uprising the Prudential building was hit by approximately a thousand artillery shells. On the following day I carefully climbed up a few floors of the Prudential building with some friends. The bomb damage meant that we had a good view in all directions from part way up the building. We gazed down upon the devastation all around us; Warsaw was in flames.

DEATH AT THE BARRICADE

While on WSS patrol I would frequently cross between City Centre North and South, which were divided by Jerozolimska Boulevard. Due to their width, Warsaw's boulevards acted as natural division lines between sectors of conflict. Crossing them was particularly dangerous due to the length of time one was exposed to sniper fire and could only be done through the barricades. I think the barricade on Jerozolimska Boulevard was where Bracka Street crossed over. The exit from the barricade on the south side was through a house. A shallow ditch had been dug along the middle of the barricade and protective walls had been built of earth, sandbags and paving stones. Still, these crossings were always perilous: even if one kept one's head down, the barricade provided only partial protection. Sniper and machine-gun fire frequently penetrated the ramparts, which made it ultimately a matter of luck whether one made it across or not.

The barricade on Jerozolimska Boulevard was particularly exposed. The Germans controlled the enormous BGK building, the Bank for Internal Affairs, which stood about 200 metres east on the corner of Nowy Świat and Jerozolimska Boulevard. This provided a vantage point from which the Germans could shoot down directly at the barricade. On the other side, about 300 metres to the west, was the Central Railway Station from which my mother had embarked upon her smuggling journeys to the country. In the area of the station at the intersection of Jerozolimska and Marszałkowska Boulevards the Germans had additional positions from which they could also fire at the barricade. The barricade on Jerozolimska Boulevard was strategically important to both sides. For us it was the only link between between City Centre North and South. For the Germans the boulevard was a potential link between their forces across the Poniatowski Bridge in Praga and those on the western side. We only controlled a few buildings in between immediately around the barricade. As a result the boulevard was constantly fought over, house by house, and the barricade was permanently under fire.

An AK guard was always positioned on either side of the barricade checking documentation and signalling when to start across, which was normally whenever there was a brief lull in the shooting. The waiting time varied depending on the time of day, the level of German activity and the number of people trying to cross. Sometimes I waited the better part of an hour for the signal to cross, other times only a few minutes. It seemed to me that the Germans were most active in shooting in the late afternoon, perhaps because of the higher numbers of people crossing. We would set off one by one, a few steps apart, hunching down as low as possible all the way through the barricade, hoping and praying that the shooting would not recommence quickly. The Germans would often pretend to stop shooting and then restart suddenly, trying to catch us midway.

The end of August brought another traumatic experience which I will never forget. I was returning with Danusia from a patrol in City Centre South. We waited for a while at the barricade on Aleje Jerozolimskie until we received the signal to cross. As the shooting subsided we heard the shout "You can run now!" I quickly said to Danusia, "Be careful, they might start shooting again." She replied, "Don't worry, let's stick together. Soon it will all be over and we will write books about what we did." We still believed that one day life would return to normal...

Danusia ran first and I followed a few paces behind her. Suddenly the shooting restarted. I looked up from my stooping position: she had been hit and had fallen in front of me. Danusia was dead. I wanted to go to her and lift her up, to hold her, but the shooting did not stop and everyone was shouting at me to run back. I managed to scramble back to cover; others behind me did the same. In a state of shock I waited for the next signal to cross again and this time I ran past my friend's body to safety on the other side. There were many difficult days but this was one of the worst for me.

We had special AK groups charged with the task of collecting and burying the bodies of our fallen colleagues. By now all coffins and any wood for making new ones had been used up, in fact it had all gone within the first few days of the Uprising. Bodies were first wrapped in blankets and when those ran out in anything else that could be found. Shallow graves were dug and the dead laid to rest wherever there was space. The parks became full of fresh graves in the first few days. After that, bodies were laid to rest wherever it was possible to dig, including in squares, courtyards and pavements where the paving stones had been taken up and used to build barricades. It wasn't until the evening that my friend's body was recovered and laid to rest in my absence. I can't answer why I didn't go back to see where Danusia was buried. It wouldn't have been straightforward but I do wonder now whether I should at least have enquired about her resting place.

Losing my friend – seeing her shot right in front of me – was another terrible shock in my young life. It was one of many occasions when I had a strong sense that my mother was protecting me from above and yet I also felt increasingly cut off and on my own.

KANAŁ

At the start of September we started seeing AK fighters and civilians emerging from manholes in the City Centre. They looked utterly exhausted; in many cases they were traumatised. They emerged covered from head to toe in sewage which they could only partially wash away due to our limited washing facilities; as a result many contracted unpleasant illnesses and infections. Many of their colleagues had died in the sewers and those who made it needed time to recover before they could talk about their experiences while others simply remained too traumatised to talk. These people were survivors of the savagery in the Old Town.

After the Germans had secured Wola and Ochota they had directed the main thrust of their assault against the Old Town. This historic part of the city would become the scene of the most intense battles of the Uprising, with our fighters bravely and selflessly resisting overwhelming German firepower. By the end of August, after three weeks of ruthless German onslaughts, the Old Town could not hold out any longer. The decision was taken to evacuate and to attempt to join us in the City Centre North. With the Germans holding the ground in between the Old Town and the City Centre, the perilous evacuation had to be made underground through the sewers (*kanały*). These journeys through the sewers would become synonymous with the Warsaw Uprising and have been immortalised in the 1956 Andrzej Wajda film 'Kanał'.

I spoke with some of the survivors at my base in the Prudential and they described the conditions below ground. The sewer routes took retreating fighters under enemy lines and the Germans quickly became aware of this. The first escapees would chalk markings on the walls for directions but in the darkness many got lost in the tunnels and reappeared above ground in German-controlled areas where they were shot on the spot. As the Germans became aware of these escape routes they booby-trapped manholes with explosives and dropped grenades, poison gas and petrol into the sewers to kill those trying to pass below. However the Germans never entered the sewers themselves – they were too afraid. The intense claustrophobia and constant fear drove many to something like madness, and deaths in the sewers were numerous. Speaking with these survivors after they emerged from the sewers, it was clear that we who had lived and fought in the City Centre had so far suffered little compared to those in the Old Town and other parts of Warsaw.

In future years I would get to know Maria Scheybal, pseudonym 'Marzena', who gave me an account of her journey through the sewers. She was in one of the last groups to leave the Old Town via the sewers on 2nd September. Large numbers queueing with her did not manage to get down in time as the Germans closed in. There were 39 people in Marzena's group, led by a guide. After entering the drain through the manhole she climbed down eight to ten metal steps, about five metres down to the base, at which point she had to kneel down and push herself into the sewer. She describes the sewers as being pipes of 70 or 80 centimetres in diameter in places which is barely high enough to be able to kneel. There was putrid effluent running along the floor all the way, everywhere was silent and pitch black. There were some directional signs at the foot of the drains but otherwise no way of knowing which way to go, hence there was a heavy reliance on guides. She was told the journey would take around two hours but it ended up taking 16, from 8pm until noon the following day.

Many of the group were in a state of fear and panic, and the terror of the dark, enclosed tunnel made them hysterical. They would start shouting wildly while others tried to calm them down to avoid spreading the panic and being heard by the Germans above. Some wanted to give themselves up to the enemy, anything just to get out of the sewer, despite the likelihood of being immediately shot. At one point the guide disappeared ahead and, believing themselves lost, the group were considering turning back to the Old Town when, fortunately, the guide returned. Whenever they approached a drain they had to wait for a while to make sure there were no Germans listening above ground. At one point a dead escapee from a previous run lay ahead blocking the route and so the group had to push the body along as a chain until they reached the next drain, where the opening was a little bigger and they were able to squeeze past.

Eventually, after 16 long hours in the filth below ground, the group reached the exit on Chmielna Street in City Centre North. At the drain Marzena and her group had to wait to be pulled up individually by ropes as the sudden exposure to fresh air caused people to faint and fall back down. Marzena herself fainted on being pulled out and needed some time to revive. Exhausted and covered in effluent, she was given an address where she could wash, but when she arrived there the water had run out. She was then directed to another address where there were still some barrels with warm water. When her group conducted assembly later that day she was missing. After a search Marzena was eventually found unconscious in the barrel, due to an infection she had contracted from the sewer.

In total around 5,300 people were evacuated from the Old Town to the City Centre through the sewers. Left behind them in the Old Town were

2,500 severely wounded AK fighters and 35,000 civilians, of whom 5,000 were also wounded. Most of the wounded were forced out of the hospitals onto the street and executed. Others were shot in their hospital beds or burned to death along with the medical staff. The fate of the remaining 30,000 civilians in the Old Town was determined by their fitness for work. Those judged incapable of work were shot.

HELL ON EARTH

Following the fall of the Old Town, the Germans turned the focus of their attack on to City Centre North, bringing all their superior military strength to bear against us. At first we were subjected to ceaseless pounding by heavy artillery. Building after building tumbled and the cellars offered no protection against a direct hit. The shelling was so imprecise and indiscriminate that there was no telling where the next rocket would land or which building would be reduced to rubble. In addition, gunners rained bullets down on us from Stuka planes, targeting people with precision. There was nowhere to hide and survival was a matter of pure luck. I can truly say that those early days of September in City Centre North felt like hell on earth.

Soon the Germans launched massive ground assaults against us from all sides. Fighting was savage and on a house-by-house basis. Those first days of September were the most intense of my life. Talk started that we might have to abandon the area. I never stopped being afraid for a moment but I did have a sense of group security and all the while I felt my mother was watching over me and keeping me safe.

Despite the situation I couldn't just sit there waiting to die, so I continued with my work, patrolling the cellars. As the Germans gained more ground they occupied our hospitals and routinely murdered all the patients. Increasing numbers of wounded AK soldiers were brought down into the most accessible cellars for treatment. I would do my best to attend to the injured until specialist nurses could be found. Sometimes I would be required to fetch a priest when death was near. On one occasion I was looking after six injured boys; one in particular was in a bad way and his friends begged me to find a priest. I scrambled over mountains of rubble, which used to be our homes and streets, stumbling and grazing my knees. I reached a church, only to find it deserted. I continued searching, begging anyone I saw for help to find a priest. Finally I found one; he was very old and he agreed to come with me. As we made our way back to the cellar we held hands and supported each other. The priest must have sensed my fear because he halted, held my hand and said, "Do not be afraid, young scout, God will look after us." I felt safer in his company. Finally we reached our injured soldiers and the priest was able to give the sacrament of communion and hear the boy's final confession just in time. Moments later, the boy passed away.

Throughout the Uprising priests were synonymous with the struggle. They were everywhere among the Uprisers, even amidst the heaviest fighting. Many priests were members of the AK. They were afraid and hid like everyone else but they were always available to talk, give spiritual support and guidance and to take confession. Priests worked tirelessly, conducting frequent daily masses, taking countless confessions, reading the last rites, conducting funerals and even weddings among the ruins. In the early days priests also provided practical help such as recovering works of art from burning churches. Most importantly, the priests took care of Warsaw's spiritual needs and helped keep up morale. But they also died in large numbers, so there were fewer and fewer of them. I have to confess that my faith in God wavered at times.

On 4th September the main Post Office in Napoleon Square was bombed to the ground. Two days later, after much bloody fighting, the Powiśle region along the riverside where I had been sent a few weeks earlier fell to the Germans.

On 8th and 9th September the Germans agreed ceasefires, each lasting two hours, in order to allow civilians to leave Warsaw. Prior to this the Germans airdropped leaflets addressed to the civilian population with the headline 'Ultimatum', urging them to leave the city without reprisal or face severe consequences. I didn't pay too much attention to the leaflets which were not intended for the AK and I regarded any message from the Germans as propaganda. Although many civilians felt safer staying in the

city with our army, a few thousand did take this opportunity to leave. I
heard how these civilians emerged from the cellars holding white flags they
had made from rags and sticks. They huddled together in fear, nobody
wishing to get separated from the group. They must have been petrified, not
knowing whether they could trust the Germans and what might happen to
them. The ceasefire was observed and the civilians were taken out of the
city but we did not know what happened to them once outside. Subsequent
reports suggest that their treatment was harsh and many were transported
into forced labour. In Warsaw, meanwhile, within minutes of the ceasefire
ending, the German onslaught restarted with renewed intensity.

I felt a suffocating sense of being totally surrounded as the German
stranglehold continued to tighten. We were becoming increasingly concentrated in the City Centre as the enemy closed in. Despite this, I never
stopped believing and hoping for a good outcome. Maybe this was due to
my youth and naivety, maybe due to my natural sense of optimism.

By the early days of September food was in short supply and getting
water became more difficult due to bomb damage to the water system.
Water had to be brought to the civilians from more distant sources, which
was a job for the boy scouts also affiliated to the WSS. I continued patrolling
the City Centre cellars, helping the civilian population as much as I could
and reporting back about morale.

The growing hunger and incessant heavy bombing caused civilian
morale to rapidly deteriorate. As fear and hardship mounted the general
demeanour among civilians understandably changed. People were growing
more miserable and increasingly frustrated. Many civilians started to
display dissatisfaction as time went on and hunger, death and destruction
escalated. Some civilians understood what we were trying to do and stayed
resolute but others started blaming the AK for what was happening and
began to take their frustrations out on us. I have to say that this resentment
tended to be directed more towards the boys than the girls. Only once did I
experience a particularly unpleasant encounter.

Early one day while on patrol I entered a crowded cellar and immediately felt an unfriendly atmosphere. A lady was sitting on the floor in the
corner. She sat by herself and looked agitated. I approached her and asked,

"Is something wrong? Do you need anything?" She replied in a loud and unpleasant voice, "Yes, I'm angry, I am hungry, there is nothing to eat, I have nothing to sleep on or to cover myself with. Am I supposed to be happy about this?" I tried to calm her. "I understand, that's why I am here, to help if I can. I'll try to get you what you want." "Yes, very well, and can you, girl scout, stop this war for me? You started it knowing the Germans are well armed and you don't have what they have. They shoot us here like dogs because there are almost no dogs left!" I answered, "Nobody could foresee how the Uprising would turn out, the situation was changing." "But you have commanders who should have foreseen what could happen." Speaking calmly, I replied, "I have lost my entire family and am alone. Instead of waiting for the Germans to murder us all I prefer to fight for freedom and my right to live because nobody can take this away from me! We have to support each other in order to achieve something!" At this the anger and sorrow in her seemed to subside. She apologised to me calmly and hugged me before saying, "Dear child, may God help us all!" I felt the atmosphere in the cellar lift and other people who had been listening to our conversation spoke sympathetically to both of us. What I could find I brought back to the lady. When I submitted my report to Jurwiś later that day he complimented me on my response to her criticism.

ON THE FRONT LINE

A week or so into September I was told that I would be crossing permanently to City Centre South. City Centre North was under intense pressure and we were ordered to evacuate. Despite heavy attacks the AK were still holding the Jerozolimska Boulevard barricade, enabling us to make the crossing.

I was told that I was being assigned to the combat group Battalion Miłosz in City Centre South, along with one of my colleagues from the Executive Group, Krystyna Zbyszewska. Krystyna has mentioned this subsequently in her written recollections. I presume we were given some instructions about how to reach our battalion.

We worked our way through the sidestreets and crossed into the City Centre South across the Jerozolimska Boulevard barricade. Continuing southwards we reached the north of Three Crosses Square, in the middle of which stood the church of St Alexander. On the other side of the church, leading further south from the square, ran Ujazdowskie Boulevard. Here, a little way down, the Germans were amassed behind what seemed like a huge carpet. This was draped across the boulevard not far from the point where it joined the square, the carpet acting as a screen. Diagonally to our left on the eastern side of the square stood a large building which was the now deserted Institute for the Deaf and Blind. We ran across the square heading behind the church for cover, watching out for snipers from the direction of Nowy Świat to our left. We dashed into the Institute building as quickly as we could. I recall running inside the Institute in the darkness through a massive hall. I felt full of fear, particularly as there were only two of us young girls and I didn't know if there was anybody else inside. The hall was filled with chairs but otherwise empty. We climbed over chairs in places and reached an exit at the far end of the hall. Once outside again, we worked our way through some other buildings until we reached our destination, which I think was on Konopnicka Street.

Having reached Battalion Miłosz I was assigned to Company 'Bradl', named after the pseudonym of the Company commander, Kazimierz Leski. Later that month on 22nd September my AK pass card had added to it: "I confirm that liaison person 'Wira' serves in Company Bradl in Battalion Miłosz". The signature below these words seems to be that of Bradl himself. I do not recall whether Krystyna also joined Company Bradl or a different Company within the Battalion. From that point onwards over the following weeks, my activities became much more front-line related.

Battalion Miłosz was part of Sector East 'Bogumił' and was divided among three Companies called Bradl, Redy and Ziuka. The area fought over by these Companies had at its heart the Three Crosses Square but also covered part of Książęca Street, Na Skarpie Boulevard, Prusa Street, Marii Konopnickiej (Konopnicka) Street, Wiejska Street leading south to the parliament building and the northern part of Ujazdowskie Boulevard. Leading south from Three Crosses Square along Wiejska Street and Ujazdowskie

Boulevard was territory which had been held by the Germans throughout the Uprising and which therefore remained less damaged. Company Bradl had made its name on 2nd September by taking the German stronghold at the YMCA building on Konopnicka Street, which we managed to hold until the end of the Uprising. At some point while I was with Company Bradl I was based on Konopnicka Street, either in or near the YMCA complex. One image from inside the YMCA has remained with me. It is of a large swimming pool. I imagined Germans swimming in the pool and how good their lives must have been in our city...

At first City Centre South seemed to me relatively undamaged. In the North I had experienced mass destruction caused by mortar bombs and rockets as well as regular aerial bombardment. I had barely survived the heavy bombing in Powiśle when I was buried in debris, deafened and suffering from memory loss. But so far the City Centre South had avoided the worst of the bombardment. This would rapidly change as the Germans intensified the assault on the South and increasingly encircled us. Very quickly the South started resembling the North which I had so recently left, with desperate fighting taking place between well-armed Germans and the poorly equipped AK units. The fighting was always close by.

The nature of the fighting was similar to the North: skirmishes and operations that were rarely in the open and usually over individual buildings. Each building held by us was a foothold and was desperately defended. Usually one side would defend the building from the top while the other attacked from below, ending up face to face in deadly hand-to-hand combat. Often buildings would change hands a number of times. If we were able to gain a few buildings adjacent to each other we could consolidate the area and it would become ours.

The Germans frequently brought in tanks to attack our buildings. The tanks would roll slowly towards us from Nowy Świat or from the sideroads behind Konopnicka Street. Once they were in view they would shoot directly at the buildings controlled by the AK, often at short range.

We were heavily reliant on homemade weapons. I would frequently see our boys throw petrol directly onto encroaching German tanks, normally from a building above, followed by a petrol bomb to set fire to the tank.

Sometimes they used homemade flamethrowers against tanks or when attacking buildings controlled by the enemy. Unlike German flamethrowers, however, our homemade ones had a very short reach. In addition petrol, like ammunition, had to be used sparingly due to our diminished resources.

I was no longer in my home territory and I knew fewer people. With few familiar faces around me I felt even more frightened and alone. Despite this, I was proud that I could be involved more directly and on equal terms with others in an AK battle group. I felt much closer to the real battle and had plenty of work to do, interspersed with plenty of scary moments.

One of my tasks with the Company was to deliver reports from the Company leadership including Bradl himself to other platoons. These often took me to buildings our boys were defending against constant gunfire. Other times our boys would be on the offensive, attacking buildings. Due to casualties and territorial changes the security situation with personnel was constantly in flux, so on reaching the platoon I would be asked for the password to ascertain my identity. Sometimes I was given a response to take back to Bradl. Occasionally during the Conspiracy messages had been delivered verbally but during the Uprising everything was written down. I was under orders not to allow anybody other than the intended recipients to read the message. This included myself, so I had no knowledge of the information I was passing.

At times I was instructed to deliver ammunition which was either in a box or a package and not too heavy to be be carried easily and at speed. I generally travelled on my own in those days. Despite the risks these deliveries were essential as our soldiers depended on them.

The worst of my routes was from the top of Wiejska Street to the Three Crosses Square. This area was exposed and constantly under sniper fire. The German shooting from the top of the BGK building only a few hundred metres away was particularly fierce. The area was also an open target for snipers we called *gołębiarze* ('pigeon people'), marksmen who hid in attics or perched on building roofs. Many of these *gołębiarze* were often *Volksdeutsche* who had lived in the German area around Ujazdowskie Boulevard before the Uprising. We avoided these open areas except when absolutely necessary and therefore they were usually empty. Whenever possible I would stick to the narrower side roads where I had more cover and the buildings adjoined so that I could run below ground through the cellars. If I saw a tank I would immediately try to hide in a building or a cellar. The Germans were good shots and I ran in constant fear, always on my guard, praying for help. I felt that somebody was always watching over me from above.

When I wasn't needed as a messenger I would continue with WSS duties, attending to civilians. The cellars were full of frightened and hungry people. By the middle of September the situation had become even more difficult, particularly regarding food and water. There was a severe deterioration in living conditions for all, both physically and mentally. By now the cellars were filthy and everybody was hungry. Everybody knew that Germans were murdering people in hospitals as they closed in. Those were dark and difficult days and they would only get worse.

One day while I was travelling through the cellars I came across an old lady lying on the floor, hungry and crying. Her grandchildren had gone and she had no idea where they were. Back at my base on Konopnicka I asked for some food for her. I was only able to get a few scraps but I took them to her. I had spent many days helping civilians in my time with the WSS so this now came naturally to me, particularly in such a situation. The gratitude the old lady showed me was incredibly moving: she was unable to thank me enough. I felt good that I was able to help a little. I have no idea what became of her because I never travelled that way again.

Despite our limited resources, in the first part of my time in City Centre South I still felt that I was fighting for Warsaw and that we might yet somehow prevail. All the time we were suffering terrible casualties but our spirits and discipline remained high and we were willing and able to keep fighting until the very last drop of blood. The Germans also were suffering severe casualties and the prolonged fighting was tying up a lot of their vital resources.

From the middle of September there was a brief flicker of hope. News filtered through that the Red Army had finally moved forward against the Germans on the east side of the Vistula in Praga. We heard that the

Germans had withdrawn to our side of the river and that the Soviets were bombarding their positions from the east. There was talk that some of our people were swimming across the river to discuss assistance with the Red Army and that some Soviet contacts were being parachuted into Warsaw to liaise with the AK. Soviet planes started appearing in the skies: we called them *Kukuruzniki*. Soon I could tell Soviet planes from German and Allied planes as they each made a distinctive sound. People reported that the Soviet planes were dropping supplies. Once or twice I received some powdered milk which I was able to distribute to mothers with children. We also heard that groups of Polish soldiers fighting under General Berling within the Red Army had made crossings to support our fighters on the riverbank. On 18th September I heard reports that the US Airforce conducted a huge air supply mission over Warsaw involving 174 planes after the Soviets had finally granted Allied planes permission to land for refuelling on Soviet-controlled airfields.

During this period desperate battles continued unabated in my area and there wasn't too much time to dwell on potential outside help. Nevertheless the news raised morale a little. Personally I wanted to believe that help was coming but I never truly did. I dared not hope. Soviet support at this stage didn't make sense. If the Soviets had really wanted to help us surely they would have done so before? They had stood by for 44 days. They knew perfectly well that we had almost nothing left. The underlying suspicion in my area was that all this activity was merely Soviet propaganda. After everything they had done – and not done – how could they be trusted?

This flicker of hope didn't last long. Sentiment about Soviet air supplies soon turned negative. The supplies were poorly protected and dropped without parachutes so that the contents generally disintegrated on impact with the ground. Our fighters regarded many of the arms drops as worthless. The US Airforce mission also amounted to very little as the drops were made at high altitude. The combination of prevailing winds and our dwindling territory meant that only 288 of the 1,280 containers reached our fighters – the rest fell behind German lines. The Soviets did not grant permission for any more landings. Within a few days we were also hearing that the Red Army soldiers were being evacuated back across the river. It quickly became clear that no significant help was coming and any vague hope faded.

I had little thought of political intrigues at the time but these days I have no doubt that these shortlived and belated efforts to relieve Warsaw were no more than propaganda. They served only to enable Stalin to claim that he was giving military aid to Warsaw. By offering false hope the Soviets probably extended the fighting in Warsaw. Apparently there had been rumours, of which I was unaware, that we might capitulate, but these had died down when news of possible Soviet help appeared. It seems that Stalin's strategy was to facilitate the total destruction of the AK by the Germans in order to smooth the eventual subjugation of Poland by the Soviet Union. Stalin may have considered conducting his policy through the Armia Ludowa (People's Army) who supported a pro-Soviet communist government. Although the AL participated fully in the Warsaw Uprising alongside the AK, they were not officially attached to the AK. As they represented only about five percent of those fighting in Warsaw, the AL were simply too small to be promoted by Stalin for propaganda reasons. While Warsaw continued fighting to the death, Stalin concerned himself with manipulating world opinion.

NEARING THE END

There was almost no food left. I was so hungry I could barely think of anything else. Occasionally the boys would still manage to recover a few scraps from raids, which we would devour. I recall one particularly strange dish after the boys had found some flour, flakes of some sort and chocolate. They were cooked together and made into what seemed like a cross between cake and noodles mixed with chocolate, a kind of croquette. It tasted unpleasantly sweet but was gratefully received. A soup which became synonymous with the Uprising and hunger was called *Zupa plujka* – literally meaning 'spit soup'. It was so named as it contained hard grains that could not be digested and so had to be spat out.

Meat became a rarity from the earliest days of the Uprising and on the rare occasions that I had some it was not from the usual sources. While eating horse in City Centre North a few weeks earlier I recollected how, before the war, my mother had argued with Henia and me about the suitability of horsemeat. One day my mother had secretly prepared a horsemeat dish. Henia devoured the dish with enthusiasm and was only told it was horse afterwards. My mother had proved her point.

By the middle of September it had been quite some time since I had last tasted meat of any kind so I was amazed when I was handed a plate with some meat on it one evening. I wondered where it had come from. "This is so good," I said. One of the boys sitting opposite me laughed and joked, "It's a special delivery from Paris." After I had devoured the last piece of meat the same boy said, "So did you like it? It's not really from Paris, it's Polish dog!" I immediately felt sick, and I said, "How could you make me eat dogs, I would never have eaten dog!" The boy replied, "You would never eat dog, but you did eat it and you liked it." I felt so sad as I loved pets. Throughout the Uprising owners guarded their dogs keenly for they knew that strays would be eaten. Some days later, as food shortages became even more acute, I forced myself to eat the meat from a stray cat. Cat is distinctly different from dog. I preferred dog meat as I found cat meat too sweet and unpleasant.

My clothes had been in tatters for some time and my summer sandals had fallen apart many weeks earlier. I don't recall what I had found to replace the sandals but the replacements were also beyond use by now. The boys tried to find me something to wear and one managed to get some high-heeled shoes. I soon showed him how ungrateful I was for such useless aid as I snapped at him, "Are you crazy, do you think I am going to wear these running over mountains of rubble and break my legs?" The boy replied, "So put them aside, you can wear them for the ball." Finally another boy brought me some rubber wellington boots. It seemed these were the best I was going to get and so I wore the wellington boots from then on, in constant agony from the chafing and the many blisters they gave me.

It was becoming clear that something would have to change, that we could not go on like this. I think the turning-point for me was when I realised how utterly inadequate the Soviet support had been. From this point my hopes for a successful outcome to the Uprising began to fade. Many people have subsequently said that they knew that the Uprising was doomed after the first few days when it became clear that the Red Army advance had stopped but I had never thought that way. Until this point I had always hoped and believed that something good would come out of it all – with or without help.

The mood among the starving civilians had also changed. People who had grown angry about the Uprising no longer displayed any antagonism. Instead they had succumbed to a pervasive air of resignation and defeat accompanied only by a fear of what might happen next. They had been through every emotion. I would say that overall there was no unanimous opinion about what had taken place. In the long run there would be many different views of the Uprising, both supportive and critical.

At the end of September it became hopeless. Mokotów had fallen on the 27th and Żoliborz on the 30th and we were the only sector left. Company Bradl was winding down and I was told to go to Wilcza Street, where the Szare Szeregi had our main base. I think the building was at number 41 and a former school of commerce. Some of the boys came with me but only to see if they could get some food before returning to their platoons. There were lots of girls and boys at the base and I vaguely recall seeing some kitchens and a group of girls from the PZ which we called Pezetki. PZ stood for 'Pomoc Żolnierzy' ('Help for Soldiers'). I think that Pezetki provided food, laundry services and moral support for soldiers from bases near the front line.

By the time I got to Wilcza rumours were already circulating that our leaders were discussing capitulation terms with the Germans. Wilcza was bursting with nervous energy and tension as these rumours gained more credence and different people reacted in different ways. When more concrete news came that our leader, General 'Bór' Komorowski, was actually in discussions with the Germans, not everybody wanted to believe it. Some received the news with relief as they could not see how we could continue fighting. Others reacted with anger and renewed determination to fight until the bitter end. Some continued to shoot until the final moment.

At first my mind was empty and I didn't know what to think. Then my head started spinning and questions began to multiply. What had all that death and destruction been for? For a while life lost its meaning for me. There had been so much joy when the Uprising began, so much belief that we would finally achieve a new and better life with our families in a free Poland. After the first few days of the Uprising, when reality dawned I always thought that I might die during the struggle but it had never entered my mind that I alone would survive while my family would suddenly be lost. I was filled with grief that our Uprising was ending along with any hope of removing our subjugation. What would happen to us now? Again I recalled the visit to the fortune-teller and her words to me, "Young lady, you will leave everybody and travel far away over the sea." At the time I wondered how could this be, that I would go far away on my own? It was unimaginable.

By this stage people generally thought it was better to negotiate an end with the Germans rather than with the Soviets. The Germans were clearly keen for an end to the fighting as we were still tying up some of their vital resources. Although our losses were massive, German losses were also high and we still held some parts of the City Centre. If we fought to the very death – which we were still prepared to do – then we could maintain the fight, albeit defensively, for some time yet. Therefore it seemed likely that reasonable terms could be negotiated with the Germans. We knew what we were dealing with with the Germans, while there was absolutely no trust in the Soviets by this stage.

Point by point the text of the capitulation agreement was hammered out. On 1st October a brief ceasefire enabled more civilians to evacuate the city, although it seemed to me that the majority chose to remain. The 24-point agreement was signed in the early hours of 3rd October 1944. Signatories from the AK were Colonel Kazimierz Osmecki and Lieutenant colonel Zygmund Dobrowolski, with authority from Bór. The signatory from the German side was SS Obergruppenführer and Police General Erich von dem Bach. A key condition for the AK was that soldiers of the AK, both men and women, would be regarded as combatants and therefore granted Prisoner of War status. This would entitle us to the human rights inscribed in the Geneva Convention. This granting of POW status for us women was unprecedented in European history. The other key condition was that the remaining civilians of Warsaw would not be charged with collective responsiblity and that they would not be persecuted. It was also agreed that Polish POWs would be handled by the Wehrmacht and not by the SS or their collaborators.

When we officially received the news about our capitulation at Wilcza there was an outpouring of mixed emotions. Some were happy, many cried, but we were all in utter despair that the Uprising had failed. For me the emotions were overwhelming. While I had a sense of relief that the nightmare was over and pride that we had kept fighting for 63 days against great odds and expectations, I also felt great sadness, both at our defeat and at the fact that we were going into captivity. I drew some comfort that we were surrendering to the Germans, and as POWs, as I was more frightened of what the Soviets might do to us. As my fear subsided I began to feel extremely lonely. Again I drew some comfort from the fact that I would be with the AK girls and boys; I looked apon the army as my family now. But what later? Questions started swirling around in my head. I was still only 15 years old, I was deeply confused and there was nobody who could help me. Once again I felt completely alone; for the second time, my life fell apart and I broke down in tears.

Soon after the capitulation, one of our commanders led discussions about what was to happen. Warsaw was to be evacuated. We were told that the army was going into captivity and that we would be leaving Poland. If, however, any individuals chose to stay in Poland, they could try to mix in with the civilians and there would be no recriminations from the AK if they did. Many of the AK did decide to remain in Poland in order to take part in the next conspiracy that inevitably lay ahead against the next occupier. I found out subsequently that many of my former female colleagues including Miki chose the civilian option. In later years many AK members who remained in Poland would be subjected to severe treatment by the communist authorities. Some disappeared, others spent a long time in prison and many would be excluded from normal life indefinitely.

It was a difficult decision for me to make. In despair I decided to leave
with the army. I had nobody left to stay for, having lost my entire immediate
family, and I couldn't imagine how I could look after myself on my own. I
was attached to the Uprising and the AK; this was my family now. I also saw
it as a matter of honour that having gone into the Uprising with my people,
the soldiers of the AK, I should also go with them now into captivity.

I heard that various units began burying records, archives and films
taken during the Uprising to be preserved for retrieval at a later date, as
a permanent record of our fight. Most were lost for ever but decades later
some were still being recovered.

View from Świętokrzyska Street across Napoleon Square to the main Post Office building captured by the Kiliński battalion on 2nd August. The Polish flag flies above.

AK patrol running across an intersection in City Centre North. 3rd August.

Wira, 2nd from right, in the postal sorting office on Świętokrzyska Street, standing next to Przemysław Górecki, 'Kuropatwa', head of the Field Post. 3rd August.

German Stuka dive bomber plane over Warsaw near Nowy Świat. Silhouette of the Prudential building is in the background.

Civilian men and boys help build a barricade in the Old Town. 5th August.

Barricade near Wira's school on Moniuszko Street. 5th August.

Areas held by the Uprising, showing how they changed over the 63 days. The distance from Sadyba in the south to Marymont in the north is approximately 13 km.

*Central Warsaw. The blue areas were held by the Uprisers from the beginning. The red
areas were German held positions from the beginning and the red arrows indicate the direction of
German attacks. The darker blue were the areas still in Polish hands at capitulation. The lighter
coloured roads were Wira's area of operation during the Uprising.*

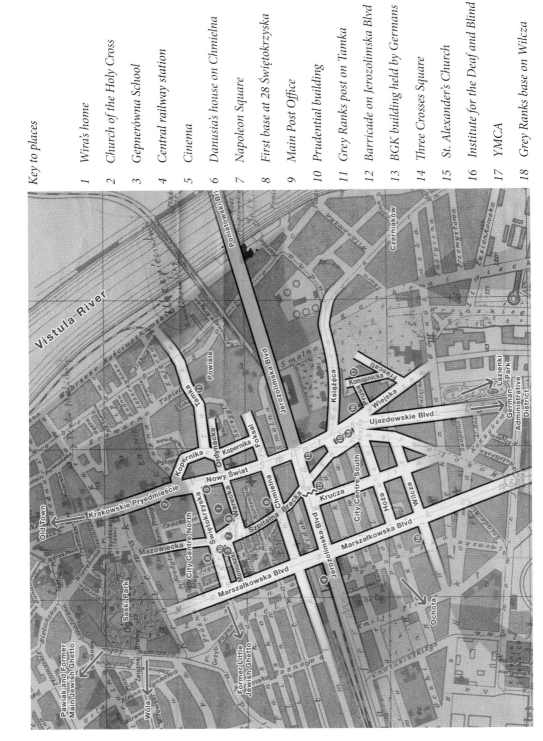

Key to places

1   *Wira's home*

2   *Church of the Holy Cross*

3   *Gepnerówna School*

4   *Central railway station*

5   *Cinema*

6   *Danusia's house on Chmielna*

7   *Napoleon Square*

8   *First base at 28 Świętokrzyska*

9   *Main Post Office*

10   *Prudential building*

11   *Grey Ranks post on Tamka*

12   *Barricade on Jerozolimska Blvd*

13   *BGK building held by Germans*

14   *Three Crosses Square*

15   *St. Alexander's Church*

16   *Institute for the Deaf and Blind*

17   *YMCA*

18   *Grey Ranks base on Wilcza*

Boys of the Uprising patrol the streets while civilians run for cover in City Centre North, near Napoleon Square.

Warsaw became a graveyard. Mazowiecka Street, City Centre North, two minutes walk from Wira's base. Written on the cross to the left is simply 'The cleaning lady from the 2nd floor'.

Borgward IV tankette after the explosion which killed 300 AK soldiers and civilians.

Wira's AK passcard from the Uprising

The barricade of death. AK soldiers crossing Jerozolimska Boulevard from City Centre North in September. This is where Wira's friend, Danusia, was killed.

Underground maze of passageways created
by knocking down the walls between cellars.

Nebelwerfer releases its rockets in Warsaw, six at a time.

German Karl-Gerät mortar firing 600mm shells in Warsaw during August.

German prisoners from the battle for the PASTA (telephone exchange building). 20th August.

Battle for Wira's Church of the Holy Cross. AK soldier looking out through the ruined wall of the church. Circa 25th August.

Wira's base, the Prudential building, being hit by a shell from the Karl-Gerät mortar. 28th August.

AK fighter measuring an unexploded 600mm shell from the Karl-Gerät mortar in the basement of the Prudential building.

View along Szpitalna Street in early September. The Prudential building can be seen in the distance. This was Wira's route on her first day of the Uprising.

St Alexander's Church on Three Crosses Square. The Institute for the Deaf and Blind is to the left.

An unfortunate AK soldier from the Mototów district emerging from the sewers into German-held territory. He was executed soon after along with 120 AK colleagues. 27th Sept.

Tadeusz 'Bór' Komorowski, Commander of the Warsaw Uprising reporting to SS Obergruppenführer and Police General Erich von dem Bach after capitulation.

German demolition squads using flamethrowers after the Warsaw Uprising had ended.

Napoleon Square looking from the other side of Swiętokrzyska Street. The Prudential building is near right. January 1945.

*Remains of Wira's Church of the Holy Cross (left), and the Old Town main square (right).
February 1945.*

Remains of the Old Town main square from above.

Chapter 5

PRISONER OF WAR

Around 5th October, a few days after the capitulation, I marched out of Warsaw with our army. We had been ordered to gather on the edge of the Mokotów Fields, a massive common area, and we made our way there in small groups. At the gathering point, under the watchful eyes of the Germans who stood at the front, we organised ourselves into lines. Groups of civilians had come to watch and look out for family members. Suddenly I heard my name being called out: "Danusia!" I looked around to see my Aunt Janka. Despite the crowd she had managed to spot me. She did not approach me but we both now knew the other was alive and we gestured our farewells.

We lined up six abreast – the boys of my Company with weapons in hand at the front and the women soldiers, including me, behind them. There were about a hundred of us in my group and we were leaving within the newly formed 72nd infantry regiment. We held our heads high, all wearing red-and-white armbands. I was still wearing my wellington boots. I watched as the boys at the front started marching first; they laid down their arms in large containers before moving through Mokotów Fields, and we followed behind them. As we marched past the standing Germans, some of them saluted us. Later I heard that Heinrich Himmler had described the fighting during the Warsaw Uprising as the fiercest since the beginning of the war, comparable to the street fighting in Stalingrad, which had been conducted between two well-armed professional armies. We had lasted for much longer than anybody could have expected. We had also treated German prisoners humanely. All this had apparently gained us a degree of respect among their soldiers.

In total about 15,000 AK soldiers left Warsaw, taken into captivity from different assembly points over those few days. Among this number were

2,000 women soldiers of the AK and 5,000 wounded, who were evacuated separately.

Despite the heroism of the Uprising, however, it was a failure with catastrophic losses. The exact numbers of casualties of the Uprising remains unknown but subsequent estimates place AK casualties at about 50 percent of the 47,000 AK soldiers who had started the Uprising. Sixteen thousand were known to be dead and 6,000 badly wounded. On the German side, despite their overwhelming military superiority, casualties matched those of our soldiers, with 16,000 killed and missing, 9,000 wounded and 2,000 taken prisoner. However the greatest tragedy was on the civilian side. Up to 200,000 Polish civilians died during the 63 days of the Uprising, mainly due to mass murder by the Germans and their associates.

As the AK departed from the city the remaining 200,000 civilians still in Warsaw were forced to leave. Among them were 3,500 AK soldiers disguised as civilians. Contrary to the capitulation agreement, about 55,000 thousand civilians were categorised as 'dangerous elements' and sent to concentration camps including Auschwitz. The remaining civilians were driven into the countryside with no means of support. This added to the 150,000 civilians who had left Warsaw throughout the Uprising and were taken to Germany into forced labour in factories or on farms.

Following the evacuations, on Hitler's orders and also in contravention of the capitulation agreement, the Germans razed what remained of the entire city of Warsaw to the ground. Before this everything left was looted from the city. I have read subsequently that 33,000 railway wagons filled with furniture, paintings, artefacts, personal belongings and factory equipment were taken out of Warsaw by the Germans. In later life I watched film footage on television of German demolition detachments with flame-throwers burning down building after building of my city, not checking whether anybody was hiding inside. Buildings of historical importance were not spared. By the time the Soviets finally entered Warsaw in January 1945 about 85 percent of the city's buildings no longer stood. The Germans had destroyed 25 percent prior to the Uprising, mainly during the 1939 bombing and following the Ghetto Uprising, another 25 percent during the fighting and a further 35 percent after the capitulation.

The march out of Warsaw to the combatant transit camp at Ożarów was about 15 kilometres eastwards and took a few hours. Warsaw's civilian population were marched to a different staging post at Pruszków which was not far from Ożarów. German guards marched alongside us every step of the way although it was a civilised march and we were treated appropriately as POWs. For me, however, the march was agonising as my wellington boots gave me yet more blisters. Some civilians came out to see us walk by. They were not allowed to approach us and so they stood to the side of the roads a few metres away. Occasionally someone managed to throw us the odd piece of fruit, bread or biscuit, ignoring the German orders. I could see sadness and pity in people's faces and a desire to help even though there was nothing they could do.

During this march out of Warsaw my mind was fixed entirely on the future. I did not dwell on the Uprising; it was now over and in the past. There would be time for reflection later.

We were told that we were heading into captivity in Germany but not where. I was going into the complete unknown. I drew some comfort that I was in a group; there were older people with me and I felt that whatever happened I would not be by myself. There was nobody with me whom I had known from before the Uprising, in fact nobody I had known for more than a couple of weeks; nevertheless I felt a strong sense of solidarity with those around me.

We reached Ożarów early that evening. I was in tears due to my wellington boots. We were squeezed into two enormous halls where we made our beds for the night on the concrete floor. It was very cold in the halls and I was hungry. Our stay at Ożarów lasted for two or three days, after which we were boarded onto tightly packed cattle trains. It was possible for a few among us to sit down where they stood but we were too tightly packed for everybody to sit down at once. Despite the discomfort the atmosphere in our wagon was good. Many of us were still teenagers and, with the threat of imminent death now gone, humour came to the fore.

It was in this train wagon that I came across two young sisters. At first I was surprised to see them among us as they did not look like members of the AK. The older of the two was Mancia who looked about 15 years old: she was squat and slightly underdeveloped physically. Mancia's sister, Kajtus, was a lot younger, about nine years old and particularly slight. I vaguely remembered having seen Mancia and Kajtus before when some of the other girls told me the sisters had been well-known street singers during the occupation, for which they received handouts from the public. I couldn't believe that the girls had managed to get past the Germans to join us as they were clearly Jewish and Kajtus in particular had striking Jewish features. To this day, given their appearance, I cannot imagine how the sisters had avoided capture by the Germans throughout the occupation while being so visible in public places when performing. I recall briefly speaking with Mancia a couple of times although we did not have a long conversation. Both sisters were extremely likeable and they looked so feeble and lonely that the AK girls were protective towards them. Maybe by this stage of the war the ordinary Wermacht soldier was less bothered with singling out Jews. Nevertheless it was still a concern and over those few days that we spent together in the train wagon all the AK girls took particular care to prevent the Germans becoming aware of the sisters' ethnicity.

Mancia and Kajtus must have been faced with particularly difficult choices as Jews after our surrender. They could have stayed hidden among the ruins of a city deserted by its population. However after our departure the Germans would destroy the remaining buildings in Warsaw, killing anyone they came across. Some people did remain in hiding in the city after the Uprising. One of these was Władysław Szpilman, who was vividly depicted in the 2002 film *The Pianist*. These Robinson Crusoes of Warsaw were mostly Jews who feared being identified by the Germans although many Poles also chose to remain. The girls had two other options; leave with the civilian population, or with the AK. I seems they thought their best chance of survival was within the ranks of the AK.

After a few days the train stopped at what looked like a depot area rather than a station. Here we were separated into various groups; the girls were also separated from the boys and we were boarded onto different trains. I don't know what the selection criteria were, apart from gender, but I presume our senior staff were involved. I found out later that some of the girls were taken to German munitions factories as forced labour in direct contravention of the Geneva Convention. I was put onto a train with a group of about 300 women. I do not recall seeing Mancia and Kajtus again but I would hear about them some years later.

We were stopped in the German countryside for delousing. We had spent two months living in the rubble and we were filthy and infested with head lice. I recall a line of German women beside the train, about seven of them, each sitting on a stool behind a metal household bowl filled with disinfectant. We queued in line to dip our heads into these bowls. The women helped make sure we dipped fully. Some of us who were particularly grubby, like myself, had to dip our heads into a number of bowls. Nobody spoke to these German women and they did not speak to us. Once the delousing was finished we reboarded our train and moved on.

After a few more days we reached the station at Bremervörde in north-west Germany. I was now about a thousand kilometres from my home. We disembarked and began marching. By now we had been informed that our destination was the international POW camp Stalag X-B near Sandbostel. The POW camp was about ten kilometres away and we were hungry and exhausted after an uncomfortable journey. During the march, which took most of the day, spirits were low. People lacked humour and some girls collapsed along the way. I was still wearing my painful wellington boots which certainly clouded my mood.

My first memory of Sandbostel camp is of our approach. Sandbostel had been used for the internment of POWs from the start of the war and already contained many Polish soldiers, held there since 1939. By now some of these prisoners had a certain amount of freedom and were even allowed to go beyond the camp perimeter at times. It seems that some of these Poles knew we were arriving because as we approached they rushed out to help us over the last stretch. They carried many of our girls who were struggling with illness or exhaustion. It was a wonderful surprise to see our countrymen and it gave us much comfort to know that we were not alone.

We entered the camp through a large gate into a courtyard surrounded by barracks. There were other nationalities at Sandbostel including French, Hungarians, Italians and Romanians, but we were the only women.

We were allocated two barracks near the far end. The first barracks was labelled number 90 and the officers moved in there, each with one adjutant. The rest of us were next door, a few metres away. Our barracks did not have a number; instead the word *Aufnahme* was written on the front, which I believe means reception in German. We quickly set about improving our personal hygiene. I had a thick head of hair in those days and I recall some of the girls picking out lice eggs, which took them quite some time. For one girl the disinfecting en route had not worked. She was too embarrassed for others to know and so she had travelled to Sandbostel with her head covered in a headscarf of sorts. By the time we got to Sandbostel the lice had grown so big and plentiful that they started crawling out onto her forehead. Our commandant was soon called and the girl was taken away for a thorough clean-up.

The Poles at Sandbostel took exceptional care of us and tried hard to make our circumstances as tolerable as possible. Food rations were brought to our barracks, where our senior girls allocated them. The rations were meagre, which left us all constantly hungry. Each day we received only one piece of bread with some margarine and a bowl of soup. Many of us were still developing teenagers, some as young as 14 years old. The resident Poles used the fact that they were on reasonable terms with the Germans to get an additional daily bowl of milky soup with noodles for us younger girls, which made a huge difference. Our countrymen also shared half of their Red Cross parcels with us, which contained tins of meat, fruit, sausages and always cigarettes. We did not start receiving Red Cross parcels ourselves until some months later. We remained constantly hungry but with the help we received we got by.

Unlike many of the male prisoners at Sandbostel, who were allowed to wander beyond the camp perimeter, we were much more restricted. I presume this was for our protection as we were the only women in the camp. The importance of this restriction was soon to become clear.

Not long after we arrived most of our officers and their adjutants were moved to an Oflag, a camp for officers. About 200 of us girls remained in our barracks with only a few officers to look after us. I recall my commandant being a tall lady with a nice figure and a pretty face; she wore a black eye-patch to conceal an injury sustained during the Uprising. After the officers had been moved out, a group of Russian male prisoners were brought in to the empty barracks next to ours. The Germans surrounded the Russian barracks with barbed wire, leaving them barely any room to move around outside. As Stalin had not signed the Geneva Convention, the Germans treated the Soviet prisoners harshly. A man who is treated like an animal will surely grow wild, and on seeing women in the next barracks they tried to get to us. Around Christmas – I think it was Christmas Eve – some Russian prisoners managed to cut their way through the barbed wire and came into our barrack. We were all petrified when these wild men walked in. Fortunately they were only in our barracks for a few minutes. The alarm was raised and the Russians were soon chased out by the Polish male prisoners. The Germans forced the Russians back into their barrack, where we could hear them being severely punished.

There were also happier episodes at Sandbostel. The French prisoners had attained certain privileges, which they used to establish a camp theatre. These were very elegant events and they tried particularly hard to put on impressive performances for us women. It was the first time I had been to a grown-up theatre; it felt real and the sights and smells were wonderful. I recall thinking that, having come through the tragedy of the Warsaw Uprising, this was a truly pleasurable moment.

Although the few months we spent at Sandbostel were hard, in truth all the other prisoners were especially helpful towards us girls and we were treated favourably. Overall I felt quite safe and unafraid. Despite the horrors of Warsaw I did not feel traumatised. I also did not give too much thought to the future. I had absolutely no idea what might happen and it seemed pointless looking ahead. We seemed quite removed from the war in our camp, a feeling somewhat enhanced by the camp being surrounded by trees. We knew little of what was going on in the wider world, other than the odd encouraging rumour that things were not going well for the Germans.

We were at Sandbostel for around three months. Some of our girls were moved to another camp in December, and in January 1945 we followed on. We were marched back to Bremervörde, where we boarded another cattle wagon. While waiting in the wagon in Bremervörde station I had my next brush with death when we were caught in a heavy Allied bombing raid. The Allies regularly bombed German transport links and Bremevörde was a large railway hub. As the bombs started falling, our wagon was quickly shunted into some sidings and we were left locked inside while our German guards dashed for cover elsewhere. The raid lasted for what seemed like an hour. We could hear planes flying low overhead and the sound of gunfire and huge explosions as the bombs fell all around, some only metres away from us. Each time there was a loud explosion nearby we trembled and prayed. Eventually the explosions gave way to calm. Our wagon had escaped being hit and I knew that my mother was still protecting me.

We travelled about 200 kilometres to Lathen from where we walked the 14 kilometres to our new place of internment, Stalag VI-C subcamp in Oberlangen. Oberlangen, as we called the camp, was originally built in 1933 to intern German political opponents to the Nazi party and from 1939 it had been used to detain POWs. The camp's location was in the remote marshlands of North-West Germany in the Emsland district near the Dutch border. The area was mainly used for the production of peat for fuel, which made the local air heavy with a high concentration of dust particles that caused various lung diseases. In addition, internal camp conditions were sub-standard. As a result Oberlangen was deemed unsuitable for the internment of POWs under the Geneva Convention. All the male POWs were moved to a more suitable camp in October 1944 and Oberlangen was delisted as a POW camp and ceased to appear in any German POW camp statistics. Yet from December 1944 we were brought to Oberlangen as POWs without the Red Cross being informed and with no officially recorded dates of our arrival.

When we arrived at Oberlangen the camp still felt quite empty, but at least the other girls who had travelled before us from Sandbostel were there, as well as a small number of Italian male prisoners. The Italians lived in the German section in the forecamp, where they worked in the kitchen block. Over the following days other women from the Uprising started arriving from various camps and forced labour establishments. Our headcount soon grew to over 1,700, all women soldiers of the Warsaw Uprising. There were about 13 barracks with bunk beds running along both sides with a walkway in-between. I slept on the top bunk.

For me the worst aspect of life at Oberlangen was the complete lack of food. Rations were the barest minimum to keep us alive in the short term and some of the girls occasionally fainted from hunger. A typical daily ration would be tepid tea and wet bread for breakfast, sometimes with a bit of butter or marmalade. The bread was distributed on the basis of weight, and by soaking the bread in water to make it heavier the Germans were able to give us less. For lunch and dinner we received some watery soup made from leftovers such as kale, a type of bitter cabbage, to which the odd piece of potato peel was added. Our hunger was intense throughout our stay and what food there was always tasted awful.

One of the women who arrived in the following days was called Hania. She had spent the previous few months in forced labour at a German munitions factory. When Hania first saw me I was sitting on my top bunk crying. She asked sympathetically, "Why are you crying?" I replied, "Because I am hungry as hell." To my surprise she took some rusks out of her pocket and gave them to me, saying, "Here, eat some of these. Don't worry, it will get better... If it doesn't get worse first." That's how we first got to know each other. Hania took the bunk next to mine and I would remain friends for life with this generous girl who always looked at life cheerfully.

Hania had grown up in Warsaw. Her father had perished early in the war leaving Hania with her mother and one brother. Hania's brother was active in the AK and had persuaded Hania to join in the run-up to the Uprising. Her pseudonym was 'Panterka' (Panther). As Hania was leaving home to join the Uprising, her mother cried after her and begged her to stay. Hania reassured her she would be back soon and ran off to war. She never saw her mother again. Hania's brother died on the first day of the Uprising and her mother soon afterwards. Our similar family tragedies made us close and we were always together. Hania always said she regarded me as her sister and I felt the same way about her.

Finally, after about a month, we started receiving our first Red Cross parcels. Apparently the Red Cross was only informed about our presence at Oberlangen when prisoners still at Sandbostel found out where we were and spread the word. But I have also read contrary reports that the parcels were merely diverted from other camps by the Germans. Receiving the parcels was wonderful although barely enough to supplement our inadequate food rations. However, the American cigarettes which came in the parcels made many of the girls particularly happy. Some, like Hania, were so hooked that they were willing to trade food from their parcels for more tobacco. When that ran out they would roll dried grass in scraps of paper and smoke it. I did not smoke and I held my tobacco in reserve for trading in the future. In total I received three Red Cross parcels while at Oberlangen.

Many of the older girls in the camp had established careers back in Warsaw, some as teachers. They offered some limited education classes in the barracks for us younger girls. We were taught subjects which had been banned by the Germans in Warsaw including history, Polish and foreign languages. We also played sports and engaged in scout activities. I recall readings and lectures about philosophy and literature, as well as poetry and song evenings. One of the AK women among us was a well-known Polish actress called Maryna Buchwaldowa and she organised a group that put on various artistic performances for us in the evenings. These performances would include plays, dances and recitals and were aimed at keeping spirits up as well as providing cultural education for the younger girls.

It was a severely cold winter and our somewhat aged wooden barracks were freezing, except for one small wood-fired heater in the middle that produced more smoke than heat. The nights were extremely cold and we would often wake up with frost in our hair. In the morning our washroom floors were covered with ice and the darkness made this treacherous. We had to open the washroom windows in order to get some light from the permanently manned German watchtowers outside. This made the washrooms even colder. I believe that washing in these freezing conditions made many of us susceptible to illnesses in later life. Visiting the latrines was also an unpleasant experience. They had minimal privacy and consisted of a plank of wood over on open ditch. Some girls occasionally slipped off this gangplank into the mire below.

The German guards would sometimes take some of the girls outside the camp to gather scraps of wood for burning. The braver girls would take this opportunity to sneak off into the fields in search of the odd potato, carrot or broccoli although there wasn't much around at this time of year. Sometimes they also found discarded clothes, which helped us to keep warm. These finds had to be sneaked back to the barracks as they were not permitted and although some Germans turned a blind eye, others reacted harshly and punished the girls severely. Because of such punishments, I was too frightened to sneak off on the one occasion I was taken to the woods. When one of the girls was successful in scavenging the odd vegetable it made a wonderful treat; we would all sit around our wood-fired heater in the barracks and cook our single potato.

Relations with the Germans at Oberlangen were much worse than at Sandbostel. Although some of the guards behaved quite decently towards us there were others who treated us with cruelty. One SS Feltwebel (sergeant), I think his name was Treiber, was particularly unpleasant. He constantly spied on us and eagerly reported any transgressions to his superiors. This often led to the withholding of food rations, which was life-threatening given our circumstances. He enjoyed screaming aggressively and would occasionally punch one of the girls in the face. When the Red Cross parcels eventually started arriving he confiscated some out of spite. He was later held to account for his actions.

We had little communication with our German guards beyond the bare minimum. Any important discussions were undertaken by our commandant Lieutenant 'Jaga'. I liked Jaga, she was a strong leader who inspired confidence. However she was better at dealing with the senior ranks and was less approachable for us in the lower ranks.

Overall our living conditions at Oberlangen were totally inadequate and I have always regarded it as a concentration camp rather than a POW camp. I have since read that we were possibly sent there as punishment for our refusal, despite repeated threats, to renounce our POW status. Had we done so, our captors would have been able to use us as forced labour in the German war effort without having to take heed of the Geneva Convention. These days I also hear rumours that the plan was to liquidate us before the war was over. Perhaps fortunately, I was unaware of all of this at the time.

LIBERATED BY OUR OWN

We had little information about the outside world, just what little titbits we could glean from the Italians. However, as the sounds of warfare got louder and the explosions ever closer, hopes were rising that the war was coming to an end.

Little did we know that General Maczek's Polish 1st Armoured Division, which had previously been based in Scotland, had arrived nearby in April 1945. This Division was attached to the Canadian army and had fought its way East from Normandy after the opening of the Western Front. After they established a base in the German town of Haren, only about ten kilometres from us, the Division started hearing rumours about a mystery POW camp in the vicinity. They could not have imagined that they would soon be liberating women soldiers from their own country...

It was the morning of 12th April 1945. An unusual stillness had descended on the camp and it seemed that some of the Germans had left. I could only see about a dozen Germans including the command-ing General and the Feldwebel. Something was clearly in the air. In the distance we could hear the sound of heavy explosions. Many of the girls spent the morning wandering around the camp while others just stood by the fence staring into the distance. All of a sudden they saw some vehicles approaching the camp from afar. When we heard their screams all of us still left in the barracks came rushing out to see what was happening. As the vehicles got closer we could see that this was a military convoy. There was a motorcycle moving quickly at the front, followed by a Jeep, then two scout carriers, with a tank bringing up the rear. They were close now, we could see soldiers but we could not tell who they were. The girls started shouting, "English? *Français*? American?"

Suddenly a soldier in the Jeep, noticing the eagle emblem on our forage caps, shouted, "They are Polish girls!" Other soldiers shouted, "We are Poles, the 1st Armoured Division." This didn't make any immediate sense to us as in captivity we knew nothing about what was happening on the Western battlefront. We had not heard about the 1st Armoured Division or that it had been fighting so close by. We girls shouted, "We are women of the AK! From Warsaw! From the Warsaw Uprising!" Everybody was now shouting – "It's a miracle!" This was an unbelievable moment, an overwhelming feeling of unbridled joy.

The tank drove over the camp gate into the forecamp where the Germans were based. The soldiers fired a few shots into the air as a warning and soon the Germans scuttled out of their barracks to surrender. The girls mobbed the tank, many shouting with joy, some crying. Everyone was greeting and hugging. One of the soldiers spoke with deep emotion: "Our beloved compatriots. You are free."

This was a day of great celebration for us AK girls. After two long months of fighting in Warsaw, humiliation in captivity, enduring hunger and dirt, we had been liberated by our own. A Polish flag which had been made in secret and presented to us by the Italian prisoners was soon hoisted up the flagpole. Commandant Jaga immediately called an assembly as a show of discipline, which was observed impeccably. We felt proud and wanted to make a good impression in front of our soldiers. The head of the convoy, a Lieutenant Colonel, received Lieutenant Jaga's report, which stated that we were the Ladies' Battalion for the Defence of Warsaw and that our numbers were 1,716 present, 20 in the sick bay and seven babies.

The fact that ten babies in total were born in the camp has always amazed me. I always wondered how these mothers who had participated in the Warsaw Uprising, obviously in early pregnancy, had managed to cope with the many months of hardship in captivity.

The Lieutenant Colonel asked Jaga how we had been treated by the Germans and her response was included in her report. Soon afterwards the cruel Feldwebel Treiber was led away under escort. The sound of a single gunshot could be heard some moments later.

After making an assessment of our food and sanitary requirements, some of the soldiers left to report back to base. They took with them the remaining German prisoners and their General who was treated according to his rank. Later that day supplies started arriving from the Divisional base, which included food, toiletries and other essentials along with greetings and good wishes. The older girls were taken for rides in Jeeps or on the tank late into the night.

The Italians cooked a wonderful dinner that evening and we ate well for the first time in a long while. The Italians stayed and enjoyed the evening with us for they too had been liberated. That night we felt free and safe under the protection of the Polish army. Some of the older girls felt particularly excited about a happier life now that the Polish army was around. I went to bed late and slept like a baby. It had been the most wonderful day and one I would cherish for the rest of my life.

I had not been aware of the Italian alliance with Germany under Mussolini earlier in the war. When I discovered it later it did not alter my good perception of our fellow Italian prisoners. Many Italians had been opposed to this alliance and had not supported Mussolini. The Italian prisoners had been very kind to us and had helped us when they could. We liked them and regarded them as our friends and they were treated as fellow liberated prisoners.

The next day a priest came and said a thanksgiving mass at our liberated camp. Many more soldiers from the Division would visit us in the coming days including General Maczek himself. Jaga organised another assembly, at which General Maczek spoke to us of his delight that his Division had been able to liberate the Polish girls who had defended Warsaw. Everybody immediately warmed to him and we quickly realised that General Maczek was well liked by his entire Division. In the following weeks General Anders, who led the 2nd Polish Corps, also visited us from his base in Italy. Many soldiers who came to our camp were hoping to hear news of relatives. One Colonel found his daughter, another soldier his sister and many others their cousins. The reunions were very emotional.

We remained at Oberlangen for another few weeks while decisions were made about where to take us. Although the war was not yet over the German army had retreated from the vicinity and we were able to wander freely outside the camp. There was, however, little to see in this remote peat land – no towns or villages. Some of the older girls visited the Division's base in Haren but I had not turned 16 yet and was considered too young for such trips.

On 8th May 1945 Germany surrendered unconditionally and after five years and eight months the war in Europe was finally over. Over 60 million lives had been lost, including almost six million Polish citizens, of whom three million were Jewish.

DISPLACED

After a few weeks we were transported six kilometres to the former concentration camp Neusustrum which became known to us by the name of its municipality, Niederlangen. Many of the male prisoners had previously been moved there, before our arrival at Oberlangen, due to the vastly superior conditions. It was a much larger camp, the barracks were in a better state and the beds even had mattresses, which actually made them quite comfortable. Hygiene levels were higher and we now had more personal space. Inside the camp was a large, picturesque pond in which I learned to swim. I also learned to ride a bike there.

Other Polish units in the area quickly found out that there were women at Niederlangen and started visiting. The Polish pilots based a little further away at Quakenbruck started arriving frequently in addition to the regular visits from the Division. Soon we were being invited to parties and I discovered how much I loved dancing.

When I danced with the boys they would offer me a cigarette. I didn't smoke but the older girls would tell me to accept the offer and, after taking a puff or two, to put it out and hide it so that they could smoke the rest later. So I danced with the boys and took their cigarettes. After taking small puffs for a while I started to get a taste for smoking so when I was back in the barracks I decided to keep a few cigarette butts for myself. As I lit a match some of the older girls shouted at me, "Hey, give them back, you don't smoke!" "But I want to smoke as well," I replied. The girls rounded on me, saying, "Oh, you're too immature to smoke." In defiance I retorted, "If I'm too immature to smoke, then I'm too immature to accept cigarettes!" and I turned away, determined that I would not take cigarettes for them again. I thought they were being ungrateful and that the least they could have done was give me a piece of chocolate in exchange. I can see now that if I hadn't been so stubborn I could easily have taken up smoking at that time. Whatever their motives, it was because of those girls that I never started smoking.

I turned 16 years of age that July in Niederlangen and in those few weeks we were there I began my first relationships with boys. I fell in love with a handsome boy close to my age called Czesio. Unfortunately Czesio left quite early for France, where he planned to study. Then there was Januszek, who fell in love with me and wanted me to go back to Poland with him. Januszek was always happy, he liked to sing and wrote many love poems for me. He always generated a jovial atmosphere. Januszek came from a very different part of Poland from me and in the end I couldn't imagine myself living there. I felt I was too young to make such a commitment and perhaps I also didn't feel strongly enough for him. I felt so sorry for him when I told him my decision.

I also became friends with an older pilot, Zygmund, who became a kind of father figure to me. Mary, Zygmund's fiancé in London, was also very kind, and whenever he made flights back to England she would give him some treats to bring back for me. I stayed in touch with Zygmund and Mary – whom he married – for the rest of their lives.

I had been longing for some comfortable shoes and finally an opportunity presented itself. I still had 150 cigarettes from my reserves from Oberlangen and they were still in short supply. I did a deal with one of the boys, my 150 cigarettes for a new pair of shoes on his next trip away from base. He measured my feet before departing and brought me back the most beautiful brown leather shoes from Belgium. They fitted me perfectly and were blissful to wear. I kept those shoes with me for many years afterwards. Meanwhile the other girls just smoked their assets away.

Those early days of freedom soon brought a change in attitudes among some of us young girls as the strain of living under intense conditions was lifted. My barracks at Niederlangen was filled with mainly younger girls and we started behaving like the teenagers we were. Hania was one of the naughtier ones. Despite the war being over, and perhaps in response to our behaviour, our commandant tried to enforce a disciplined regime. The commandant was formerly a senior Polish literature teacher, pseudonym 'Rakieta', and we young girls often fell foul of her rules. We regularly missed morning assembly; Rakieta would castigate us and we would protest when oversleeping was not deemed an acceptable excuse. My son has recently found a written appraisal of me dated 15th June 1945 by one of our female seniors. In the appraisal I am described as 'disobedient, lazy and easily led astray'. I agree that I was insubordinate at that time but even after all these years I was somewhat annoyed by the rest of the description.

Plans were being prepared for us to be transported to Italy and Rakieta warned us that if our discipline did not improve we would be left behind. Initially we disregarded the threat and the bad behaviour continued. Eventually she told us firmly that we were staying in Germany and we started to believe it. Nevertheless, when the transport trucks arrived we packed our things and sneaked onto a truck near the back of the convoy. We took with us the long German coats we had recently been given, which were lined with fur and very warm. What we did not know was that Rakieta was seated in the cabin of the truck immediately behind us.

After about 900 kilometres we reached Oflag VII-A Murnau, a German POW camp in Bavaria near the Austrian border. Murnau had housed a thousand Polish officer POWs since 1939 and was now a transit camp. On arrival at Murnau we were ordered to report to Rakieta. She told us that as we were not on the list we would have to return to Niederlangen. We pleaded with her to put our names on the list; she said this was impossible, although I suspect she could have done so if she had wanted. She suggested that we return to Niederlangen, where we could register for the next transport back again, and naively we accepted, believing that we would be back at Murnau soon. Of course it didn't occur to us teenage girls that as this was the last transport to Italy from Niederlangen there would be nobody to bring us back. Worst of all, Rakieta told us to leave our warm, fur-lined German coats behind and that they would be waiting for us when we returned. And so we went back to Niederlangen, having wasted about four days travelling over 1,700 kilometres. We had lost our coats and Rakieta had served us her punishment.

Rakieta was certainly not my favourite commandant! She wasn't good at dealing with us younger girls. She had no warmth or sense of guardianship and everything had to be done her way. Appropriately her pseudonym translates as 'Rocket'.

When we arrived back at Niederlangen camp it was in the process of being emptied and closed down. Within a few days we were moved to a nearby convent called Hange, where we would spend the following year. Only a few senior girls had stayed behind to look after us including Jaga and my new commandant 'Nika'. There was also the Kwarta family. Mr Kwarta had been a well-known painter in Warsaw where he had drafted the image used for the famous Warsaw mermaid statue, which was the city's coat of arms. We would remain in contact for many years. A few of the nuns at the convent had also remained and they helped by cooking and generally looking after us. They were polite and pleasant but we never became close to them. There were about 50 of us in total including around 30 of us younger AK girls. The convent was a lovely big building, we shared three large bedrooms and each of us had her own bed. There were no more bunk beds.

Hange was only a short walk from the 1st Armoured Division in Haren. With the war in Europe over, there were about three million displaced Polish citizens in Germany who had been liberated from camps and forced labour. In May 1945 the thousand-or-so German inhabitants of Haren were moved to surrounding communities and the town became a staging post for many thousands of these Polish DPs. The town was officially renamed Maczków after the Division's leader – a name it would retain until eventually the last refugees left in 1948.

That 18 months or so following our liberation from Oberlangen was the happiest period of my life. I had no responsibilities, I felt free and I was growing into a young lady with lots of friends and boys around me. I expect this is true for most people in their teenage years but for me this was in particularly stark contrast to my life so far.

I attended school with the girls in Maczków, which was a 30 minute walk away. One of our teachers, Mrs Trenkner, had been a Latin teacher at Haliny Gepnerówny, my school in Warsaw. While still at Oberlangen Mrs Trenkner had provided me with a certificate vouching that I had already completed my second year of school, so I was able to enter the third year of high school at Maczków. We walked to school each day in a group and the weather was almost always good. We all bonded well and there was much laughter. Silly little things stay in my memory – like how we coloured our hair with the bark from oak trees. We would boil the bark in water then rinse our hair in the liquid which gave it a lovely oaky colour. For those who wanted a slightly lighter colour, bulrushes were used instead.

We attended frequent parties where there was always plenty of dancing and laughter. Our commandant at Hange, Captain Nika, was very understanding. She was a sympathetic person and I could always turn to her for help; as a result she commanded respect and was able to maintain good discipline. If we got back from a dance later than the agreed time, she would often be waiting up for us. She would order us to get ready for bed immediately and then calmly inform us what our punishment for the following day would be. We knew where we stood with Nika and respected her for it. She and Jaga both returned to Poland quite soon after the war.

JANUSZ

Despite these happy times and early freedoms, food in Germany remained scarce and we continued to be hungry. Fruit in particular was almost non-existent. Our provisions were brought to us by land from the 2nd Polish Corps, which was based in Italy. The transport unit was headed by Janusz Szlachetko. I recall him arriving for the first time, in a Jeep, at the head of his unit of about five vehicles, and I immediately took a shine to him. Over time I got to know Janusz quite well. At 38 he was considerably older than me. He took a protective attitude towards me as well as bringing me the odd little luxury from Italy. During one of his visits I was unable to greet him, having been grounded for two days after arriving home late from a dance. Somehow he managed to pass the stockings he had brought for me through a window, despite my great embarrassment at him seeing me being treated like the schoolgirl I still was. On another visit I managed to talk Janusz into teaching me to drive his Jeep. He drove us a little distance from Hange before letting me take the wheel. Jeeps are very responsive vehicles and it wasn't long before I drove it into a ditch on the side of the road.

Some nearby soldiers were highly amused by my performance although they tried to remain respectful because of Janusz's senior rank. Of course he was deeply embarrassed by this and we had to wait until the soldiers had gone before manoeuvering the Jeep out of the ditch.

Janusz came from the ancient village of Buszcze in the *voivodeship* (administrative district) of Tarnopol in Eastern Galicia, where his family had lived for generations. He was the youngest of three siblings. Tarnopol had been part of Poland for 400 years until Poland ceased to exist in 1772. At the time of Janusz's birth on 28th May 1908 Tarnopol was part of the Austro-Hungarian Empire. Following Poland's rebirth as an independent country in 1918 Tarnopol became part of the eastern borderlands of the Second Polish Republic referred to as 'the Kresy'. As a young man Janusz lived in the large historic town of Brzeżany about 16 kilometres south of Buszcze and a little over a hundred kilometres south-east of the storied City of Lwów. After his education Janusz initially worked in the Tax Office from 1925 before joining the army as a non-commissioned officer in 1928 assigned to the 51st Infantry Regiment based in Brzeżane. The Regiment was part of the 12th Infantry Division headquartered in Tarnopol.

ENLISTING BY STEALTH

Although I was still preoccupied with enjoying my freedom thoughts inevitably turned towards the future. It was becoming clear that Poland had already lost her independence again to the Soviet Union. Soon after liberation we had all heard about the Yalta Conference, which had consolidated the Soviets' hold over our country. There was growing concern about how the Soviet regime would treat soldiers of the Polish Armed Forces who'd served abroad and the soldiers of the AK. Our early experiences were not encouraging.

In early 1946, two of our group at Hange, Ela and Babi, received letters from their families in Poland begging them to return. We were fearful of what might happen to them and desperately tried to convince them not to go, but to no avail. They left us in the spring of 1946. That was the last we ever heard of Ela and Babi. For years we wrote letters to Poland asking for information but nothing ever came back. Some years later still, when I was in Poland with one of the other girls, we placed advertisements in newspapers seeking information but not a single word came back. Years later Hania told me a similar story about a girl called Halina (pseudonym 'Tomek') she had known from their time at the munitions factory. Tomek had also decided to return to Poland from Germany around this time and was also never heard of again; she was only 14 years old.

General Anders had strong views about the new Poland under communist rule and he cautioned against returning. He had first-hand experience of life under the Soviets during his two-year incarceration in the infamous Lubyanka prison in Moscow following his capture during the 1939 campaign. Anders suspected that Soviet hostility towards Poland and the Polish government-in-exile also extended to all those loyal to this government, including the Polish army overseas and particularly the AK. Our army had not been demobilised yet but individuals were given permission to make their own decision as to whether to return to Poland. In those early post-war days in Germany only a few chose to go back knowing the considerable risk.

Because the Polish force was under British command it had somewhere to go, at least initially, as the army would be going to Britain before demobilising. There was particular concern about us AK soldiers; we were not part of the British army and therefore not eligible to go to Britain. Meanwhile we were at risk if we returned to Poland, where the puppet Soviet government would consider us enemies of communism. In order to protect us General Anders tried to enlist as many AK soldiers as possible into the Polish army while under British command. He had already managed to enlist some liberated Poles who had been forcibly conscripted into the German army but the British were making things difficult. They didn't want additional costs and made it clear there should be no further enlistments other than the very close relatives of serving soldiers. From his base in Italy General Anders ordered both his 2nd Polish Corps in Italy and the Division in Maczków to find ways around these impediments. Thus began a sizeable enlistment operation by stealth.

Some of the older girls managed to get jobs with the Division working in canteens, messes and other areas and so were able to enter the Polish Armed Forces that way. Other girls married Polish soldiers and many others were falsely registered as sisters or cousins of soldiers. The British constantly complained about the rising numbers but somehow Anders was able to smooth things over. Personally I was oblivious to these clandestine manoeuvres at the time – I was too busy enjoying my freedom and having a good time. I just assumed that wherever the Polish army went, I would go too. I had lost my family in Poland and had no one to go home to. I was now becoming part of an increasingly close-knit group of Poles who were a second family for me. I only became aware later that Janusz had taken responsibility for me. I still have Janusz's British service record in which I am listed as his first cousin. This paved the way for my eventual entry into England.

ITALY

After a year at the convent it was time for us to rejoin the other girls in Italy. In the early summer of 1946 we travelled in one of the last transportations to Italy from Germany. Janusz was in charge of the transport; the 50 or so girls including Hania squeezed into a couple of troop carriers, while I managed to get a seat at the front in Janusz's Jeep.

The route to Italy was circuitous, covering almost 2,500 kilometres. The first day took us through Germany and much of France. We stopped for the night on the edge of the French Alps at Grenoble and it was here that I had my first taste of Champagne. While a wonderful dinner was being prepared, the boys opened a bottle and gave me a glass to taste. The Champagne tasted so gorgeously sweet that I wanted to finish the whole glass. Janusz was trying to tell me to drink slowly and only try a little but it tasted too good for me to stop. Soon the glass was empty, I was on my back and Hania and the girls were carrying me up to bed. That was the end of my dinner that evening; I had no idea Champagne could have that effect on me.

The following day's journey through the Alps was treacherous as we headed for the Brenner Pass and drove head on into the biggest storm I have experienced in my life. The sky above was black, the rain slapped down like falling bricks, the lightning and booming thunder were incessant. Our road took us alongside a steep drop into a deep gorge and I couldn't bear to look. We could see very little ahead of us. Suddenly I saw what seemed like the whole mountain crumbling onto the road just in front of us. We had avoided the landslide by the narrowest of margins; yet another near escape. We had spent that night in our trucks until groups of men were able to clear the road.

The next day we crossed the pass and drove south to Ancona on the Adriatic coast where Janusz was based. After another gruelling day of travelling I was grateful that we would be resting there for the night. Ancona had been taken from the Germans in July 1944 and the 2nd Polish Corps had established its headquarters there.

That evening Janusz and I discussed our experiences during the war and I learned much about his personal journey since Germany attacked Poland in September 1939.

After two weeks of heavy fighting against the invading Germans the weakened Polish army sought to regroup in the south-east of Poland in the hills along the borders with Romania and the Soviet Union, near Janusz's homeland. This became known as the Romanian Bridgehead. The plan was to organise a successful defence of the region and await the expected French attack on Germany from the west. This attack never took place. When the Russians unexpectedly attacked Poland from the east on 17th September the remainder of the Polish army was caught between the two most powerful armies in the world and all hope was lost. The Polish government ordered all remaining troops to evacuate with the objective of regrouping abroad to continue the fight. Thus begun a massive evacuation from Poland in small groups, each man for himself, as the net tightened.

Dressed in civilian clothing Janusz stole across the border into Romania on 22nd September evading Russian troops who had all but secured the border. In total about a hundred thousand Polish troops managed to escape into Romania and Hungary. Although Romania was still allied to Poland it was under intense pressure from Germany to prevent passage for the Polish soldiers and Janusz was interned in a camp in Buzau. Perhaps out of sympathy for the Poles, Romanian security at the various camps was weak and, like thousands of others Janusz managed to escape and avoid capture by fascist sympathisers and Gestapo agents who were swarming the country. Many escapees travelled west and joined the Polish army in the defence of France. Janusz continued south to Bucharest where he received travel documents from the Polish consulate. This enabled him to board a ship at the port of Konstanca for the Middle East. From Beirut Janusz journeyed overland to Haifa where he joined the Independent Polish Carpathian Rifle Brigade (the SBSK) in October 1940. His rank is documented as sergeant.

The SBSK was created in April 1940 as part of the Polish Army in Homs in French Syria where it entered the ranks of the French Armée du Levant. Between April and June 1940 around 3,500 Polish soldiers arrived to join the SBSK, mostly from the port of Konstanca but also from Piraeus in Greece and Split in Jugoslavia. A smaller number of officers sailed in from the French port of Marseille. In June 1940 France capitulated and the Armée du Levant decided to support the Vichy government. The SBSK refused to accept the French command to lay down arms and threatened to fight their way out if necessary. In late June the Brigade defected to British-controlled Palestine, where it came under the command of the British Eighth Army. The British had expected a band of dishevelled and dispirited men and they were surprised to witness the arrival of 3,500 well-armed, highly educated and committed soldiers.

The Brigade song gives some understanding of the various circuitous routes taken to the Middle East by the soldiers who formed the SBSK in 1940 and offers a glimpse of their strong convictions. The words translate as follows:

> We walked here from Narvik
> We from Hungary and we from Czechoslovakia
> In Syria we are countless
> And three of us blew in from Germany

We came by sea and we from Flanders
We over mountains and we through forests
Now we all to Alexandria
Now we are as one

Carpathian Brigade, far is the world
Long is our soldier's wandering trail
Far is the road, through storms and through fog
From the snows of Narvik to the Libyan sands

The Brigade marches and marches
We march with every breath
As Poland looks out from afar
Awaiting day after day

Carpathian Brigade to our houses and our huts
We are going to Poland across the whole world
We'll walk every track and every road
We'll return back to Poland, so help us God

In August 1941 Janusz was promoted to Sergeant Major, Warrant Officer Class 2. The SBSK served with distinction in the siege of the Libyan port of Tobruk from August to December 1941 and Janusz received a commendation for his part in it. The Australian troops had already adopted the name of 'Rats of Tobruk' for themselves. Impressed by the SBSK's valour, the Australians honoured their Polish colleagues by bestowing this name upon them too.

Janusz told me that he had been wounded in the head by shrapnel and also that he had lost all his hair due to an illness. After trying many doctors and treatments he eventually came across a Jewish doctor who was successful in helping his hair grow back.

In June 1941 Hitler reneged on his treaty with Stalin by launching a full-scale invasion of Russia. Taken by surprise, Stalin sought a pact with Poland which became the Sikorski–Mayski agreement of July 1941. This led to the release of some of the hundreds of thousands of Poles who had been force-fully deported to Siberia by the Soviets in 1940. Following this 'amnesty', a Polish army was formed under General Anders, made up of those who had managed to make their way from the various gulags. Ever distrustful of the Russians, Anders grasped the opportunity to evacuate this army to the Middle East, where it arrived between March and August 1942. The 2nd Polish Corps was formed from this force headed by General Anders and operating from within the British Eighth Army. Janusz's SBSK was integrated into the Corps and formed the backbone of the Third Carpathian Rifle Division, abbreviated to the 3rd DSK. Janusz was attached to the Divisional headquarters as a technical writer. The Division became known as the Christmas Tree Division due to their distinctive emblem which bore a Christmas tree set on the colours of the Polish flag.

Janusz told me that when they arrived in Palestine around 4,000 Jewish soldiers in the Corps deserted one night, fully armed. General Anders effectively turned a blind eye to this desertion, a gesture which later became known by the Jews as the 'Anders Aliyah'. This was a significant event in the future establishment of Israel as many of these soldiers went on to contribute to the defence of Jewish settlements in Palestine and to fight for a Jewish homeland. One of them was Menachem Begin, the future Prime Minister of the State of Israel.

In December 1943 the 2nd Polish Corps embarked apon the Italian campaign and made its name in the fourth and final battle of Monte Cassino in May 1944, at which Janusz served within the 3rd DSK. In September 1944 Janusz was sent to Officer Training School, as a result of which he was nominated for a commission in February 1945 and eventually achieved promotion to the full officer rank of 2nd Lieutenant (reserve) in 1946. The nomination was signed by Tadeusz 'Bór' Komorowski, the Commander of the Warsaw Uprising and future Prime Minister of the Polish government-in-exile.

In March 1945 after completing officer school, Janusz joined the 22nd Artillery Supply Company. He was in the transport platoon, which was famous for its special mascot – a live bear. Polish soldiers in Palestine had adopted an orphaned Syrian brown bear cub in November 1942 and named it Wojtek, which derives from the Polish for 'Happy Warrior'. Over the years, fond of drinking beer and eating cigarettes, Wojtek became an important part of the company. He moved with the men through Iraq, Syria, Palestine, Egypt and Italy. After some initial problems in acquiring permission for Wojtek to board a ship with the troops, the issue was settled formally when Wojtek was officially drafted into the Polish army as a listed soldier with the rank of Corporal. Legend has it that as one of the 'soldiers' at the battle of Monte Cassino, Wojtek helped to carry boxes of artillery shells to the gunners. As a result the 22s' official emblem became an effigy of Wojtek carrying an artillery shell. Wojtek would spend his remaining years in Edinburgh Zoo where he was a great attraction until he eventually passed away in 1963.

I slept soundly that night, exhausted by the arduous journey and imbued with a sense of pride in our Polish army abroad and admiration for Janusz's courage.

The following day we embarked upon the final 400 kilometres of our journey. This route took us further south along the coast through Barletta, which was only 12 kilometres from our final destination of Trani. Both towns had transit camps for Polish former POWs which were administered by the 2nd Corps. During a stop-off at Barletta, Janusz introduced me to his close army friend from his home town of Brzeżany, Jasio Bączkowski. Janusz asked Jasio if he would visit me occasionally to make sure I was well while he was away. "Don't worry, I'll take very good care of her!" he replied with a cheeky grin on his face. I joined in with Jasio and we both laughed, which visibly annoyed Janusz, who sulked for a while. Jasio never did visit me after that.

Finally at Trani we were reunited with the rest of the AK girls who had travelled to Italy the year before. Our entire leadership was now based here and a school had been set up for the younger girls. Fortunately for me, the school was closed for the summer break and I was able to enjoy two wonderful, carefree months in the sun. Our camp was only a short walk from the beach, which stretched all the way to Barletta. We had a great time there, paddling around in the sea with the boys. The weather was wonderful and we knew that we would soon be leaving for England. It was a joyous, carefree time and I had just turned 17. There were many vineyards nearby and my friends and I often sneaked in at night to eat some fruit. The locals kept close watch over their crop and we were frequently spotted and chased away. I have never again come across better, juicier grapes anywhere in the world.

I didn't see much of Janusz during those few months at Trani as his base in Ancona was about 400 kilometres away, although he did visit a couple of times and took me on a few trips in his Jeep. Once we visited Venice for a few days and he took me for a ride in a gondola. This city was still majestically beautiful despite having suffered significant bomb damage. Although post-war Venice looked less spectacular than it does today, I loved being there and enjoyed learning about the history of the city; it was a new experience for me. Western Europe was visibly different from the East, having been much less affected by the war. Janusz also took me to Rome, which was beautiful and even less damaged than Venice.

While we were in Venice Janusz told me about his old life back in Poland. He explained he was married to Józefa but that the marriage had failed, and that he had two children, Rysia and Adam. I was getting closer to Janusz but our relationship was not sufficiently developed for this information to shock or upset me and I had no basis to expect anything of him. Janusz was always very honest with me. As we talked Janusz also confided in me a matter that was upsetting him concerning his sister, Stasia. Janusz's brother-in-law Józef Kohlbek had also ended up fighting in the Middle East and Janusz had established contact with him. While in Italy Józef had fallen in love with another Polish girl and they decided to emigrate to Argentina together. Although the men had been away from their previous lives in Poland for over six years, Józef was still married to Janusz's sister. Janusz would never forgive Józef for abandoning Stasia.

Chapter 6

ENGLAND

I left with the school from Trani for Britain in September 1946. We travelled first by train to a French port on the English Channel and then by ferry around the south-west coast of Britain. It was misty and drizzly as our ferry approached Merseyside and we joked that English women must have great complexions due to the lack of sun. When we landed I was issued with a temporary 'Certificate of Immigration' identity card which stated that, as the first cousin of Janusz Szlachetko, I was a dependant of a member of the Polish Armed Forces.

Our first stop, for a few weeks, was at a transit camp in Maghull near Aintree just north of Liverpool. In October 1946 we were moved to a resettlement camp at Doddington Park, where we spent the cold winter of 1946–47. Unusually for England there was heavy snow that year. Doddington was a fine place and life was comfortable and sociable for the many Polish men and women of all ages who passed through the camp. It had been seven years since my last normal, happy family Christmas so this time was tinged with an underlying sadness. But in many respects I recall my first Christmas in England as joyous, as it was an experience I shared with many girls of my age. I did feel a sense of freedom and homeliness, and the fact that there were many teachers around us made me feel protected, which a teenage girl needs.

Doddington Park was only 13 kilometres from Crewe town centre. Some of the girls had asked me to buy them cotton wool on one of my shopping trips, which led to my first real challenge with the English language. I went to a pharmacy and kept repeating the word 'wool' but I had no idea how to say 'cotton' in English so I tried sign language instead. The girls in the pharmacy spent at least half an hour showing me virtually every item in the shop until we finally came across what I was looking for. The girls were perfectly pleasant but they had a little giggle and I felt a bit silly. I never forgot the word 'cotton' after that.

Janusz had travelled separately with the army to a camp in Scotland and visited me a couple of times at Doddington. I still had my beautiful brown shoes from Niederlangen which I had just polished meticulously and laid by my quarters before one of his visits. When he saw the shoes he was incredulous that I could have polished them up so well. It's strange how such small things stay in the memory. Afterwards Janusz took me to the wonderful cinema in Crewe, where we saw an American film starring Bing Crosby.

During the visit we talked a little more about Janusz's wife and children back in Poland. At the end of the war they too had been deported west and were now settling in Gliwice in western Poland, not far from Janusz's sister Stasia. His children Rysia and Adam were now aged nine and eight and he had not seen them in more than seven years. He wanted to be totally open with me. I would have to come to terms with his situation if our relationship were to develop any further.

I spent about five months at Doddington Park waiting for something to happen. In April I was asked if I would be interested in working in a hospital in Manchester. About five of us girls, including Hania, agreed to go, on the condition that we would be enrolled to train as nurses. We were told that the next nursing course would begin at the end of the summer and were assured that we would be put forward for enrolment.

In May we reported to Broughton House in Manchester, which was a hospital caring mainly for the war wounded. My orderly duties were quite menial and I was immediately given the night shift. This was a shock to the system as I had little time to adjust and so found it a real struggle to stay awake on duty at first. Hania soon complained about the work and it didn't take long before she resigned and left. The rest of us remained. I remember a nurse teaching us how to butter bread, we were told to scrape back twice at the end in order to save butter. This technique was known as 'spread and scrape' and I find myself still using it to this day.

Broughton House was caring for long-term injured from the war; there were even some older patients from the First World War. One of the patients

I looked after was the dashing Donald, a former pilot who had been injured in the stomach and was confined to a wheelchair. We became very friendly and talked about our lives. Donald would ask for me specifically to take him to the cinema or to push him around the large park which surrounded the hospital. He was good-looking with dark hair, perhaps in his mid to late twenties, and I felt good in his company.

Donald was from an upper-class English family and his mother and sister visited him a few times looking properly grand. This was the first time in my life that I had felt looked down upon. As I was spending a lot of time looking after Donald I expected his mother and sister to acknowledge me beyond a curt "Thank you". I was just turning 18 and still feeling unsure of myself in a foreign country so even a friendly look in my direction would have given me a boost. Instead they made me feel like I wasn't even there. I wasn't used to such a manner and it made me quite uncomfortable. It made me realise that, as a foreigner and a mere orderly, I would be regarded as intrinsically inferior by certain English people.

Summer was coming to an end and the hospital took us to the nursing college as promised. But when we got there we were told that there were no training places available. The hospital suggested we stay on as orderlies and promised that they would bring us back in a few months for the next nurse training enrolment opportunity. I wasn't convinced that this nurse training would actually materialise. I had heard that a Polish boarding school was opening at Stowell Park so I decided to leave Broughton and finish my education, which had been so interrupted. I wanted to better myself and this seemed to be my only option.

Stowell Park Polish School for Girls was based at a former American army hospital in the grounds of Stowell Park in the Cotswolds. It originated from the school in Trani, Italy. The official opening was in September 1947 and it would function for seven years until its closure in 1954. At its peak in 1950 there were 419 pupils. I would complete my fourth year of senior school at Stowell Park.

We lived in Nissen huts, semi-circular structures made from corrugated iron. At the front we had a shared room with a coke burner for heat. My class had about 15 girls including Stefa and Irka, whom I knew from

Doddington, and Celina. They would become lifelong friends. I recall Irka being one of those lucky girls who was capable of anything and didn't mind rolling her sleeves up to get things done. I very much disliked having to clean the dirty coke-burner but Irka would happily exchange this chore with me for one I found easier.

That year was taught in Polish but the following years would be taught only in English and there was pressure to make that language transition. The curriculum covered all the basics including History, Geography, Chemistry, Mathematics and Religion. Behaviour was strictly monitored and assessed, and any misbehaviour was treated seriously and punished. Despite such regulations we behaved like any other group of teenagers, often talking in class and mucking about. A blackboard cleaner would frequently fly in our direction from an annoyed teacher.

Food rations continued to be sparse, leaving us all perpetually hungry. The rations may have been enough to live on but they certainly weren't satisfying. We received five shillings from the Polish government-in-exile for other necessities but this did not stretch far, it was barely enough to buy a slice of cake and some toothpaste. Occasionally we walked quite a distance to the nearest town for some window-shopping, particularly to look at one tempting cake shop as I still had a very sweet tooth!

Most of our teachers were experienced, as they had taught previously in Poland. I remember a particularly happy day when our lady gymnastics teacher married a much younger teacher from our school; we stood excitedly outside her window from early morning just to see her dress. Some of the older pupils also went on to marry their teachers.

Janusz visited me once or twice at Stowell Park from his army base at Winfield Camp, Berwick-upon-Tweed. He would share some of his rations with me and leave a little money to help me out. He always strongly stressed the value of education and urged me to learn as much as possible.

GO HOME

Soon after the war was over the British government began to apply pressure for our armed forces to be repatriated back to Poland now that they were no longer needed. As early as March 1946, with the 2nd Polish Corps still in Italy, the Foreign Secretary, Ernest Bevin, issued a circular in Polish addressed to each individual soldier urging them to return to Poland. Statements were made in the House of Commons such as 'It is the first and last duty of a Pole to return to his own country if possible.' A few soldiers had started returning to Poland from Italy. Others moved to different parts of the world where workers were needed and there were quotas for immigration. Argentina and Brazil were taking people at the time.

Meanwhile the existence of a 'foreign' Polish army was becoming a thorn in the side for the 'puppet' Polish government that was trying to establish its authority. Delegations were sent both from this government and from the newly established military in Poland calling for the army in Britain to return to Poland with promises of fair treatment. Letters also started arriving from families in Poland encouraging soldiers to return.

But Poland was no longer free and we already had specific and detailed knowledge of what was actually happening to soldiers who returned home. The promises of fair treatment were not being kept and were not to be trusted. This was not fully understood by British politicians at first. Many of the letters from families were clearly fakes or written under coercion from the new Polish authorities. In addition many of the Polish soldiers were convinced that there would be a third world war against communism, which would lead to Poland's borders being redrawn once again. Some even kept their uniforms in readiness.

To some extent I was shielded from such politics and the aggressive propaganda against Poles in Britain. If General Anders had taken the army back to Poland I'm not even completely sure that I would have gone with them. Who would I have gone back to? I was disoriented. It crossed my mind that if I was to be left behind then it might be better for me to go to the USA or to Canada. At the time Britain seemed to have little to offer and there was a lot of talk that Canada was taking Polish DPs and offering better opportunities...

Nevertheless it was soon clear that the troops would not be returning. General Anders had already said the army would return only if fully armed and this was unacceptable to the British. I therefore assumed we would all be staying. Although we hadn't discussed the issue specifically I was also sure that Janusz would not be returning to Poland. I think he had already made up his mind while in Italy. He no longer had a home there and his marriage was effectively over, but it must have been an immensely difficult decision for him not to return to his children. As for a third world war, I didn't want to think about such things: I had had enough of war.

The Polish government's attempts to persuade us to return continued for quite a few years, even after repression against former AK members in Poland became increasingly open. At the same time communist agents were secretly placed among us to spy on the Polish community in Britain. My friend Stefa later wrote down her recollection of being visited by her history teacher with another man while she was still at Stowell Park. She was asked if she wanted to continue studying and promised a scholarship, which she declined. Some time later an English official informed her that this had been an attempt to recruit her as an agent for the communists. She would have been expected to pass information between communists in England and in Poland.

For many years every correspondence with Poland was read by the communist authorities and letters were vetted and censured. Families in Poland were even coerced into pressing relatives abroad for information that could be used to undermine the capitalist West. People tried to send informative books and news from England but little got through. High-ranking officials and officers, like General Anders and General Maczek, particularly were closely observed, branded fascists and publicly undermined. General Anders' Polish citizenship was withdrawn along with that of many of his senior officers.

Over the years the names of spies and collaborators such as Stanislaw Tatar, formerly one of the commanders of the AK, have come to light. Tatar betrayed our Polish government-in-exile in 1947 by organising the illegal handover of reserves including the remaining gold from our Fund of National Defence to communist Poland. The names of many other such spies and collaborators would be revealed decades later after the fall of communism, when we would be shocked by revelations about some of those we had regarded as pillars of our community.

Despite the propaganda and pressure from Poland and the Soviets, Britain did act honourably. General Anders later wrote in his book *An Army in Exile*: 'Britain, to her great credit, was the only country which realised that there was a moral obligation to those soldiers who had fought so long by the side of the Allies and which was therefore prepared to make provision for the future of all who would not risk returning home.'

Out of about a quarter of a million members of the Polish Armed Forces overseas in 1945, about 150,000 would remain in exile, of whom 123,000 stayed in Britain. The majority of those were from the Kresy. However, over 100,000 decided to return individually to their families in Poland. Over the years we heard a litany of sad stories relating to those who chose to return to Poland. These included arrests, deportations, even murders. The Soviets were particularly hostile to members of the AK.

In 1946 the British government formed the Polish Resettlement Corps, the PKPR, to ease the transition from military to civilian life for those in the army who chose to stay in Britain. Janusz entered the PKPR in November 1946 after six years of active military service under British command. In signing up for the PKPR, Janusz was committing to remaining under military control for two years, during which he was to fully adjust to a life in Britain. About 115,000 Polish military personnel joined the PKPR. This was followed by the Polish Resettlement Act of 1947, the first mass immigration act in Britain, which enabled the Polish troops and their dependants to remain in the UK. The Polish Army in Great Britain was disbanded later that same year.

After the completion of their two-year commitment under the PKPR, the former soldiers scattered in search of work. Britain had been hit hard by the war and needed such a large group of able bodied men. Once he had improved his English, still in the PKPR, Janusz left his military base in Scotland for London in early 1948, working at first for British Railways at Willesden Junction.

LONDON

I completed my fourth and final year of senior school in the summer of
1948. This was three years late as I had just turned 19. Each of my four
years had been at a different school or, in the case of my very first year, at
home. I was now faced with an important decision which I still regard as a
pivotal point in my life. I could continue with my studies at Stowell Park in
the lyceum or leave education behind and seek work. Many of the teachers
in Poland and at Stowell Park had frequently told me I was clever and as a
child in Poland I had dearly wanted to fulfil my mother's dreams and expectations of me.

However, most of the girls who stayed on in education had other family
members in England they could rely on, whereas I had nobody to support
and encourage me. I felt close to Janusz and hoped that we would be
together one day but I did not feel I could expect anything from him yet
and I was certainly not going to ask him to support me during two more
years of school. I suppose also that when I lost my family in Warsaw I also
lost some of my ambition. I stopped thinking about my future.

And yet it was a very painful moment for me when I decided I could
not pursue my education. To this day that decision has remained a constant
source of regret. In the end I felt I had no choice. The pain came from the
certain knowledge that I would never achieve what I was capable of, that
without education my potential would not be fulfilled. Instead I headed to
London along with some other girls, hoping to find work.

Hania had not stayed and studied with us at Stowell Park. She had met
and fallen in love with Wojtek, another Uprising survivor, in Niederlangen
in Germany. Wojtek had fallen ill with tuberculosis and was being treated
at the Polish hospital at Penley. Hania had some nursing experience from
the Uprising and so was allowed to work at Penley and help care for Wojtek.
Streptomycin was a new antibiotic then and it was still very expensive
and not widely available. One of the doctors agreed to prescribe some for
Wojtek if Hania could raise the money. Often forgoing her own food, she
saved virtually every penny she earned to pay for his treatment and saved
his life.

When I arrived in London, Hania was already there with Wojtek, who was still recovering. She was working in a factory that made ladies' lingerie: it was called Belgrave Manufacturing, and I think, was located in Strutton Ground in Victoria. She managed to get me a job there as well. The factory-owners were a Polish Jewish family and I think Hania had known the lady owner back in Warsaw. Many of the other workers were also Poles who had recently arrived in London. The atmosphere was good; the owner liked her Polish compatriots and treated us well. We were paid £3.10s per week, rising to £4 or £5 with overtime, which was considered good money at the time. I worked there for a couple of years until 1950.

Hania remained good friends with the lady owner, who helped her a lot over the years. I think she also helped towards the cost of the treatment for Wojtek. Even after the lady owner died many years later, her son paid for Hania to visit him on holiday in Israel and her daughter also kept in contact. Often Polish Christians and Jews who had arrived in Britain due to the war felt a kinship and were drawn to each other.

Janusz was discharged from the PKPR in September 1948 and became a civilian. He had accumulated savings of around £500 from his army service and decided to buy a house jointly with his army friend Mr Derendal. The house was on Portland Road, just off Holland Park and close to the famous Portobello Road market. Nowadays of course the area is wealthy and salubrious but that certainly was not the case after the war. The house had three floors with two rooms on each, the majority of which were let to Polish tenants.

I was living with some other girls in rented accommodation not far from work in Victoria. After a few months Janusz suggested that I moved into one of the rooms at Portland Road. This was an important transition in our relationship. I moved in soon afterwards and from this point we began to consider a long-term future together.

The atmosphere at Portland Road was always lively and there was a lot of socialising. Janusz had many army friends who frequently visited and this in turn meant that many of my girlfriends often dropped by. Stefa, my friend from Stowell Park, was a particularly frequent visitor after she met and fell in love with Janusz's friend, Jasio Bączkowski. Stefa and Jasio would go on to marry and I would become godmother to their first child.

After leaving Stowell Park, Stefa had initially gone to work in a hospital, which I think was in Gloucestershire. After a short while she too came to London and I was able to get her work at the lingerie company with me. Stefa was one of seven siblings left orphaned by the war. She had been taken into forced labour in Germany and was then helped by the Polish Red Cross after the war. Unfortunately the family was separated, with three of the siblings ending up in the USA and Canada and four in England. Much later I heard from Celina's historian daughter Bogusia that once while in western Poland, Stefa had been thrown off a road into a ditch by German soldiers. As she looked up she saw Adolf Hitler riding by in a cavalcade. Bogusia researched the story and concluded that Hitler had indeed visited that part of Poland around Stefa's remembered date.

Over the three years that we lived there, many tenants passed through the Portland Road house, adding to the busy atmosphere. At some point Hania and her husband Wojtek moved into one of the rooms above me. Wojtek worked at a hotel late into the night and they had a habit of cooking and eating when he got home, regularly waking me up. I also recall, with some amusement, two Polish chaps who lived on the top floor. As soon as they got paid on Fridays they would gamble at White City dog track and normally by Tuesday they were broke. Janusz would always listen out for their return so they started taking their boots off and tiptoeing down the hall and up the stairs in order to avoid a lecture.

By now there was always plenty of food around for us despite rationing. Many large families were living in our area and most of them could not afford to buy their full allocations of rations. This meant that shopkeepers always had some spare ration coupons to sell under the counter, enabling us to buy more than our allowance. There was also a thriving black market, particularly in Portobello Road, where we had the choice of many Polish and Jewish shops.

I would cook enough food for three evenings ahead as I was coming home exhausted from work. On one occasion Janusz tried to help by cooking a huge pot of vegetable soup. He was very pleased with his work until we realised he had put rhubarb in with the vegetables. The soup was inedible and we ended up throwing the whole pot away.

Along with many other Poles who were also in the early stages of settling into a new life in England, we attended Polish mass at the Brompton Oratory in Kensington. The Oratory had started hosting Polish mass during the war. Gradually Polish businesses sprang up in the area; I recall a particularly good cafeteria across the road from the Oratory that we occasionally visited with friends after mass. The now famous Polish restaurant Daquise, which had opened in 1947, was also nearby. Some older friends told me that the owner, Tadeusz Dakowski, had owned a popular restaurant of the same name in Warsaw before the war. We had lunch there once or twice on special occasions and Daquise continues to serve Polish cuisine to this present day.

Travelling through central London in those early days brought back memories of Warsaw and the devastation I had left behind, as many of the buildings were still bomb-damaged. Much of this was from the eight-month German bombing campaign of late 1940 to summer 1941 known as The Blitz, and from the V1 and V2 flying bomb attacks in the last year of the war.

BETRAYED

I think it was during those early years in Notting Hill that I began to fully understand how Poland had been lost to all of us. After the war I had been preoccupied, initially with enjoying my first taste of real freedom in Germany and Italy. Then came all the uncertainty of that first year in England and then my year at school in Stowell Park. Now that I had become a little more settled I began to understand what had taken place in my country; I ached from the malice which the Soviets had inflicted on Poland and from the utter betrayal by our Western Allies. I was finally beginning to comprehend and share the pain and the constant knocks that the former soldiers of the Polish Armed Forces overseas had endured continuously since before the end of the war.

This bitter taste of betrayal stems from the conviction that Poland's Western Allies failed to honour their military obligations under the terms of their formal agreements with our nation. Our allies had secretly agreed to give away Polish land and independence in order to appease Stalin. Our fate and betrayal were sealed at two conferences held between the USA, Britain and the USSR.

The first conference had been held in Tehran in November and December 1943. There, President Roosevelt and the British Prime Minister Churchill secretly conceded Eastern Poland to Stalin along the former 1939 Soviet-German division line. When I learned about this secret agreement I finally began to understand the Soviets' behaviour on entering Polish territory back in 1944, and in particular their treatment of our Uprising. As Norman Davies writes in his book *Rising '44*, 'Roosevelt and Churchill had failed to launch a second front for the second year running and were keen to make concessions to Stalin.' But the Polish government-in-exile had never been informed about this agreement, either when it was first reached or indeed during the run-up to the tragic Warsaw Uprising. Although in the ascendancy following the Battle of Stalingrad, at the time of the Tehran Conference the Soviet Union was heavily dependent on the Allies for material support, particularly transportation equipment, so the Allies still had considerable influence. Most Poles still regard this agreement as an unnecessary sacrifice of a major ally.

The terms of the Tehran Conference were made easier due to the convenient death of General Sikorski in a plane crash earlier that year. As Prime Minister of the Polish government-in-exile and Commander-in-Chief of the Polish Armed Forces, he was our chief Polish leader of influence. I am convinced that this was no accident. Among other factors it is common knowledge that the infamous double agent Kim Philby, at that time head of British Intelligence for the Iberian Peninsula, was in Gibraltar when Prime Minister Sikorski's plane took off. This tragedy took place soon after Stalin severed diplomatic relations with our country, following Poland's request for further investigation into the discovery of mass graves in the Katyn forest in April 1943.

In February 1945 the second of the two crucial conferences between Stalin, Churchill and Roosevelt took place at Yalta in the Crimea. In Yalta the USA and Britain formally accepted the annexation of Eastern Poland by the Soviet Union and in exchange Poland received some territory from Germany in the west. Many Polish troops hailed from Eastern Poland and in effect this agreement robbed them of their homes. When they received the news of the agreement at Yalta, 30 officers and men from the 2nd Polish Corps committed suicide in response. Stalin then stated that the Soviet Union had greatly sinned against Poland and claimed that he was now interested in a mighty, free and independent Poland. Prompted by Churchill, Stalin then pledged to permit free elections in Poland.

After the Yalta conference Churchill remembered how the British government had appeased Hitler in 1939 and remarked, "Poor Neville Chamberlain believed he could trust Hitler. He was wrong. But I don't think I am wrong about Stalin". Unfortunately Churchill was equally wrong. The wholesale deportation and liquidation of any Poles who opposed the Soviets followed rapidly while Stalin dragged his feet regarding free elections. Churchill reportedly became desperately concerned while Roosevelt remained confident, reasoning that Stalin's early priesthood training had "entered into his nature of the way in which a Christian gentleman should behave." But within weeks even Roosevelt had begun to admit that his trust in Stalin had been optimistic. On 27th March 1945, sixteen Polish opposition political leaders were invited by the Soviets to 'important' negotiations about forming a provisional government. These negotiations never took place and they were arrested by the NKVD, taken to Moscow for show trials and sentenced to imprisonment.

Despite all these betrayals, in June and July 1945 the West formally ceased to recognise the Polish government-in-exile as Poland's legitimate government. Instead the West now recognised the new Soviet-sponsored communist Provisional Government of National Unity in Poland.

This acquiescence by our allies hurt deeply, and the pain was further accentuated by the fact that Poland had fought alongside, and for, Britain. The Polish contribution to the war and to the British cause was considerable. The Polish forces as a whole are considered to have been the fourth-largest Allied army in Europe. Among a long list of Polish contributions, our troops played a significant part in defeating Germany in North Africa and Italy, especially at the battles of Tobruk, Monte Cassino and Bologna. Polish fighter pilots accounted for over 7 percent of all enemy planes destroyed in the Battle of Britain, with the Polish 303 squadron the highest-performing of all Allied squadrons. Hugh Dowding, who was the head of RAF Fighter Command later commented, "Had it not been for the Poles, I hesitate to say that the outcome of the battle [of Britain] would have been the same." After the war the Polish government-in-exile paid a bill for 68 million pounds presented by the British government, covering the equipment and operating costs of the Polish Air Force in Great Britain. This was paid for out of the 75 tonnes of Polish gold reserves which had been evacuated from Poland to Great Britain and Canada at the outbreak of war.

Polish mathematicians cracked the first-generation German Enigma code before presenting the formulae and two working Enigma machine replicas to Britain and France in 1939. Only recently did we realise the contribution this made to the further British successes in breaking Enigma at Bletchley Park. Polish intelligence located the German rocket programme research centre and test ranges and this enabled their bombing by the RAF. The AK delivered key parts of a V-2 rocket to Britain, along with technical drawings and the cracked fuel formula, all of which contributed greatly to Britain's self-defence. Of all intelligence reports received by the British secret service from Europe during the war, 43 percent came from Polish sources.

But all this now seemed forgotten. Severe political damage had already been done to Poland but in June 1946 this was followed by a blatant 'slap in the face'. That June while I was still in Italy, London hosted the British Commonwealth, Empire and Allied victory parade. Fifty-one countries who had been at war with Germany before its surrender were invited to participate. The Soviet-backed government in Poland was invited but no specific invitation was extended to the 200,000 members of the Polish Armed Forces in the West who had fought under British command. Some Britons, including the now former Prime Minister Churchill, senior figures in the RAF and a number of MPs, protested against this decision both as an affront to the Polish war effort and as an immoral concession to communist power. In response, representatives of the Polish fighter squadrons who had fought in the Battle of Britain were invited to march with other foreign detachments as part of the RAF. The day before the parade, invitations were also sent to the chiefs of the Polish Army, Air Force and Navy and to individual generals. These were all declined and the airmen also refused to participate as a protest against the failure to invite their other colleagues. In response to the invitations to the Polish pilots the Soviet-backed government in Poland also decided not to attend. As a result Poland had no representation at the parade. This fiasco remains profoundly irritating to the present day!

Along with all Poles in Britain, I felt then and I feel today that Britain and America had no right to give Polish lands and sovereignty away and I still cannot believe that they were surrendered so cheaply to the Soviets who only a few years before in 1939 had allied themselves with Nazi Germany.

OUTSIDERS

We did not integrate much into British society to start with, but we asked for and received nothing. There were so many of us Poles in exile that we were already a community. We formed Polish enclaves and looked after ourselves. We were here not of our own free will but because we had been taken or forced out of our own country. We all wanted to go back to a free Poland but this was not possible. We also felt that the country we were now living in had betrayed us during the war and that we were not particularly welcome on her streets.

The early years in England were very difficult. Those lucky enough to get funding to continue their studies at university generally fitted in more quickly. Most others, even if well educated and experienced in their former careers in Poland, now found access to professions hard. Our command of the language was undeniably a problem but could only be overcome with time. In most cases Poles had no documentation or proof of their former work experience and were therefore often not even considered for positions. Like Janusz, many Poles were already on the older side, which counted against them. However there was plenty of menial work around due to severe post-war labour shortages. Thus many former doctors, architects and other professionals ended up washing dishes at one of the J Lyons and Co tea rooms. General Maczek, so feted by the Allies as the commander of the Polish 1st Armoured Division during the war, ended up working as a bartender at a friend's bar in Scotland. Not only did these exiles have to learn a new language late in life but everything they had previously worked hard for and achieved now counted for little. The adjustment process was difficult and required considerable energy. As a result, morale among many older Poles suffered. Janusz was bright and had been well educated in Poland but after so many years in the army he now had to start all over again in his early forties. Time and circumstances were not on his side and the best he could hope for was to work towards skilled manual labour.

All Poles who had entered Britain in the post-war period continued to be classed as Dispaced Persons or DPs. We were required to carry our Aliens Certificate at all times and any change of address had to be reported to a police station and officially recorded on this document. The certificate stated that we were to produce it on demand to a police officer or member of HM Armed Forces. Under the Polish Resettlement Act we would remain Displaced Persons and not become eligible for British citizenship for at least five years.

Personally I had little direct contact with British people at first. After Stowell Park I had gone straight to work for a company owned by Polish Jews and so I was less exposed to local sentiment. But among our community as a whole there were frequent complaints about native attitudes to us newcomers. Friends would complain about comments such as 'Bloody foreigner!' and 'Why don't you go home?' Many reported being patronised and treated as second-class citizens. We all saw those signs in people's houses saying 'Room to rent, no Poles'. There was an appreciation that the better-educated were well disposed towards us but it was also clear that the general public were indifferent at best.

Public hostility to Poles was perhaps understandable. The British were not used to many foreigners on home soil and suddenly here were a huge number of Eastern Europeans, mainly Poles but also Czechs and others. In the 1931 census, the Polish-born population of Britain was only around 44,000; by the 1951 census it had risen to 162,000.

Another significant factor explaining and perhaps even actively encouraging resentment towards Poles was the British media. In the first few years after the war the British media seemed besotted with 'Uncle Joe' Stalin. As early as September 1944, George Orwell had written in the Tribune, 'At present, so slavish is the attitude of nearly the whole British press [to the Soviet Union] that ordinary people have so little idea about what is happening.' This remained the case with the British media when I arrived in London. It felt as though our wartime contribution had been completely forgotten. The public simply didn't understand why we didn't want to go home. The press called us fascists as we were anti-communist. It was not until the late 1940s that attitudes changed as Britain finally woke up to the realities of Stalin's Soviet Union. This heralded the start of the 40-year 'Cold War'.

Competition for jobs was another factor holding back integration. Despite labour shortages, Trade Unions put up barriers to Poles getting certain jobs, and there were reports of strikes because companies had employed Polish workers.

Perhaps less important but still a source of local friction was the success young Polish men had with British women. Polish men had been brought up to be charming to the opposite sex. They would always kiss a lady on the hand and be attentive, and this appealed to many British women.

Over many years these barriers broke down and we strove to develop a good reputation among the British through hard work, honesty, enthusiasm and politeness. We realised that we were in somebody else's country and ultimately we were grateful to be here. It was surprising just how different the two communities were at first. Although it took decades I sensed that acceptance and respect for us gradually grew, albeit grudgingly in some cases. The British gradually saw that we Poles were not here to take advantage of them but that we were prepared to work hard and honestly, to pay our debts, and build new lives. This hard work bore fruit and gave us the means to build solid foundations. We achieved this with absolutely no financial support from the British government; there were no welfare payments back then. We stuck together and supported one another as 'families' do.

Chapter 7

A NEW BEGINNING

In 1951 Janusz's friend was keen to sell his half of the Portland Road house. As it was rather narrow, Janusz agreed to sell and we decided to look for somewhere more spacious. In the meantime we lived in rented accommodation. At first I lived at 33 Melrose Gardens, W6, and later I joined Janusz at 141 Hammersmith Grove in the same area. The Polish community was now closely knit and we continued to make good friends who stayed with us for life. These included my neighbours at Melrose Gardens, Lodzia and Stefan.

Lodzia grew up in Eastern Poland before the war but was deported with her parents to Siberia by the invading Soviet army. Like many deportees, they contracted typhoid. Lodzia's parents died in a squalid Soviet prison camp but Lodzia managed to overcome the disease. Intense hunger made her eat anything she could find in Siberia, including snakes and tortoises. Lodzia later told me that these tortoises carried toxins which affected her for the rest of her life by damaging her intestines, making it difficult to digest food. She managed to escape Russia with General Anders during the Soviet amnesty in 1942, eventually finding her way with the air force to England, where she worked at an RAF base. During an inspection of her barracks in England a female inspector found some dried bread under Lodzia's pillow and asked her why it was there. Lodzia explained that after the intense hunger she had suffered in Russia she always needed to have a scrap of food nearby. This made the inspector cry.

Lodzia went on to marry Stefan Lipka. He was very bright and spoke Russian, so was recruited to work for British intelligence at GCHQ listening to intercepted Russian communications. Lodzia would become godmother to my first child. Sadly she was unable to have children of her own which she put down to the hardships she had experienced in Siberia.

Through Lodzia I met Jadzia, who would also become a lifelong friend. Jadzia and Lodzia shared similarly sad histories. Jadzia was deported to Siberia with her two young daughters, where she lost them both to typhoid. She too had come to Britain with the Polish air force after she met a navigator called Zygmund whom she would marry. Zygmund had been exposed to severe changes of air pressure while flying, which left him with damaged sinuses and suffering permanent headaches for the rest of his life. He eventually died from related causes. Sadly Jadzia too would not be able to conceive again.

We had been looking for a house for some time when one of Janusz's friends who worked as an estate agent suggested that we take a look at a house in Ealing, the 'Queen of the Suburbs'. Ealing had a lot of large houses while the post-war austerity period was seeing a general trend to down-sizing. We immediately liked the area and the house. It was a large, three story, semi-detached Edwardian house near Ealing Common. On the top floor there was an attic room that had been used as servant quarters during grander days. Opposite the house was a new block of flats built on a Blitz bombsite. We moved to our new house in Ealing in April 1952.

Buying the house was a major financial undertaking for us. The house cost £2,600; we had £800 from the sale of the Portland Road house and we covered the balance with a mortgage from a building society. We could only afford the repayments by both working while also renting out as many rooms in the house as possible.

Janusz got a job in nearby Acton working for CAV. The company manufactured aircraft and employed many Poles at the time. This partially explains why so many Poles were moving into the Ealing area at the time. Meanwhile I travelled to Regent Street, where I worked making dresses.

In order to rent out rooms in the house we first needed to renovate and buy furniture. As we had reached our borrowing limit with the building society, we borrowed the rest from friends. That's how the Polish community got by in those days: everybody helped one another and there was great integrity and trust between us. A debt between Poles was a debt of honour. Mind you, not all the loans were cheap! Olenka was one of our friends who lent us money and she was clearly a good businesswoman. For a £100 loan

Olenka charged us ten percent up front, the most expensive loan we took out.

Olenka and her daughter Iza from her first marriage had recently moved to Acton. Her first husband had been an army major in Poland and spent everything they had on gambling and alcohol – perhaps that's why she was so cautious with her money. While in Italy, Olenka met Stasio Wasilewski in the 2nd Polish Corps and gave up on her first, spendthrift husband. She married Stasio and over the years we became good friends: Olenka would later become godmother to my second son.

Due to our debts those first few years in Ealing were tough and we hardly spent any money on ourselves, particularly as Janusz strongly disliked being in debt. As the expression goes, we were working *swiątek do piątek,* literally meaning from holy day (Sunday) to Friday, six days a week, sometimes seven. I was still earning about £3.10s a week, Janusz a little more at CAV, and virtually every penny we made went on the house and the loans.

We lived in the back room on the ground floor and accessed our small kitchen by walking through the garden and around the coal shed to the side passage. This was so that we could rent out the rest of the ground floor. We slept on a metal bed with only Janusz's army coat as a mattress and only one blanket for cover; it was uncomfortable. We barely had enough money to feed ourselves and I often cried from hunger, which reminded me of the Oberlangen camp. Every meal was the same: macaroni with milk. We would joke about this, laughing that all we ate all week was noodles and milk, milk and noodles. I think this is why I don't like noodles today!

Soon after we moved in we converted the small coal shed into a sewing room and invested in a wonderful industrial Singer sewing machine, which stands on its own worktable and still works well today. I made every curtain and soft furnishing for the whole house on that machine. Many years later I would sew dresses from home for various companies. Two such companies were Lenmore and Lucio in Clerkenwell and they remain recorded on my alien ID card. I also recall tacking and sewing beautiful tailored dresses for an exclusive shop on Bond Street.

Finding tenants in those days was not difficult as there were many Poles still moving around trying to find somewhere to settle. Janusz still had many contacts through the Polish army and one by one we furnished and rented the rooms.

The Kucharek family, Bolek and Jadzia with their young son Bogusz, were the first to move in. The Kuchareks occupied the rest of the ground floor, taking two rooms and a kitchenette. During the war Bolek had been part of the Polish Special Operations Executive (SOE) which worked with but was predominantly independent of the British SOE. The task of the Polish SOE was to be parachuted behind enemy lines to support resistance movements in Poland. The Polish SOE were known as the Cichociemni ('Silent Dark Ones' or the 'Silent Unseen') because of their stealth. Jadzia had come to England from Ravensbrück, the notorious German concentration camp for women, where she had contracted a serious illness but was somehow among the few inmates to survive. Some years later a Jewish lawyer helped Jadzia get compensation from Germany for her suffering, eventually enabling her family to buy their own house in north London. I would later become godmother to their daughter Danusia.

While living in our house Jadzia would occasionally do some cleaning work for us as part payment of rent. Having held such a distinguished position in the Polish army, Bolek had trouble dealing with the idea of his wife having to clean. It was painful for him but he had to live with it. I remember how their four-year-old son Bogusz would sometimes help me with the cooking. He would stand on a chair next to the cooker and stir the soup and then proudly boast to his parents about his contribution.

Next to move in was Mr Kowalewski, who had the misfortune of having Adolf as a first name and who took a single room on the first floor. Having been deported from the Kresy, Adolf Kowalewski had come to Britain with General Anders' army. After the war his wife and daughter had stayed in the lands incorporated into the Soviet Union and become Soviet citizens. Contact with them was therefore extremely difficult. He made numerous attempts to bring his daughter to England but unfortunately was never successful.

Soon afterwards came Gerard Ruranski, who moved into two rooms on the first floor next to Kowalewski. Gerard had been enlisted into Anders' army at the end of the war after being liberated from his enforced conscription into the German army. This enforced conscription affected many Poles who lived in Poland's Silesian region when it was incorporated into the Reich. Under the PKPR Gerard had initially worked down a coalmine in Wales. After his release from the PKPR, the attraction of being among his own countrymen brought him to London. Both Gerard and Kowaleski became long-term tenants, staying with us for the rest of their lives.

The remaining two front rooms on the first floor were rented by one of the Swarnowski brothers and his English wife. We didn't have enough money to furnish Swarnowski's rooms so he agreed to buy his own mattress and pay a reduced rent until it was paid off. Swarnowski was an excellent cartographer and we still have a huge wall-mounted relief map he gave us as a gift.

The attic room on the second floor was rented out to a number of short-term tenants over the years. Next to this was a large, open attic space that we used for storage; Janusz was not amused when I managed to put my foot through the attic floor one day. All the tenants shared one toilet and bathroom on the first floor.

Our next-door neighbours were a very fine English couple, impeccably mannered and extremely elegant. They often invited us round for tea and we liked them very much. Sadly after a few years they decided to move, and the other Swarnowski brother bought the house with his wife, who was also English.

In those days Poles were scattered all around England and throughout London. We were all desperate to build foundations and get some security, which is why everybody was working so hard to buy their own properties. Ealing was not a particularly Polish area when we first moved in but gradually it would grow into one of the largest Polish communities in Britain. Over the years many of our friends moved into the area. Jadzia, Stefa, Celina and Marta all ended up living close by and the area became known in Polish circles as the Polish ghetto. Others like Lodzia were close by in Chiswick, which was developing its own substantial Polish community.

I first met Marta at the lingerie company in Victoria but our paths had crossed before. Marta was six years older than me and had also been in the

AK during the Uprising and at the Oberlangen camp. After Oberlangen she got a job at the nursery in Maczków while I had been at the convent in nearby Hange. Her husband had left her for her cousin before the Uprising, but Marta always said that as she wasn't too upset about this she couldn't have loved him much anyway! While in Maczków, Marta met the charming Edek, who served with General Maczek's Polish 1st Armoured Division, and they were later married in England. She too was unable to have children of her own, which always caused her great sadness.

At some point Basia Skulska from our Portland Road days bought a house around the corner from us. Basia had a daughter called Lila, then in her twenties, from her marriage in Poland. Basia was married to a high-ranking Polish army officer, which presumably meant that she had been of high social standing herself. After the war Basia's husband decided to stay in Poland within the newly formed Polish People's Army, the national army of communist Poland. Basia viewed this as collaborating with Poland's enemies and chose not to join him but she was desperate to have Lila living with her in England. As Lila was a keen pianist Basia thought that she would encourage the visiting Lila to remain with her in Britain by buying a piano. To pay for the piano she needed a loan and came round to see Janusz. Janusz told her that life was hard enough financially without her borrowing more money to buy a piano, which he considered to be inessential. I suspect Janusz made his point quite undiplomatically because Basia was very upset and never spoke to us again. To her credit Basia did go on to buy her piano and Lila settled with her in England. I still see Lila occasionally; she was very bright, attained a doctorate and now works at PUNO, the Polish University Abroad in West London.

When we moved to Ealing many of us started to attend mass at Ealing Abbey. We always referred to the church by the name of St Benedict's as it belongs to the Benedictine order and adjoins a school by that name. St Benedict's had kindly allowed our community to have mass said in Polish. The first was in August 1950, a date that could be seen as the beginning of the Polish parish in Ealing. I recall our masses were in the afternoon, which was not ideal but was preferable to travelling all the way to Brompton Oratory in Kensington.

NEWS FROM POLAND

I had not had any contact with Poland since arriving in England. My priority had been to build a new life. Tracing people in Poland in those days was not straightforward. I now wanted to know what had happened to my family after I left Poland. I wrote to Laski in the hope that Janka was there. Fortunately she replied, and so began our long correspondence.

After we had exchanged farewells at Mokótow Fields in October 1944, Janka had returned to Laski to find the area bereft of civilians and her children and mother-in-law gone. During the Uprising, AK partisans from the Kampinos Forest had fought the Germans in the area of Laski and the local inhabitants had taken to the roads on foot and scattered throughout the surrounding region. Janka's children and mother-in-law had joined this flight and taken refuge in another village. Janka searched frantically for them but to no avail. All she could do was wait and quietly suffer a mother's distress. Finally, after a few days, her children and mother-in-law came home to a joyful reunion. Janka had remained at Laski thereafter.

Janka informed me that after the war she had arranged for my mother and sister to be buried at Bródno cemetery on the eastern side of the Vistula river in Warsaw. Many Warsawians who lost their lives during the war are buried there. Bródno is an enormous cemetery, one of the biggest in Europe, having seen over one and a quarter million burials. It was good to receive this news and I felt happy that my mother and sister had been peacefully laid to rest.

I still had not heard if my father had survived the war. I thought this was unlikely but I wanted to be sure. Eventually the sad yet unsurprising news arrived. Janka managed to establish that my father had been killed while lying injured in a hospital in Wola when the hospital was bombed during the Warsaw Uprising. I have no idea if he was involved in the Uprising. In some respects it was a relief to know what had happened to him although I was deeply sad that nothing had survived of him. Eleven tonnes of ashes comprising many of the victims of the Wola massacres were symbolically laid to rest at the Warsaw Insurgents Cemetery in Wola after the war, and

I content myself that maybe a little piece of my father is there. Now I knew for certain that I was the only survivor of my family.

I still remembered how Henia and I had each planted an oak sapling before the war at Laski, and I was eager to know what had happened to the trees. Janka described how my tree had grown tall but crooked while Henia's had withered and died. This news brought back so much grief: the trees had recreated our divergent fates.

Janka also gave me details of her brother Janek and his wife Alinka, whom I had always liked so much. I never forgot that day in 1939 when we ran through the burning streets of Warsaw trying to avoid the bombs and Alinka's baby fell onto the ground in the panic. Janka informed me that the family had survived the war and Elżbieta, the baby, had grown into a beautiful young girl. As Warsaw's Old Town was gradually rebuilt after the war, Janek and Alinka moved back into an apartment near the main square. Over time I started corresponding with Alinka. She helped me greatly throughout the process of having the house in Laski transferred into my name as the sole family survivor. This took many years as there was no evidence of my father's demise to establish proof of death.

Janka also sent me the sad news that my uncle Józek from Sieraków had not returned from war. His distraught wife Genia had taken the loss of her husband badly and was being looked after in a care home. She never recovered from losing the man she loved so much.

Even today I don't know why Janka came to Warsaw at the start of the Uprising with my mother and sister. In all my letters and phone calls with Janka I never found out the reason. If I ever asked then I have absolutely no recollection of receiving an answer.

POLISH COMMUNITY

During the 1950s the west London Polish community continued to grow. We spent a lot of time socialising with friends mainly in our houses. Occasionally we allowed ourselves to attend a ball or other such event organised by various Polish societies. Many Polish social and cultural centres were springing up, where we would meet Poles from further afield. One of the first such places was the White Eagle Club, which was in a huge building at 2 Albert Gate in Knightsbridge. The French embassy was across the street and Harrods was only a short walk away. Nowadays the building is the Kuwaiti embassy.

Janusz and I both loved dressing up and I fondly recall my first experience of wearing a glamorous dress. I was working for a high-quality dressmaker on Regent Street and once a year the staff were offered a substantial discount on unsold stock. I bought a bottle-green chiffon evening dress with guipure lace trim. It was the first time I had ever possessed such a beautiful dress. I shortened it to suit my style and when I put that dress on I felt wonderful. Janusz looked proud to have me on his arm.

It was at the White Eagle Club around 1955 that I became reacquainted with my friend Irka from Stowell Park. Irka had travelled down from Cambridge with her husband Władek Gorczynski, who was studying at the university. They brought with them their first child, Erwin, who was about two years old at the time. We gradually became close friends with the Gorczynskis; I became Erwin's godmother and Władek would eventually become godfather to my second son George.

Władek came from Dżwinogród, which was not far from Janusz's home in the Kresy. As a 16-year-old in the winter of 1940, Władek escaped the Soviet occupation with a few other local young men by skiing across the frozen Dniestr river into Romania. After being interned for a while, Władek escaped and headed for Yugoslavia. At Split he boarded a French ship bound for Marseilles. In France Władek joined the Polish army and fought with the French army in the Battle of France in the summer of 1940. He received a medal for bravery for storming a German tank. After France's capitulation Władek was interned for much of the rest of the war in neutral Switzerland, where he benefited from a good education. In 1944 he attempted to join the Allied forces in France but the attempt failed when he was caught by the communist French resistance and sent back to Switzerland. Despite the resultant increased vigilance by the Swiss, Władek made another attempt, this time successfully joining British forces in the push against Germany.

The White Eagle club closed down after a fire and so we started socialising at the Polish Hearth Club, Ognisko, which still stands on Exhibition
Road in Kensington near the Brompton Oratory. Although I didn't know
him personally, General Anders was a frequent visitor and we saw him many
times at the club. He often came with his senior officers for card sessions
on the top floor. Sometimes he would give public talks, which we attended.
There were various plays and presentations at the in-house theatre on the
first floor where we would meet friends. The atmosphere at the Hearth Club
was wonderful in those days; the place exuded an air of sophistication and
was an important centre for Poles in London.

I saw much less of Hania for a while as in 1956 her husband Wojtek
opened The Atlantic restaurant near the Hearth Club, which took up most
of their time. We went there once but unfortunately the restaurant didn't
last long as Wojtek was excessively generous to his friends.

We became part of a close set of friends who shared the common background of originating from Janusz's home town of Brzeżany in the Kresy.
This group included Bishop Rubin from Lwów, Jasio Bączkowski and Teresa,
the daughter of friends from Brzeżany. Teresa and I got on particularly well
as she was vivacious, about my age and lived close by. For some reason we
nicknamed Teresa's husband Józef Huczynski 'Kizia'. Kizia had also been in
the AK and through those circles I gradually got to know him better too.

After the war the many former members of the AK who had settled in
exile around the world began to form social and self-help organisations
which were closely linked to each other. There were no such organisations
in Poland due to the Soviet repression of the AK. The Polish Home Army
Ex-Servicemen's Association or AK Association of Great Britain began
in 1946 and was headquartered in London. There were also branches in
a number of countries including Canada, the USA, Australia, France,
Belgium and South Africa. Kizia became heavily involved in setting up
a related AK organisation and he asked me to come along to a meeting
when a new board was being elected. They were also looking for volunteers.
Janusz came to the meeting as well but soon got annoyed by the bluster and
political posturing of younger 'upstarts' rather than the serious discussion
he expected.

Janusz's attitude was shared by some of his colleagues and stemmed from the fact that the Independent Carpathian Brigade, with which he had served in North Africa from 1940, was made up of men with a high level of military experience and education. When General Anders' new army arrived from Russia in 1942 some of these new arrivals were initially regarded as overly formal, officious and rather self-aggrandising. However Anders' men soon lost this attitude and became an effective army, earning a powerful reputation on the battlefield. Unfortunately some of the AK people at this meeting mirrored that initially arrogant attitude. Janusz felt they seemed primarily interested in personal prestige and getting their picture taken with Princess Marina of the British Royal Family. He thought that they should show more humility, particularly as many had only two months of real fighting under their belts.

It is an acknowledged truism that Poles love organisations. There is a well-known saying that 'When there are two Poles there are three organisations'. I wasn't particularly fond of such meetings yet I couldn't help wanting to be involved, as I was genuinely interested in helping with the AK organisations and felt it was my duty. Janusz insisted that they would just use me to do all their 'running around' and forbade me to waste my time with them. As a result I didn't get involved in these AK organisations until many years later.

Janusz was a good man but he could also be difficult. He was good-looking with a lively personality. He had a spark about him. He was sociable and everybody liked him. He was able to run a conversation and enjoyed arguing after a good drink with his friends but he also knew how to smooth things over if arguments went too far. Janusz was always honest and helpful to all. In his wartime army record – as far as I can make out, given the old-fashioned handwriting – Janusz's wartime commanders describe him as intelligent, patriotic, hard-working, modest, calm and sociable.

He cared very much for his children back in Poland, actively maintaining a correspondence and providing financial support by sending saleable items to their mother. This caused some friction between us. I understood his commitment and agreed that he should provide financial support but I felt he was sending too much while we were living on a shoestring.

Sometimes Janusz could be possessive and petulant, and we often argued about this. After one such argument Janusz pulled out of a holiday at the last moment so I went on my own with friends. Another time I even registered to emigrate to Canada, although we patched things up and I stayed. Perhaps the failure of Janusz's first marriage and our age gap contributed to his insecurities, but mainly I think this was just in his nature.

CHILDREN

In 1957 Janusz left CAV in order to start his own business utilising skills he had acquired from a course in light leatherwork. He purchased a machine and stocks of high-quality leather including cow, crocodile and snake skins which he used to make glamorous handbags from home. He sold through a Polish shop in Turnham Green. I still have a beautiful crocodile handbag that Janusz made for me. At first business went well and I was even able to have my first holiday abroad in Spain with friends. Sadly this did not last and after about 18 months Janusz started looking for the greater security of employment. And so, at the age of 51, he completed a mechanical draughtsmanship evening course at The Institute of Polish Engineers in Great Britain. He then began work as a machine setter, grinder and operator at Rotax in the aerospace division in Park Royal Industrial Estate, and ended up staying with the company for over ten years.

Towards the end of the decade, as my thirtieth birthday loomed, I started longing to have a family. I still missed Henia desperately and I dreamed of having a daughter I could be close to. I had never lost that feeling of loneliness: living in a foreign country increased my sense of isolation and made me even more determined to have my own family. At first Janusz was not keen; money was still tight and he was in his fifties. Many couples I knew were having similar arguments as the men worried about being able to provide for their children. I would listen to the anguish of one particular neighbour and we were able to comfort one another. Janusz tended to avoid talking about children but with time I think he came to realise that the issue would not disappear, that I would not give up and that I needed a child.

Janusz's divorce finally came through in 1959 and we got married soon after in a civil ceremony at Ealing Town Hall. As a divorced Catholic, Janusz was not allowed to remarry in church. It was a low-key wedding without much fuss.

I miscarried my first pregnancy, which was a devastating blow and took some time to get over. I had the inevitable fear that I would never have children. Incompatible blood groupings were given as the prime reason for the miscarriage but I was also diagnosed with an incompetent cervix, so when I eventually got pregnant again the risks of another miscarriage were considered high. My brilliant Australian doctor at Queen Charlotte's Hospital in Chiswick suggested a pioneering surgical technique which involved sewing up the cervix followed by confinement in bed. I spent seven long months just lying in bed at Queen Charlotte's, desperately hoping that my baby would survive. Janusz was with me as often as he could be. I had many visitors during that warm summer and I remember the tune 'Theme from a Summer Place' playing regularly on the radio. I shared the ward with about five other women who were all having birth problems and we got to know each other well. As it was a warm summer the hospital windows were constantly open and one day a bird flew into our ward. We all watched with interest to see what it would do. After a short while it landed on my bed where it made a mess. The other women erupted with laughter and one said it was a good omen.

While I waited anxiously, I had a dream that I have never forgotten. In it I found myself in the darkness of night surrounded by houses. I kept walking among the buildings, desperately searching for a way out. It was so hard and depressing. Eventually I emerged into an uplifting scene. It was bright daylight and before me was a luscious green field with a stream running through it and some trees on the other side. There were two beautiful white swans slowly floating along the stream, one bigger than the other. I awoke feeling content, as though the dream was a premonition, and it gave me a big boost. Even today if I close my eyes I can still see that stream and green grass.

Andrew was born on 4th September 1960. It had been a long and hard labour as my muscles were weak after lying in bed for so many months.

I collapsed with exhaustion and fell asleep within minutes of the birth. Despite his earlier reservations, Janusz was overjoyed and bought cigars for all his friends to celebrate. When, a few weeks later, Janusz drove me home, I was overwhelmed by all the presents that his best friend Józek and his wife Dzidzia had bought for the baby: there was a pram, lots of toys and baby clothes all in blue.

Andrew had been born prematurely and badly jaundiced. We were told it was quite serious and that he would need a blood transfusion, something that worried me greatly and I prayed we could avoid. For months I had to take him back to hospital for injections in his heel. It broke my heart watching him screaming with pain. The entire experience was traumatic but my prayers were answered when I was told that there were signs of improvement in his condition.

Nothing has come easily to me in life: I have had to fight for everything. Because everything has been a struggle I treasure things so much more. Andrew will always be special to me not only because he was my first child but also because we both had to fight so much for him to be born and survive. Whenever I hear 'Theme from a Summer Place' it always reminds me of Andrew.

He was baptised at Ealing Abbey and afterwards we held a large dinner reception with 30 close friends. My friend from the German convent at Hange, Mr Kwarta, attended. After the war he had continued painting in England and was even commissioned to paint Winston Churchill's portrait. At Andrew's baptism party Mr Kwarta gave us a beautiful picture he had painted of the Palace on the Isle in Warsaw's Łazienki park. The painting still hangs in my living room and reminds me of my childhood home. We chose Lodzia and Józek Florczykowski as Andrew's godparents.

Janusz and Józek had been friends since the early days of the war; they both came from the Kresy and were together in the Independent Carpathian Rifle Brigade in North Africa prior to the arrival of General Anders and his army from Russia. Józek too had been previously married in Poland. He married his second wife Dzidzia in Rome before they came to London. Later his son from his first marriage came over to London but decided not to stay. Sadly the marriage with Dzidzia was not blessed with children.

We spent a lot of time with the Florczykowscy chatting and playing cards late into the night. The men would often drink too much and argue; Janusz enjoyed holding forth and speaking his mind. Sometimes they would fall out and not speak for a while. Dzidzia would tell them to grow up and eventually they would make up. It was the sort of relationship that could only exist between two people who are extremely close.

My pregnancy with my second son George was much easier, although I still needed the precautionary surgery and spent the first two months confined to the house. Marta's husband Edek managed to get me some work through his employer assembling pieces of jewellery from home. George – whose name appears on his birth certificate in its Polish form, Jerzy – arrived on 2nd June 1964. We chose Olenka and Irka's husband Władek as his godparents.

Before I came home from the hospital we lost a dear friend, Stefa's husband Jasio Bączkowski. Jasio was in hospital with heart problems; I was planning to visit him when I came out. Sadly on 15th June, the day he was due to leave hospital, Jasio sat on his bed, keeled over and died. This was a major blow for us all and particularly for Janusz as they both came from Brzeżany in the Kresy and had spent five years fighting in North Africa and Italy together.

George was baptised at the St Andrew Bobola church in Shepherd's Bush. The church had been purchased by the Polish community in 1961 and was another important milestone in the foundation of the Polish community in west London. Andrzej Bobola was a seventeenth-century priest and missionary in the Kresy region of Poland, which is now in Belarus. While he was being sadistically tortured by Cossacks, Bobola prayed aloud for his torturers until his death. The church had an overtly military character; it was adorned with insignias and significant dates were commemorated there. The church's name has particular resonance for Poles in England, many whom came from the Kresy.

THE KRESY

Although Poland was still firmly under communist control, after Stalin's death in 1953 politics in Poland went through a period of mild reform known as the 'Gomulka thaw' after the then leader of the Polish communist party. Travel restrictions were eased and families started to be reunited. Finally in 1962, after 23 years, Janusz was able to see his sister Stasia when she came to visit us in Ealing.

Janusz was excited about seeing his elder sister again and he showed her all over London. I was happy for Janusz but at the same time I was aware that there was nobody to come and visit me. I imagined how wonderful it would be if Henia came to visit, I would have taken her everywhere and given her all that I could. But it could never be. Even then, with a child of my own, I felt a pervasive sense of loneliness that has never really left me.

Stasia was quite burly and a very fine lady. I can still picture her bouncing Andrew up and down on her knees in our garden. We got on well and chatted at length, particularly about the family's tragic circumstances in the Kresy during the war. I have been able to expand on the details through knowledge acquired subsequently.

Stasia had stayed in the Kresy in East Galicia with her parents, Leon Szlachetko and Katarzyna Zalewska. An elder brother, Kazimierz (Kazik), had moved to western Poland before the war. The two eldest siblings, Jadwiga and Jakub, had died in infancy.

Stasia chillingly described how Soviet soldiers arrived at the door to deport her family to Siberia in 1940. As the soldiers entered the house they were greeted with the sight of two bodies. Just a few days earlier Stasia and Janusz's mother Katarzyna and Stasia's ten-year-old daughter Zofia had both died and now lay in their coffins. They had succumbed to one of the many epidemics of the time. Stasia was pregnant and hid in the cellar with her eight-year-old son Nusek. She held her hand over Nusek's mouth to stop him from making a noise as they both cowered in the dark. When the Soviet soldiers saw the two coffins Stasia heard one of them say, "There's no need to deport them as they have their own Siberia here already." Thus Stasia avoided detection and deportation. Their father Leon died a few months after his wife.

The scale of deportations of Poles by the Soviets was incredible. Between 1939 and 1941 around a million and a half Polish citizens were forcibly deported to camps, mainly in Siberia and Kazakhstan. These included almost a million people forced out of their homes in four waves during February, April and June 1940 and July 1941. Soviet soldiers, Ukrainian militia and local communist committee members would arrive at night and accuse their victims of being 'enemies of the revolution'. These Poles were then given just a few minutes to pack their belongings before embarking on the journey in cramped cattle wagons. It took weeks; around 500,000 of these deportees are estimated to have died en route or were dead by the end of 1941.

The arrival in the Kresy of the German army in 1941 was to prove even more tragic for Janusz's wider family. Leon was one of 12 siblings, some of whom owned a glass factory five kilometres from Narajów near Rohaczyn. The factory had been purchased from the noble Potocki family, for whom Leon worked as a forester before the war, while also travelling abroad to Romania and Slovakia to sell the glass products made at the factory. Some of these siblings lived in a small village adjoining the factory called Huta Szklana w Narajowie ('Glassworks'). The population of the village numbered about 400, most of whom worked in the factory and were of either Polish or German descent, although the majority of the latter considered themselves Polish.

In late 1943 and early 1944 14 families of German descent left the village for nearby towns. This was a bad sign. According to a published eyewitness account by Marian Nehrebecki, on 20th March 1944 a number of armed, Ukrainian-speaking men from Rohaczyn arrived in the village. These men were presumably Banderowczy (UPA). They forced their way into the home of Franciszek Szlachetko, Leon's brother, and took him to the nearby woods. Franciszek had been helping a number of Jewish families who were hiding in the woods after escaping from a local ghetto. There were about 70 Jews in total. Marian Nehrebecki describes how he followed at a distance and saw a trail of blood in the snow as Franciszek was badly beaten, presumably to make him reveal the Jewish hiding places. It seems likely that he succumbed. The Banderowczy then took the Jews by surprise;

they made them stand in a single file with heads bowed against their chests so that a single bullet would kill more than one person. Thirty-five of the Jews including women and children were murdered. The Banderowczy then took Franciszek and the daughter of a rabbi from Narajów to other woods nearer Rohaczyn, where they were both murdered.

The same day Leon's 22-year-old nephew Tadeusz Szlachetko, the son of Jan Szlachetko, was taken by Ukranians along with another villager to Rohaczyn. Their hands and feet were bound with barbed wire and they were sadistically tortured to death with knives.

On 25th March eyewitnesses describe how a large, armed group of Ukranians arrived at the village at 4pm. Over two hours virtually every home was burnt to the ground and most of the inhabitants unable to escape were murdered, including Leon's brother Jan and other relatives. Six more were taken and hanged the following day, apparently by a female Ukranian. The flames from the burning village were visible and the noises of shooting and screaming could be heard five kilometres away in Narajów. The head of the German army stationed in Narajów, who must have heard and observed this massacre, reportedly said that he was not proud of what was happening but that he would be signing his own death warrant if he were to intervene to stop it. Thus the Szlachetkos and their relatives became a small number of the many murdered by the Ukranian Insurgent Army (UPA).

The UPA was the military wing of the Ukranian nationalist movement (OUN) which the Poles refer to as Banderowcy after Stepan Bandera, one of the early nationalist leaders. After the German attack against the Soviet Union in 1941 the Kresy was occupied by German forces. Between 1941 and 1944, the Germans murdered most of the area's Jewish population and promoted unrest between Ukrainian nationalists (OUN) and the Poles. The Ukrainian nationalists collaborated with the Germans in the hope of gaining independence after the war, and the UPA pursued a policy of ethnic cleansing, directed mainly against the Polish population. The UPA was specifically responsible for the Volhynia and East Galicia massacres in which some of Janusz's family were murdered. In an explosion of unbridled hatred between March 1943 and late 1944, as many as 100,000 ethnic Poles and members of smaller minorities including Czechs, Russians and Jews were slaughtered. Eyewitness accounts describe numerous acts of sadism during these massacres. Many Ukranian civilians who helped their former Polish neighbours or who merely objected to this murderous policy were also killed for 'treason'.

Another two of Leon's brothers, Piotr and Marceli, had earlier died at the hands of the Germans. Piotr had been living in Warsaw when he was arrested in August 1941 for involvement in the underground Conspiracy. After being interned in the Pawiak prison Piotr was taken to Auschwitz, where, according to his death certificate, he died on 17th April 1942, aged 45. A year previously, in August 1940, Marceli Szlachetko had also been interned at the Pawiak prison. There was no further news of him.

The suffering in the Kresy did not end with the war. The Kresy was annexed by the Soviet Union and most of East Galicia was integrated into the newly formed Ukrainian Soviet Republic, and approximately 750,000 of the remaining Polish population were deported west to territories annexed from Germany. Stasia and her two young sons boarded a train with all their belongings in one trunk and left their land and former lives behind. On the train Stasia was given the option to alight at one of two stations in southern Poland, either Gliwice or Opole. She chose Gliwice and the family eventually settled in an apartment vacated by Germans in the nearby village of Bojków. They were penniless.

Some of the 1,736 AK girls at the last roll-call at Oberlangen camp on the day of liberation, 12th April 1945. Commandant 'Jaga' is in the foreground on the right.

Wira in Germany, 1945.

Portrait of Janusz taken during his internment in Romania in 1940, before his escape.

Janusz, top right, next to his sister Stasia and brother Kazik. His parents, Katarzyna and Leon, sit in the front row. Picture taken before the war.

Christmas at Doddington Park ressettlement camp in December 1946. Wira in the foreground.

Wira in London, 1950s.

Janusz in London, 1950s.

Wira's friends in her garden in Ealing. From left to right: Lodzia, Jadzia, Kizia and Teresa, Tadzik, Gerard, Teresa's mother, Zygmund, Olenka, Kowalewski and Zosia. 1960s.

First trip back to Poland in 1966. Janusz in front of his cousin Waczek and brother Kazik. Janusz's nephew, Adam Kohlbek, on the left. Two-year-old George is sitting on the car.

Second trip back to Poland in 1974. From left to right: Uncle Janek, Wira, Alinka, Elżbieta (the falling baby), Janusz and Andrew. At the front are Irka (Elżbieta's daughter) and George.

Wira with her sons at Andrew's graduation, 1986.

Wira with close friend and travelling companion, Frank, in Thailand, 1998.

*Wira at the Katyn monument in Gunnersbury cemetery in 2000, left,
and at an understated memorial at the site of the massacres in the Katyn Forest in 1996, right.*

*Wira, front left, with AK coleagues at a commemoration at Gunnersbury cemetery. Marta is in
the centre, not in uniform, and Hania is on the right.*

Friends after 60 years. From left to right: Wira, Hania, Celina and Stefa.

Wira with her son, George, at the 60th anniversary of the Warsaw Uprising commemorations in 2004.

Wira with her family in 2015. Andrew is on the left with his wife Edyta, George is on the right with his wife Jacqui. Wira's four grandchildren are in the

Chapter 8

RETURN TO POLAND

Twenty years had passed since the Germans had forced me out of Poland and 25 since Janusz had left. We longed to see our beloved country again, so after George was born we started making plans to visit Poland for the summer. Janusz had recently become a British citizen, mainly for the benefit of the children. This meant that he had a British passport offering full protection as a British citizen when abroad. I was still a DP and had only a 'travel document' issued under the United Nations Geneva Convention of July 1951. My appearance was described in my document as "dark blonde with a straight nose, an oval shaped face and with no special peculiarities". This 'travel document' gave certain rights as a political refugee, conferring the protection of participating nation states. As Poland was not a participating state, any visit would be at my own risk. I needed the security of British citizenship and so I finally applied and ceased to be a DP in 1966, shortly before our departure.

There was some last-minute uncertainty before we set off as Józek was suffering from cancer and his condition seemed to be deteriorating. Janusz wanted to cancel the trip but both Józek and Dzidzia insisted that we go and assured us that everything would be fine while we were away.

We drove the long distance through France and Germany by car. It was an arduous journey of about a thousand kilometres; cars were much less comfortable in those days and we had the two boys with us. I was struck by the difference as we crossed from West to East Germany, how sparse East Germany looked and how empty the roads were. As we approached the Polish border we were both overwhelmed by emotion and my eyes were filled with tears.

Entering Poland and driving through the countryside along Polish roads was initially a euphoric feeling; it felt as if at last we were back in our own land.

The feeling didn't last long. When we arrived in a town we were obviously in a very different Poland from the one we had both known. Each week we were obliged to report to a police station to confirm our whereabouts and we had to report every time we wanted to travel to another place. Virtually every public official seemed to be hostile towards us and it was clear that we were unwelcome foreigners. Poland had changed a lot under communist rule and we were made to feel like enemies of the state. Even shop assistants showed disrespect and were unhelpful although perhaps they treated everybody that way. They certainly didn't care whether we bought anything or not: they acted as if they were doing us a favour by opening up at all.

It was joyous but also deeply poignant for Janusz to see his family again. His brother Kazik organised a large gathering at his home in Chełmno, near Bydgoszcz, where they were reunited after more than 30 years. Kazik had built a loving family with his kind wife Jadzia and their five children, Ola, Basia, Krysia, Miecio and Zbyszek. Their sister Stasia also travelled up with her sons Adam and Nuszek from Bojków near Gliwice in southern Poland.

At the gathering Janusz was also finally reunited with his two adult children Adam and Rysia after 27 years. He introduced me to them, which was a very awkward experience. Although Adam acknowledged me a little and we chatted, Rysia completely ignored me. I was not nervous about meeting Janusz's children but I did feel uncomfortable after the meeting and as an outsider a little embarrassed. Janusz presented Rysia with one of his two solid 24-carat-gold serpent bracelets which he had bought during the war in Egypt; the other he had given to me. This would be the only time I ever met or had contact with Janusz's children.

I got to know a little more about Kazik during our time there and his wife Jadzia was particularly happy to discuss their lives during the war. Their daughter Ola has since been very helpful in adding to this knowledge.

Kazik had followed in his father's footsteps and trained as a forester. In 1929 he had moved to the Pomerania region of northern Poland to take up a forester position in Jelenia Góra in Bory Tucholskie. He belonged to the patriotic and apolitical organisation called Towarzyszenie Powstanców i Wojaków (Society of Uprisers and Soldiers) and attained the rank of Captain.

In 1939 Jelenia Góra was within the part of western Poland annexed by Germany. There were mass executions of Poland's intelligentsia, estimated at 50,000 in the annexed region alone. Many of these executions were carried out by the Selbstschutz paramilitaries formed from local ethnic Germans. With the help of local people, Kazik went into hiding – and thus narrowly avoided becoming one of the victims of the execution of hundreds of local Poles, including other foresters and patriots, which took place at the Rudski Bridge in October and November 1939. Kazik then spent most of the war in Machor where he and his father-in-law bribed German soldiers with vodka and pork to release Poles who had been rounded up in *łapanki* and were being transported into forced labour in Germany. He also played a part in the Warsaw Uprising.

After the war Kazik resumed his role as forester at Jelenia Góra. The forests became home to large numbers of Poland's Żołnierze Wyklęci (Doomed Soldiers), whose history is only now being recognised. Following the Soviet annexation of Eastern Poland and the imposition of Soviet rule, many members of the Polish underground continued an anti-Soviet partisan struggle that would not end until 1963. The term 'Doomed Soldiers' reflects the fact that these resistance fighters had no hope of a good outcome. Hounded by the communist regime they could either surrender and die or fight and die. Offers of amnesty turned out to be mere tricks which led to many Doomed Soldiers being murdered by the UB, Poland's Communist Department of Security. Kazik helped these partisans in Jelenia Góra by leaving food and medicines near his house to be collected at pre-agreed times.

Kazik and his sister Stasia both received national identity cards issued by the communist authorities in Poland stating that their place of birth was the ZSRR (USSR). They had been born in the Kresy, which was now part of the Soviet Republic of Ukraine. Both despised this. Kazik in particular found it insulting, and it pained him greatly.

As a postscript, Kazik went on to make a mark in forestry: and today there is a ten-acre forest reserve of yew trees in Jelenia Góra named in his honour.

I was desperate to see Warsaw, my childhood home, again. I had so many memories and images in my head. The city had been largely rebuilt since the war and now looked very different from the Warsaw of my childhood. Large, ugly, Soviet-style apartment blocks sprawled around the outskirts. Central Warsaw still exuded grandeur, having been rebuilt in its former style, but overall it seemed less lavish and ornate. Nowy Świat, where I had grown up, had also changed. The building arrangement was different and my beloved courtyards were now less open. I had hoped that Nowy Świat would evoke warm feelings from my past but I was disappointed. I think my mental images were still dominated by the days of occupation, with familiar faces and buildings surrounded by rubble. Things had inevitably changed; my hopes that I would feel at home again had not come true and instead I had my familiar sense of loneliness.

I decided to attend mass at my former Church of the Holy Cross which had also been entirely rebuilt. An urn containing the heart of Frederic Chopin had been preserved and was encased again in one of the pillars. At the beginning of the mass I finally heard some comforting news as the priest commenced with a dedication to Father Jan Paszyna "on the first anniversary of his death". I finally knew that the pastor, who had been such an important part of my early life and had helped me with my schooling, had managed to survive the Pawiak prison and the war. My heart warmed at last.

While in Warsaw I visited my uncle Janek and his wife Alinka, who were still living in the Old Town. It was lovely to see their first daughter Elżbieta again, who by then was 27. I also met Irka, Elżbieta's younger sister by about three years, for the first time.

I finally saw Auntie Janka after so many years. She was still living in my family house in Laski, which she shared with her brother Franek and his wife Jadzia. Seeing Franek, the youngest of my uncles, reminded me with amusement how my mother used to treat him – more like a son than as her brother. Janka prepared dinner for us one day and I finally tasted my beloved blueberry soup once more on Polish soil. I had dreamt many times of this moment but regrettably it could not match the blueberry soup from my mother's kitchen.

On the way back to England we stopped off at Janusz's brother's house again to say farewell. Kazik had hunted a young deer for us and his wife gave us a variety of venison dishes and sandwiches to help us on our long journey home. While we were there Janusz bumped into the wife of a good army friend of his, and before I knew it he had agreed to give her a lift back to London with us. We were about to drive over a thousand kilometres in a 1960s car with two young children and ever-expanding luggage, and now Janusz had agreed to take another passenger and additional luggage without asking me! I was not happy.

We drove towards the border crossing into East Germany at Słubice. In those days, in order to cross the Polish border one was given a specific time to report at the checkpoint. Our allotted time was very early in the morning and we arrived slightly late. The border guards kept us waiting for hours in the cold while they made numerous telephone calls to "check everything was in order" before finally permitting us to leave Poland. It felt as if they were saying "Don't come back" and for my part it was with some relief that we left communist Poland.

We drove across East Germany and as evening approached we stopped to eat our venison cutlets and sandwiches. We parked beside a wood not far from the border with West Germany. It was turning dark as we prepared to move again but the car wouldn't start. I felt frightened – here we were, stuck in an unfriendly country in the middle of nowhere with two young children. It soon turned completely dark. Suddenly a truck pulled up beside us, filled with Russian soldiers. Fortunately for us they were just passing and had stopped to help. Janusz knew a little Russian and was able to explain what had happened. One of the Russians took a look under the bonnet and played around a little before jokingly saying in Russian, "Try filling the engine with mustard seeds and it will be alright." His colleagues enjoyed the joke. They then gave Janusz some vague directions to a nearby garage and left. It was too late to walk anywhere and by now it had started raining so we tucked in for a night in the car. I spent that night frightened and angry at the same time; it was an unpleasant and sleepless night with the two boys stretched out all over me in the back.

In the morning Janusz had no choice but to leave us and walk to the garage. He reappeared some time later in a truck with a man from the garage; I was relieved that we finally had some help. He started to tow us and we thought we were going to the garage but after a few minutes we reached the border where there was an enormous queue of cars. Fortunately, once the border guards saw that we were being towed they let us through without queueing, which was the one stroke of luck that came out of our horrible night. Once we'd crossed the border, and to our surprise, the tow truck simply abandoned us.

With the car eventually repaired, we raced through West Germany and France but missed our ferry across the English Channel. Another long wait ensued with George suffering with diarrhoea. I had run out of nappies, which made the wait even more frustrating. Finally after midnight we were squeezed onto another ferry, and arrived in England in the dead of night. It had been an exhausting journey. I had put up with Janusz's friend's wife who was pleasant and had been very polite throughout the trip but the final straw came when she left her bags in our car to be collected later by her husband. As we unloaded her luggage we discovered that our bottle of raspberry juice had spilled all over her clothes and I had to wash them before her husband came to collect the luggage!

This nightmare journey back to England soon paled into insignificance as we received tragic news: Józek had died while we had been away. Dzidzia told us he had suffered terribly without morphine and even attempted to jump out of the hospital window as the pain was unbearable. Janusz took Józek's death badly and never stopped blaming himself for going to Poland when Józek was so ill. Janusz had lost his dearest and closest of friends.

Soon after Józek's death Dzidzia went to stay with relatives in Canada for a few months. Within six months of her return Dzidzia invited us and some other friends to dinner and introduced us to a male friend of hers. Later that evening the friend stood up in front of us, declared his love for her and asked her to marry him. Dzidzia accepted. Janusz was incensed and couldn't understand how she could accept his proposal so soon after Józek's death. Janusz was very much from the old school and felt Dzidzia had not grieved for Józek for long enough. He forbade us to attend the wedding and barely spoke to Dzidzia again.

Chapter 9

TASTING NORMAL LIFE

For us the rest of the Sixties and early Seventies centred on raising a young family in an Anglo-Polish environment. The Polish community in Ealing and the surrounding areas continued to expand, creating the need for educational, cultural and religious centres.

In 1968 our local Anglican church of St Matthew's, which overlooks Ealing Common, kindly allowed the Polish community to have Catholic mass said there on Sunday mornings. This supplemented the afternoon mass long held at Ealing Abbey. Later that same year the Polish Catholic Centre, POK, opened in West Ealing after the community purchased a large property in Courtfield Gardens at auction. POK provided some living quarters for priests, a chapel for additional Sunday masses, space for cultural and charitable activities, and a large outdoor garden for gatherings.

On Saturday mornings the boys attended Polish school. The school had been set up soon after the war in 1950 with the purpose of helping the many second-generation Polish children learn some of their culture and heritage. Originally based at St Gregory's school, the Polish school moved to Grange School and then to the premises of Ealing Green High in 1965. Lessons were conducted in Polish and all the teachers and support staff, of whom Janusz was one, were volunteers from the Polish community. The boys were not particularly keen to attend yet more classes on Saturdays but we felt they should go. Later on, we allowed George to miss Polish school to play football for his English school team after he'd worn us down with his constant complaining.

The boys also belonged to the Ealing Polish Cubs and the Second Polish Scouts Group, which regularly used the POK facilities for meetings. The Polish scout organisations in Britain and across the world were often set up by former members of the wartime Grey Ranks and kept Polish scouting traditions alive. Although the post-war Polish scouts were not paramilitaries like the Grey Ranks of wartime Poland, they were adventurous and some of their activities would certainly be considered questionable by health and safety regulators today. Boys as young as 12 took part in overnight war games with little adult supervision while at scout camp in the countryside. One of the scout badges the boys attained was called Three Feathers and required not eating or speaking for 24 hours at camp. Once they had passed this test they were sent on their own into the woods overnight with nothing but their clothes. The boys spent many summer and winter weeks away with the scouts on camping and hiking holidays or participating in endurance events such as Ten Tors on Dartmoor.

We also got involved in various community groups and I helped out at events for elderly Poles, including regular tea or dinner gatherings, and staged performances that were mainly hosted at POK. The Marian Sodality began in England in 1952; as I had been involved with the same sodality in Warsaw as a child, I attended a few meetings, but it did not feel right for me to be fully involved at that time.

In 1972 Janusz and many other fellow expatriates contributed some funds and became members of the Polish Social and Cultural Centre that was being built in Hammersmith. POSK opened its doors in 1974 and is still a thriving centre for our community. These days POSK has a reasonably large theatre, a bar and restaurants, a gallery, function rooms and a bookshop. A variety of events are hosted at POSK including dances and classes. There is also a lot of office space which is used by various Polish organisations. A whole new generation of Poles in Britain is now benefiting from the investment and commitment of the older generation.

Meanwhile economic and living conditions had deteriorated in Poland under communist rule and many basic necessities had become hard to obtain. Many Poles living abroad were busy sending back packages filled with clothes and other useful items. Mr Laskowski, one of our friends, worked for a company in nearby Brentford where he could buy items of ladies' clothing such as petticoats, blouses and waterproof overcoats at a discount. Mr Laskowski and I entered into a business arrangement whereby he would deliver these items to my house in Ealing and I would informally sell them on to expatriate Poles to be sent home to their families in Poland. Demand for these goods was huge, with people visiting the house regularly throughout the day. I kept a small commission which enabled me to supplement the family income for a couple of years.

Sending aid to families still in the Kresy, which had been annexed by the Soviet Union, was much more difficult. Our tenant Adolf Kowalewski told us that this could only be done through designated shops in London at hugely inflated prices.

The Poles in England never abandoned their patriotism. Everybody sought to acquire and display carvings of the Polish eagle wearing a crown. This was Poland's pre-war coat of arms. The communists had removed the crown from the eagle in Poland. The crown symbolised the sovereignty which we dreamed would one day be restored to our country: an aspiration and a conviction we would never abandon.

During those years we met other Polish families with children of the same age with whom we became friendly and occasionally went on holiday, like Cesia and Andrzej Uszycki, their son Kazio and daughter Basia. Cesia was a pharmacist in nearby Ealing Common, where she lived above the shop. I got on very well with Ciesia and the boys shared a lot of playdates. By coincidence I had already met Cesia's husband Andrzej at Portland Road. Andrzej had been in the Warsaw Uprising, where he played a part in the preparations for the famous assassination of SS-Brigadeführer Franz Kutschera. During the occupation his family had harboured Ron Jeffery, a British POW escapee, who married Andrzej's sister Marysia and wrote a book about life in occupied Warsaw, *Red Runs the Vistula*.

Another such family were the Zdziarscy with whom we spent a holiday in Eastbourne one year. Although it was a good holiday my overriding memory is of George going missing. The older boys ran ahead towards a shop along Eastbourne promenade and George, still only five years old, ran after them and got lost. The beach area was packed with people enjoying the funfair and we searched for him for what seemed like an eternity. The police were called and I sat there inconsolable, praying and in tears until George was eventually found. He was wandering in the nearby fairground looking for us when my friend finally spotted him, a small figure in the crowd. He still looked terrified when he was placed in my arms and I held him tightly for a long long time. I don't know if this was just the natural reaction of a mother or if I overreacted, but the experience of losing a child tore me apart. This trauma also helped me better understand how my mother must have felt when I ran away from home to join the Uprising.

Around this time I bumped into Celina, who also came from Warsaw and whom I had not seen since leaving Stowell Park. After the Uprising Celina had been deported into forced labour in Innsbruck in Austria, where she had to shovel coal onto train wagons while hoping to survive frequent Allied air raids on the railway station. Celina's journey to Innsbruck took her via Dachau concentration camp, where she was forced to work on the land and in a paper mill. Other members of Celina's family never returned from Auschwitz. After the war Celina married a Polish man in England and spent a few years at Fairford Polish Hostel near Cirencester, where her husband Bolesław was Chairman of the residents' association.

Our chance meeting took place after Celina had moved to London to live in Harrow with her husband and three daughters – Ursula, Bogusia and Dorota, the youngest, who was the same age as George. Our families started seeing each other quite often and George still bears a scar between his eyes where the seven-year-old Dorota threw a wooden toy brick at him from the top of the stairs. Eventually the family moved to Ealing and we spent many happy Christmas Days together, a tradition that continues to this day.

Bogusia went on to become a historian and has written a book, *Waiting to be Heard*, about the experiences of Poles displaced by the war who remained in exile.

As a family we were fond of hosting large dinner parties, especially on Christmas Eve, which we call Wigilia ('vigil'). Wigilia is the main Christmas holiday for Polish Catholics and traditionally consists of 12 courses without meat and alcohol. After midnight mass the men finally get to open a bottle of vodka. For our children's sake we also celebrated Christmas Day and so they had the benefit of both holidays.

The boys had huge appetites, which as a Polish mother I was always happy to encourage and indulge. As a family we ate vast amounts of fruit which we bought cheaply by the sackload from a large open-air market somewhere on the outskirts of London. I became hopelessly addicted to oranges. Fruit these days tastes nothing like pre-mass-market produce.

Janusz had various food foibles, particularly a dislike of butter and lamb, which were all in his mind. Once I served him lamb without telling him what it was and he ate it all up but then was furious when I told him what he'd eaten. This episode reminded me of my mother secretly preparing horsemeat for Henia and me all those years ago in Warsaw.

Janusz had smoked almost all of his adult life and I didn't see the point of him stopping now, in fact I rather enjoyed seeing him smoking. He made a few attempts to give up over the years but they all ended up with him gorging himself on sweets instead. One time I couldn't bear seeing him eating all those sweets any more. To our mutual relief I went out and bought him a pack of cigarettes.

I had wanted a dog for a long time, particularly as the boys were growing up. They were also desperately keen but Janusz was firmly opposed to the idea. In 1971 he finally offered the family a choice: one of the newly developed colour television sets or a dog. No doubt he expected us to go for the TV but my pedigree pug dog arrived by train from Scotland a few months later. I went to pick him up from King's Cross station, taking with me a bag and some warm milk. The passengers kept smiling as they saw his little head popping up in the Tube train. "My God, what an ugly dog!" was all Janusz could say when he got home from work. The boys immediately loved the dog, whom I named Daniel, and eventually Janusz grew fond of him too. With the boys now at school Daniel became like a new baby for me.

In the early 1970s Janusz was made redundant by Rotax and received around £500 in settlement. Rotax sent a financial advisor to help us invest the redundancy money. He recommended that as we had experienced such troubled lives we should use the money for a long family holiday and "Live a little!" Janusz rejected this advice and insisted that we should pay off the remainder of the mortgage. I hope that while 'living a little' the financial advisor got around to buying his own house too, as this was the beginning of an unprecedented period of house-price appreciation. Since the late

1960s house prices have risen by more than 5,000 percent whereas average
earnings have only risen by about 2,000 percent.

Janusz was over 60 years old by now and still had two young boys
aged eleven and seven to support. My wages from sewing were certainly
not enough to live on so he had to find another income from somewhere.
He had always been resourceful and good with his hands, so he became
a self-employed painter/decorator. Although we'd paid off the mortgage,
money was tight again.

ALONE AGAIN

I recall the day in 1973 when my wedding ring broke. I put the ring into
my handbag intending to take it to be mended but forgetfully left the
handbag in the car that night. By the morning it had been stolen. Not
long after this Janusz began feeling unwell. At first his illness didn't seem
too serious and he only took some basic medication. Early the next year
he underwent treatment in hospital which seemed to make him better.
I didn't discuss his condition with him, I think I was in a state of denial,
just as when I ran away to the Uprising; I naively never considered
the worst. However, Janusz must have known that this was something
more serious because he became determined to revisit his family and
his homeland. That summer of 1974 we bought a new Hillman Hunter
car and drove to Poland. I think now that this was Janusz's undeclared
farewell.

We visited our families again but this time the reunions were much
more subdued. Janusz's visit to his brother, Kazik and his sister Stasia were
particularly poignant. Stasia informed us that her former husband Józef
Kohlbek sought a reunion with her following the death of his second wife
in Argentina. She was reluctant not only because of Józef's betrayal but
because Stasia could not forgive her former husband for his lack of help
after the war. Nevertheless Józef had returned to Poland and was living
close by. Some years later when Stasia and Józef were both in the final days
of their lives in the same hospital, they were finally reconciled.

We also visited Warsaw again where I can recall two small incidents. While we were waiting at a set of traffic lights to cross the road, a lady turned around and said to my ten-year-old George, "Why is your Polish so bad?" Another time I had a blazing row with a lady in a café after she made some dismissive remarks about Poles from overseas. Janusz had to calm the situation down. I suppose that by now I had grown accustomed to the tact and diplomatic manners of the English.

Janusz started feeling ill again during the trip and the drive back across Europe was difficult for him. As we arrived at the ferry port in Holland in the early evening I looked out over the sea at the sunset. The firmament was a mixture of red and yellow colours which made the shape of what seemed like a deep, distant well. The image seemed unnatural, like a passageway into another world. I suddenly felt deeply fearful, with a sense that something was coming to an end.

Janusz continued working for the rest of that year but by January the pain had become too great and he was confined to bed. Daniel, our dog, became a good companion for him; even when he knocked porridge all over the bed Janusz did not get annoyed. The painkillers were not working and Janusz asked me to ask his doctor for something stronger. It was a visit I will never forget. Without any warning Dr Koziel said to me bluntly, "Don't you know what's wrong with your husband? He has cancer and doesn't have long left." I was in complete shock; I had no idea that Janusz had cancer until that moment. I stopped at the Zdziarski's on the way home and broke down. Eventually I composed myself enough to put on a brave face and went home hoping that Janusz wouldn't see the turmoil I was feeling. He took the new drugs but they were of little help and he remained in great pain.

I turned to my doctor instead, thinking that there must be something we could do whatever the cost. "If there was a treatment for cancer I would wholeheartedly recommend you sell the house and try it, but there isn't," Dr Cienska replied.

Dr Koziel came to visit Janusz at home. From the kitchen I could hear Janusz crying as he described his intense pain. I cried myself. As he was leaving I begged Dr Koziel to refer Janusz to a specialist, anything to help him. "This will not help, any money you have you should keep because you will need it," Koziel insisted. "It's Janusz's money as well as mine, I don't care about the future," I replied. I wanted so much to help Janusz and I wasn't prepared to give up. Dr Koziel relented and referred him to a private doctor in Harley Street.

I was still affected by Dr Koziel's harshness and so I wrote ahead to Harley Street requesting that, if there were only bad news, it should not be delivered in front of Janusz. I also requested that the doctor say something to lift Janusz's spirits. As we made our way to Harley Street that day I saw a slight change in Janusz, who seemed more at ease as if he had a renewed sense of hope. The examination took a while and was thorough. Afterwards the doctor said only that he would give a prescription for some medication and write to the GP. Nothing else was said and we left. Our sense of deflation was immense and Janusz was a different man on the journey home.

In early April two of Janusz's friends, Zygmund Piechura and Edek Rymaszewski, came to witness the signing of his will and final testament. In the will Janusz wrote that he was leaving everything to me and that I would 'know what to do with it'. I took this as a great endorsement of his trust in me. It was a traumatic day but the signing of the will seemed to lift a weight from his shoulders.

I had been feeling totally unsupported by the Marian Fathers at our church in Windsor Road. Nobody had contacted me to offer their help, let alone visited. I turned to the Jesuits in Willesden where Jadzia Kucharek, our former tenant from the early days, attended, and they were very helpful. The following day one of the priests came to our home and conducted mass at Janusz's bed with our son Andrew acting as altar boy. I could see Andrew was in turmoil; after the mass he went out to the garden and spent ages mowing the lawn, gripping the mower so tightly that it left his hands red raw.

Janusz once told me that in the Kresy people believed dogs could sense when death was close by. The next day when I got back from the shops Janusz told me that our dog Daniel had spent the entire time howling at the window for no apparent reason. When I looked at the kitchen clock to check the time I noticed that both hands on the clock were moving backwards.

This is the only time I have ever seen such a malfunction. Yet strangely Janusz was now feeling better and even talking about jobs he wanted to do around the house.

At about 3am I instinctively felt for Janusz's hand. Its coldness shocked me and I knew something was wrong. I called for an ambulance and then for my friend Teresa. As I waited I held Janusz's cold hand while he spoke in a muffled voice, barely conscious. He asked why we were driving for so long and moaned that we could have taken a better way to the cemetery. Teresa arrived within five minutes. There was no space for me in the ambulance so I drove myself to the hospital while Teresa stayed to watch over the boys. After some time at the hospital the nurse advised me to go home and promised to call if anything changed. The boys were still asleep when I got back so I made our bed, stood in front of the wardrobe mirror and started brushing my hair. Suddenly I heard a loud sigh from the empty bed and within seconds the telephone rang. By the time I arrived at the hospital Janusz had already passed away.

My life with a complete family was over far too quickly. My marriage had lasted only 15 years and it struck me that this was the same number of years that I had had with my first family in Poland before they were lost to me. At least this time I was not completely alone as I had two sons.

Janusz's funeral took place at Ealing Abbey and he was buried at South Ealing cemetery. George's entire class from St Vincent's attended the church ceremony, which I greatly appreciated. Later I bought all the children sweets in thanks. Janusz's death certificate is dated 15th April 1975, with carcinoma of the bladder given as the cause. One of the doctors suggested Janusz's illness might have been linked to the terrible conditions in the North African desert. Apparently there was some evidence for this explanation but I don't know any more than this.

A few days after Janusz's funeral Dzidzia called round to offer her condolences and I was very happy to see her again. Although I had stood by Janusz's rejection of Dzidzia's after her swift remarriage following her husband's death, I did not share his disapproval. She told me she had been at the service and we had a long chat, after which we resumed our friendship.

I was 45, and widowed, with two young boys aged fourteen and ten and very little money. I think there was £300 left to my name. Crucially, however, Janusz had made sure we owned our house. Somewhat unexpectedly, one of Janusz's clients, a local Jewish man, visited me shortly after his death. He had come to pay for some work Janusz had done on his house. Janusz had been working on a few other houses for local Polish people but not one other client came to settle their outstanding account. The payment from the Jewish man gave me a big boost and I much appreciated his honesty and integrity.

I needed to find work to support the family and so I started a one-year secretarial course in Acton in the autumn of 1976 at the age of 47. It was a busy and tiring year, yet rewarding and enjoyable. There were about twenty girls of all ages in our class. We all got on well and regularly lunched together in the canteen. There was a wide range of nationalities among us and our English teacher suggested we each contribute a recipe for an international cookery book at Christmas time. I still have the book today: in it my recipes for beetroot soup with mushroom ravioli and for poppy seed cake sit proudly alongside those for Welsh cakes, pakhoras, *nan khatai* and jollof rice. I got on particularly well with the West Indian girls who were always warm and friendly. I attended college from 9am until 4pm before rushing home to cook dinner for the boys, tidy the house and do the laundry. After the boys went to bed I would start my homework. My strongest skill was office practice but I was less good at shorthand.

After a lot of hard work, at the end of the year I managed to pass all five disciplines and received my secretarial qualification. I now began to look for work and approached a recruitment agency in Acton. The girls there told me they had nothing on the books at the time but that their manager's secretary would soon be on holiday for two weeks. They asked him whether I could fill in temporarily for her, to which he agreed. I had to type the manager's letters but his handwriting was so bad that the other girls and I could barely read it. Somehow the girls helped me muddle through. Then a typist position at Lucas Electronics in Acton came up, which I took as my first real office job.

The Area Manager was an older man, elegant and well educated. I told
him that my shorthand wasn't that fast but he still agreed to take me on.
Those months working for him were good; he was courteous, helpful and
showed a genuine interest in my past. I liked the creaking of his new shoes
and I told him. He liked the compliment and was particularly delighted
when I gave him some Polish vodka for Christmas. He reciprocated by
buying me flowers on special occasions. Conscious of my poor shorthand,
he always dictated very slowly to me. He was truly a fine man of the 'old
school'.

Alas, this was not to last. Lucas wanted him to accept early retire-
ment and when he decided to take it he apologised to me personally. His
replacement could not have been more different. He was an arrogant
younger man, perhaps 40 years of age. I had the sense that he wanted a
younger secretary and of course it didn't help that I was a foreigner with
a strong accent. Perhaps I was a bit slower than he required as English is
my second language. It was an unhappy time for me; he treated me badly,
criticised my work and frequently talked down to me. He certainly spoke
differently to the other girls. I finally snapped and exclaimed, "Just because
I am a foreigner does not mean I am worse!" I told him I realised I was not
as efficient as a younger person might be but that I was doing my best and
that he shouldn't treat me so badly. To some extent this had a positive effect
and he calmed down somewhat and even began to treat me with some
respect. As a foreigner one is already always a little less at ease in a work environment; it makes things much worse if someone behaves unpleasantly,
particularly when they are in a more powerful position.

Meanwhile Andrew had taken Janusz's death very badly. His father had
died at a crucial stage in his educational life; he started playing truant and
his performance deteriorated badly. It came as quite a shock to me when
the headmaster called me to ask why Andrew was absent from school so
frequently. I needed help so I called George's godfather Władek, who was
a lecturer at Sheffield University. Władek dropped everything and immediately came down to London. We went together to see Andrew's headmaster and Władek helped explain the impact his father's death had had on
Andrew. He also spent some time talking with Andrew, which seemed to

help as things improved from then on. Władek was a great help to me as I had hoped.

I had missed out on my education but I was determined the boys should have every opportunity. George had started upper school at Cardinal Vaughan in Holland Park, not far from Janusz's first house in London. The headmaster was a fine Italian man called Mr Pellegrini and he was particularly keen for his pupils to do well. George was in the lowest set at school which meant that he could not study geography for O Level, a subject he particularly enjoyed. I spoke to Mr Pellegrini and he arranged for George to be moved up. The move worked as George would later take geography for A Level also which helped him get into university. I heard later that Mr Pellegrini had referred to me as a 'formidable mother'.

I was juggling, trying to be both mother and father to the boys as well as provider and landlord, which was not without drawbacks. On one particular occasion I had to take a tenant to court in order to evict him. This tenant was a middle-aged Englishman who was always polite but occasionally had some strange visitors. One night I was awoken suddenly when a young blond lady wondered into my bedroom, totally naked and clearly in another world. My boys were still quite young and I didn't want them exposed to such behaviour, which I was morally opposed to myself. I asked my tenant to leave, which he refused to do. In court he stated that he didn't want to move as he felt comfortable and free in my house. The judge replied, "If you felt so good in the house then you should have behaved better!" and promptly ruled that he had to leave. Even after that, bailiffs were required to physically evict him, rounding off a thoroughly unpleasant experience.

Some years later I would close my door to tenants for the last time. Kowalewski and Gerard were still living in my house. Neither had any family in Britain and so the responsibility for looking after them in their dotage fell on me. As Kowalewski aged and various ailments afflicted him, somebody must have told him that smearing garlic over his body would help. It didn't, of course, but for a while the first floor and almost the whole house became a no-go area due to the smell. Meanwhile Gerard had become so messy that his kitchen was increasingly crawling with insects, which I had to complain about frequently. On one occasion an opportunistic thief broke into our house during the day and wandered into Gerard's room while he sat there reading his newspaper. Both got a terrible shock and the burglar quickly ran away.

I nursed Kowalewski and then visited him in hospital until he passed away in 1990. Gerard sadly died in 1992 while sitting at his kitchen table. Fortunately Andrew was around to help me when I found his body there. By then I was well into my sixties and after Gerard's death I decided that renting was causing me too much anxiety. Kowalewski and Gerard were my last tenants, having also been two of the first some 40 years before.

Occasionally something would happen to bring the whole trauma of the war back again. One day my friend Jadzia Kucharek came over to discuss a serious matter. Jadzia's daughter and my god-daughter, Terenia, had met and fallen in love with a young German while studying abroad and now they wanted to get married. Jadzia was distraught, given her personal suffering in the concentration camp and our wartime history. It was a difficult discussion and I struggled to take a balanced line myself but eventually I told Jadzia that we had to move on and that we couldn't stand in the way of love. I am pleased that the marriage has been happy and long-lasting.

On another occasion Andrew's school was organising a German language student exchange. I didn't know how to deal with this. I was given the details of the German family but I could not bring myself to write to them. It was the boy's mother in Germany who wrote to me first. She didn't know my personal history but she knew that we were Polish and therefore that we had come to England because of the war. Her letter was so sincere and good-hearted; she explained that she understood what we must have been through during the war. In many ways she was apologising for what her country had done and extending the hand of friendship. She also assured me that Andrew would be warmly received. When Helmut arrived he was pleasant and helpful and brought with him a gorgeous German loaf of bread and another gift. I greatly appreciated these gestures and the warmth conveyed; they helped put my mind at rest. Later Andrew went to Germany where Helmut and his family looked after him very well.

In 1978 Pope Paul IV died and the conclave met to select a new pope. As a committed Catholic, I was always interested in papal succession and I waited with interest for the white smoke signifying that a new pope had been elected. I recall my immense excitement, pride and joy when I heard that the next pope was to be Polish. I had absolutely no idea beforehand that a Pole might be chosen, let alone one who had experienced the German occupation in his home city of Kraków. Karol Wojtyła assumed the name Pope Jean Paul II. From his initial visit to Poland in 1979, he was a catalyst for Polish political change that would eventually lead to the collapse of communism in Europe. A few years later, in 1982, we joined 24,000 other members of the Polish community in England and Wales at the Crystal Palace National Sports Centre to see John Paul II on his visit to Britain. It was a great day which filled us with pride and hope.

I had worked at Lucas for a few years when the company decided to relocate my division to Reading. My boss asked me if I would continue to work for him and Lucas offered to pay my travel expenses. I tried this for a few weeks but quickly realised that, with George still at school, commuting daily to Reading was not sustainable. As a helpful alternative Lucas allowed me to stay in Acton as a typist for as long as I wanted, an offer I accepted. My boss even bought me a bouquet of flowers to say goodbye, which was a thoughtful and conciliatory gesture.

George's A-Level results arrived while he was recovering in hospital after having had his tonsils removed. I felt nervous as I watched him open the letter. Angst about my own shattered dreams for a higher education welled inside me as I waited impatiently. His sorry face suddenly broke into a broad smile and my fears seeped away. He had got the required grades for his first choice, Birmingham University. That evening I had a few Polish vodkas at home, mainly to celebrate but also out of sheer relief!

With Andrew already away at university and George soon to follow, I decided to look for part-time work. In 1981 I joined the energy-metering company Landis & Gyr in North Acton, working in the accounts department on employee overtime payments. George came to work with me during a summer break from university. He made no errors and was much faster than I was, which I had to hide from my superiors.

It was at Landis & Gyr that I met Frank Cross. Frank had recently lost his wife and was clearly grieving for her when we met. We got on well and over the years we became more friendly until he eventually asked me out on a date. I recall asking my friends what they thought about this as I was worried about how Frank would fit in with my Polish society. My friends reassured me and encouraged me to accept.

I had always wanted to go to the Passion Play at Oberammergau in Bavaria and 1984 was its 350th anniversary. I was getting to know Frank quite well and so I asked if he would like to go with me. It was heartwarming to see how happy he was to be asked and he accepted immediately. So began our many happy years of companionship and travelling together.

The holiday in Oberammergau was a wonderful time and we got along very well. The mountain setting was beautiful and the play stunning. While visiting the town I sat down on a sofa in an enormous hall to rest and I must have left my purse there. A little while later, when I tried to pay for something in a shop, I realised it was missing. My purse contained my passport and all my money and I was certain it would be gone. We ran back to the sofa: despite the huge crowds my purse was still exactly where I had left it. This incident boosted my confidence in the intrinsic goodness of people but also proved to me that I had been protected by God once again.

Our Polish community had always wanted our own church in Ealing. We had hoped to buy St Matthew's but the Church of England decided not to sell, so the search began. After much negotiating and hard work we finally opened our very own church right in the heart of Ealing Broadway on Windsor Road in 1985. I attended the opening of The Church of Our Lady Mother of the Church, which was so well attended there were people spilling out onto the streets.

In the summer of 1986 Janka's daughter Krysia visited us from Poland. Economic conditions had deteriotated sharply under the communist regime in Poland and London's well-stocked food shops vividly brought home to her the contrast between the two systems.

I had been feeling a bit lifeless while Krysia was in London but I hadn't paid much attention to this. On a routine visit to hospital the doctor noticed a lump on my neck and took a sample for analysis. He seemed concerned, which of course scared me. Those two weeks of waiting for the test results were intensely stressful and I lost over a stone in weight. The memory of losing Janusz was still strong, I was still only in my fifties and the boys were only young men. The results came and were inconclusive so I was sent to see Dr Lynn, a thyroid specialist at Hammersmith Hospital. Frank accompanied me. Dr Lynn looked through my notes and said, "Yes yes, it is cancer. We have to operate to remove your thyroid glands. But don't worry, everything will be fine, I will conduct the operation personally." After the operation a follow-up examination with another doctor concluded that the cancer had spread into the lymph nodes and things did not look good. Again I endured a stressful time until, fortunately, this assessment was reviewed and turned out to be incorrect.

Around this time Landis & Gyr began the process of computerising the office. I was accustomed to a calculator and I struggled to adapt. Then it was announced that my department was moving from an office onto the shop floor, which I found unpleasantly noisy. Taking all this into account I decided to take voluntary redundancy. My redundancy payment was £1,000 which seemed to me like a huge amount and was certainly the first time I had had anything like this sum of money. Frank advised me to put it into the bank and let it grow. My friend Teresa then got me a part-time job with her at a clothing-label manufacturer, which I took for a couple of years before retiring at the age of 60 in 1989.

Over the years my relationship with Frank became much more than a friendship; he was a warm and loving person and I felt relaxed and comfortable in his presence. We never exchanged a cross word or had any tension between us. From our first date we spent almost twenty years travelling the world together, something I had always longed to do. Our travels included a number of visits to Spain and journeys to Crete, San Marino, Hungary, Malta, Cyprus, the USA, Canada, Singapore, Hong Kong and Thailand. Of all the trips, the one to Canada and the USA was the most memorable, and I found Canada particularly beautiful. Going up the World Trade Centre in New York was also an exciting experience that I look back on with nostalgia and sadness these days.

Frank and I also went to Israel, where we visited Yad Vashem, Israel's official memorial to the Jewish victims of the Holocaust. We entered a huge, dark hall with a walkway around the side and stars on the ceiling while a speaker announced an endless list of names of Jews murdered during the Holocaust. The whole experience was profoundly moving. We also visited the Garden of the Righteous Among the Nations, which is part of the Yad Vashem complex. The trees here bear plaques with the names of non-Jews who risked their lives to save Jews for no material gain. Of over 24,000 individuals honoured with the title of Righteous Among the Nations to date, over a quarter are Polish, the most of any nation represented.

Frank proposed marriage on a number of occasions and finally I accepted, although we agreed that I would speak to my sons first. Unfortunately Frank was so happy that he couldn't wait and told his whole family the news straight away. His daughter-in-law called to congratulate me. However I was worried about upsetting my children and retracted my marriage acceptance. I was a coward and I regret this now.

Chapter 10

LASKI

Laski was a special place for me, but it seemed I would have to let it go. In 1962 the land had been registered in my name as the sole surviving member of my family, but when I was there with Janusz in 1974 I was informed that it could be taken away from me as I now lived abroad. My choices were to sell the land, give it away or risk ownership defaulting to the current occupier or to the government. It was not straightforward to divide the land up among the remaining family and if I sold it I could not take the money abroad.

When we returned to London that summer Janusz suggested that I donate my land to the adjoining blind institute. We were no longer starving, we couldn't take the money out and the institute needed room to expand. I had great sympathy for this cause as the nuns had told me about a German atrocity there during the Uprising. An outlying building, which housed some of the older blind boys, was secretly being used to give medical treatment to AK partisans from the Kampinos Forest. When the Germans discovered this, they locked the doors and burned the entire building down with the boys trapped inside. The few who escaped were shot in cold blood. I liked the idea of my land being used to rebuild what had been so cruelly destroyed. I therefore began the process of donating my land to the blind institute.

It was a convoluted business and took many years. There was a complication with the registration into my name as there had been insufficient documentary proof of my father's death and therefore I was the legal owner of only half the land. I was helped throughout this process by Zofia Morawska, a remarkable 75-year-old lady who was global fundraiser for the institute. Zofia spent years helping me to overcome the various legal issues until finally, in November 1979, the process was completed, also allowing Janka to remain in the house until the end of her life.

Over the years Zofia Morawska became a true friend and one of my greatest sources of inspiration through her kind nature and selfless work for the institute. She worked tirelessly for the blind and shunned any form of luxury. She finally passed away in 2010 at the incredible age of 106.

It would take many more years for the institute to decide how the land would be used. Although I had hoped they would replace the building destroyed by the Germans, I wanted it to be their decision and they chose to build a new church and a parish hall. I was sad that the rustic old church built from tree trunks would play a lesser role. It was special to me as it was part of my childhood, but I could see that it was too small.

The actual building process then took yet more years until finally in 1987 the Church of the Holy Mother, Queen of Mexico, was completed. I found this new church to be a rather ugly structure and more practical than inspiring. I was invited with Andrew and George to attend the inauguration which was conducted by the Cardinal-Archbishop of Warsaw and Primate of the Catholic Church in Poland, Józef Glemp, and his equivalent from Mexico, Ernesto Corripio Ahumada.

I had requested a plaque to be hung inside the church in memory of my mother, father and sister. Krysia had one made up for me in Warsaw but it was tiny, with the dates written in Roman numerals and barely legible. To add to my disappointment the priest had the plaque mounted outside the church on the door. I complained but the priest claimed it wasn't practical to have the plaque inside. I approached the Bishop of Warsaw who supported me and agreed that my wish should be fulfilled. Five years later I finally had my new, larger plaque placed inside the church to the side of the altar. It measures 76cm x 46cm and reads in translation:

"In memory of my parents, Maria and Andrzej, and my only sister Henryka who died in the Uprising of 1944 at the hands of the Hitlerites. This plaque is hung in the church on our family land in memory that they were here. We pray for their souls."

Daughter Danuta Szlachetko, Soldier of the AK 'Grey Ranks'

As we were staying in Poland for a few more days, George was keen to
visit Auschwitz, and I also was interested to see the camp. We left very early
in the morning by taxi, driving over 300 kilometres for about five hours
along poor roads. Auschwitz lies about 60 kilometres due west of Kraków
in southern Poland in the territory already annexed by Germany. Seeing it
in person was an intensely moving experience.

First we visited Auschwitz I, the former redbrick Polish army barracks
used from 1940 to imprison and murder Polish political prisoners. I
shuddered as I walked through the now infamous gateway with the sign
over it proclaiming *Arbeit Macht Frei*, (Work will set you free). Auschwitz
I houses the museum for the entire camp complex. A short drive away is
Auschwitz II, Birkenau, which was built in 1941 for Soviet POWs before
being adapted in 1942 into the biggest death camp for Jews in German-occupied Europe. We walked into Birkenau along the platform beside a
seemingly endless stretch of railway line. Here the trains had deposited their
helpless human cargo. The vastness of the complex of barracks surrounded
by barbed-wire fences brought home to me the scale of the murder perpetrated here. Current estimates of the death toll at Auschwitz are 1.1 million
people. Almost a million of those were Jews, around 75,000 were ethnic
Poles; the rest were a mix of Gypsies, Soviet POWs and others.

On our drive back to Warsaw we stopped for a moving mass at the
monastery of Jasna Góra in the historic town of Częstochowa. During the
service a curtain behind the altar was drawn back to reveal the famous
painting of the Black Madonna of Częstochowa, a revered Polish icon. It is
surrounded by legends of how the painting and monastery were saved from
destruction when besieged by vastly superior armies. This service and the
painting seemed a fitting end to an exhausting and distressing day.

Chapter 11

KATYN GLASNOST

The constant threat of Soviet military aggression had kept the Communist Party in power in Poland since the end of World War II. During this era communism had plundered Poland's wealth and tried to destroy her history.

Throughout the 1970s economic conditions in Poland deteriorated severely. Following a series of strikes culminating in the Gdansk shipyard strike in 1980, the first union in the communist bloc that was not controlled by the Communist Party emerged. It was called the Independent Self-governing Trade Union 'Solidarity' and was was headed by Lech Wałesa. At its peak a quarter of Poland's population were members. In late 1981, in response to the threat of growing opposition, the Communist Party imposed martial law, a state of military rule with wartime powers. Martial law restricted civil liberties in numerous ways: curfews were imposed, national borders were sealed, access to main cities was restricted, telephones were disconnected, mail was censored, independent organisations were made illegal, and schools and universities were closed. The dominant image that reached us in the West was the presence of tanks back on the streets of Poland. Martial law lasted for about 20 months during which the Solidarity union was made illegal, thousands of people were arrested and some were killed. For the next seven years the union functioned underground in an echo of the Polish Underground State during World War II.

The 1980s were therefore another decade of great suffering for the Polish nation. The Polish community in Great Britain mobilised to provide humanitarian aid. In August 1981 Lech Wałesa sent a letter to the Federation of Poles in Great Britain appealing for medical aid and they responded by setting up the charity Medical Aid for Poland. MAFP began by renting warehouse space in Park Royal in Acton. The substantial donations of medicines, clothes, blankets and other items were sorted here and packaged for delivery by road. The first three aid trucks arrived in Poland in January 1982. I took Andrew and George to work at a parcel-packing session where George got his first 'back of the head' appearance on BBC television. I considered volunteering to travel to Poland with a consignment of lorries, which sounded exciting, but in the end I just helped with sorting and packing at the warehouse. Some years later I became much more actively involved with MAFP and I remain so to this day.

Sue Ryder was a great friend to Poland in the decades following the end of the war. Having served in the British SOE Polish Section during the war, she had then volunteered for relief work in Poland. She started the Sue Ryder Foundation in 1953 and worked tirelessly to help the Polish in particular. She was offered a British peerage in 1979 and was appointed Baroness Ryder of Warsaw, a title she chose because of her "great admiration, respect and love for the Polish people. I feel I belong to Poland". Baroness Ryder also arranged transport of medicine, food and clothing to Poland during these difficult times in the late 1980s. Her comments perhaps best capture the importance of helping Poles in those difficult days: "A tin of food from outside means more to the Poles than just nourishment. It shows that they have not been isolated and forgotten. They know the rest of the world is thinking about them."

There was concern about the political situation in Poland and the boys joined me at various Polish protests in London including those outside the Polish embassy. Following nationwide strikes in Poland in 1987 and 1988, the Polish Government opened dialogue with Solidarity. I was grateful to Margaret Thatcher for playing an active part in reaching out to Russia. Mikhail Gorbachev became President of the Soviet Union in 1988 and finally introduced some progressive policies. Perestroika, reform of the economic and political system, and Glasnost, more open government and dissemination of information, began a series of reforms that would finally bring some relief.

After seven years underground, the Solidarity union was made legal again in April 1989, ahead of scheduled semi-free elections in June of that year. Significantly President Gorbachev refused to employ military intervention in Poland, thus removing the main threat which had kept the Polish Communist Party in power. Subsequently Solidarity candidates won every seat up for election. In 1990 Lech Wałesa became President of the first freely elected Polish government since the war. The Solidarity movement heralded a succession of peaceful anti-communist revolutions in Central and Eastern Europe, most visibly the dismantling of the Berlin Wall in November 1989 and the eventual dissolution of the Soviet Union in 1991.

The movement had effectively led a successful and peaceful Polish uprising and can be viewed as part of a long history of Polish struggles for freedom. I believe that the tragedy of the 1944 Warsaw Uprising had fostered a sense of strategic discipline within Solidarity activities as the movement knew that, despite massive moral global support, it ultimately stood alone against the might of the Soviet Union. I would like to think that the Warsaw Uprising was at least in part an inspiration for the Solidarity movement.

Immediately after the election of Lech Wałesa as the President of Poland, the presidential insignia was returned from London to Poland by Ryszard Kaczorowski, the last president of the Polish government-in-exile, thus ending its 50-year existence. Ryszard Kaczorowski would later be on the tragic 2010 plane flight to Smolensk with the then President of Poland, Lech Kaczyński.

The following year President Lech Wałesa came to Britain on a state visit, during which he requested that all official AK insignias and archives in England be transferred back to Poland. Official AK verification stamps and other insignias were taken back, along with some funds, although it was decided to keep the AK archives in London and The Sikorski Institute also kept their collection of artefacts and archives. I think this was a good decision because the transfer was not handled properly and various items ended up being lost. Ultimately I was not a great fan of Lech Wałesa. He was a good figurehead, but the success of Solidarity in the overthrow of communism was down to the efforts of many activists in Poland and he seemed to take all the credit.

Poles had been striving to make the truth of the murders and the mass graves at Katyn from 1940 known to the world at large. Not only were the graves symbolic of the wrongs perpetrated against our country by the Soviet Union during World War II but the perpetrators of these crimes were still dominating, if not actually ruling, Poland. The Soviets were still denying guilt, calling our accusations the 'Katyn lie', while the world remained silent. The Polish community wanted to erect a monument in London to those who died in Katyn but Soviet pressure on the British government to prevent this caused many years of delay. Finally a significant monument to the victims of Katyn was unveiled in Gunnersbury Cemetery, west London, in September 1976. The monument bears the inscription "The conscience of the world calls for the truth." There is no specific reference to the Soviets on the monument but we all knew they were responsible. Thousands came to the monument's official unveiling. My sons stood to attention with the scouts in their uniforms. In order not to offend the Soviets no Labour government representative attended although there were some representatives from the Conservative opposition. This was a small victory for us in our exile but the struggle for the truth would have to continue.

Finally in 1990 we had the first, albeit partial, admission of Russian guilt for the Katyn murders. With the Soviet Union in its final days of existence, President Gorbachev confirmed that the Soviet NKVD had executed Poles at Katyn on Stalin's orders. A Russian investigation was initiated which would take 14 years to conclude. Two other mass burial sites were revealed, one at Mednoye in Russia, the other at Kharkiv in Ukraine, and exhumations were begun.

A few years later Janka's daughter Krysia sent me a book published in 1991 entitled *Mord w Katyniu* (Murder in Katyn). The book listed almost 10,000 names out of 15,500 Poles then known to have been murdered at the various locations in the crimes which have become generically known as the 'Katyn massacres'. Janka's husband, Feliks Dybowski, is listed in the book as having been interned at the Oshtashkov camp before being murdered and buried at Mednoye.

In 1996 I joined one of the earliest groups from abroad to visit the burial site in the Katyn Forest. We drove by coach for many hours through Belarus into Russia to Katyn. Our guide warned us to stick together as we were being observed, which spread fear and the sense that we were not welcome.

I felt very emotional standing in the large clearing surrounded by tall trees. I could sense that something terrible had happened on this spot to which the trees bore witness. In the middle of the clearing was a simple cross over a mass grave; there were a few smaller graves to the side. No names were listed. We stood in absolute silence, the only sound the rustling of the trees in the wind. Then a priest in our group said mass and I prayed for the souls of my countrymen. I had a sense of relief when we departed.

The Russian investigation into the Katyn massacres finally concluded and confirmed the deaths of a mere 1,803 Poles. The Russians also refused to classify these deaths as war crimes or genocide and deemed that no charges could be brought as most of the perpetrators were already dead. Another 20 years would pass before the Russian lower house of parliament, the Duma, issued an official resolution in 2010 condeming the mass murder of Poles at Katyn, and declared that published documents which had been kept classified for all those years showed the true scale of the Katyn crime, which had been carried out on the direct orders of Stalin and other Soviet leaders. The NKVD had executed around 22,000 Polish army officers, policemen, intellectuals and leaders in total. All factions of the Duma voted for this resolution except the Communist MPs who continue to deny Russian guilt. But before this resolution could be issued, Katyn would be linked with another great tragedy for Poland…

Chapter 12

GREY RANKS REUNION

I always wondered what became of my friends and former colleagues from the Grey Ranks. After the war we went in different directions and many returned to Poland. I was in touch with only one of the girls, Wiesia Kanicka-Bereznicka, 'Wisełka', who also lived in London. Soon I would have the opportunity to be reunited with a few of the others.

After returning from a trip to Poland, Wiesia informed me that she had made contact with some of our former colleagues from the Executive Group. These included former Grey Ranks squad leader Teresa Pietkiewicz or Miki. Teresa had inquired about me, which led to us writing to each other. She invited me to visit, which I did in 1989 – my first reunion with my colleagues from the Conspiracy in 45 years. It was a great joy to see Teresa again; she was such a wonderful lady, she gave so much of herself and was an inspiration to me.

A small gathering was organised consisting mainly of girls from the Executive Group at a girl's house in Warsaw. There were about ten girls there; I'm not sure if the gathering was organised on my behalf. I knew some of the girls, such as Horpyna, and also Filipek, who was one of the lucky few to survive Ravensbrück concentration camp. 'Nike' was there also, having survived another concentration camp, Majdanek. However, many of the other girls I did not know.

I sat next to a very nice and slightly older lady with whom I clearly had much in common and we chatted for quite a long time, reminiscing about the past. We recalled the days of the Conspiracy and how we had both lost siblings during the occupation. When there was a quiet moment among the group I asked aloud if there was any news of Krysia Biernacka, Kali, who had recruited me back in 1943. All eyes in the room turned to me and I felt myself blushing. Then one of the girls said, "Wira, you have been talking with Krysia for the last hour!" Eventually my embarrassment subsided but I was a little taken aback by the stark change in the Krysia I had known. She used to be so beautiful, energetic and happy when I knew her during the occupation but that sparkle had gone, which was not merely down to time. When I met Krysia once more a few years later I realised with sadness that she had been ill, which had eroded all traces of that vivacious girl I had once known.

I befriended a number of girls at the gathering. One of those is the amazing Ania Mizikowska, 'Grażka', who works tirelessly for the Grey Ranks veterans' organisation. Grażka is a few years older than I am. Although I didn't know her during the occupation she had also attended my school in Krysia's year and had been a member of the Executive Group. Like Krysia, Grażka had gone on to be attached to the Grey Ranks Parasol Battalion and was based in Wola during the early days of the Uprising, where she witnessed some particularly harrowing scenes of slaughter. After the war she hid among the civilian population in order to stay in Poland and continue the conspiracy against the next occupation by the Soviets. While she was being transported from Pruszków, Grażka escaped from the train and later joined an AK offshoot called NIE, representing the first three letters of *niepodleglosc* (independence); *nie* also means no. The main role of NIE was to observe and conduct espionage against the invading Soviets while the Polish government-in-exile continued seeking a negotiated solution to Poland's sovereignty. On 1st August 1945, one year to the day after the Warsaw Uprising had begun, Grażka was arrested by the communists and sentenced to eight years imprisonment in Mokotów prison, later commuted to six months following an amnesty.

Grażka went on to complete her training to become a judge but there was always someone who would identify her as a former AK member and so she struggled to find work under the communist regime. In the 1980s she devoted herself fully to the Solidarity movement, which she saw as an extension of the AK struggle for Poland's independence. Grażka and I struck up a strong relationship and have been in close contact ever since. I also began friendships with two other girls from the Uprising, Zosia Zaborska and Dr Idalia Kubicza. Idalia worked as a doctor in tropical diseases in Iraq and the Middle East for many years after the war.

Somebody has subsequently put together a montage of photographs taken during the occupation showing all 54 of us members of the Executive Group. It is striking how young we all look – I was only 14 when my picture was taken.

It had been a wonderful trip to Poland and felt like the closest I could ever come to being reunited with my family. As always, however, there was cause for sadness too. As Teresa's husband was driving me to the airport he told me that she was terminally ill with cancer: they had both kept this from me during my trip and it was such an unhappy way to end the visit. I did not see Teresa again as she died the following year. When I returned a few years later I went to her grave and paid Miki my last respects.

OBERLANGEN CONCENTRATION CAMP

In 1991, following the collapse of the communist regime in Poland, the Polish Office for War Veterans and Victims of Oppression was established by Act of Parliament. The Office conducted an investigation into Stalag V1 C camp, Oberlangen, and concluded that conditions there were on a par with those of a concentration camp and not suitable for POWs under the Geneva Convention. This came as no surprise to me, having been there. In the years following, some of the girls applied for compensation from Germany; former concentration-camp prisoners were eligible for compensation, unlike former POWs. I chose not to do so as I regarded my status as a POW as a matter of honour. I have never taken a penny in compensation from Germany. I do not consider myself to have been a victim but a soldier fighting for a free and independent Poland.

MANCIA & KAJTUS

Another important turning-point which would have a deep impact on me and also related to Oberlangen came with news of the two Jewish girls

Mancia and Kajtus who had left Warsaw in our ranks. In the early Seventies Joseph Zieman's book *The Cigarette Sellers of Three Crosses Square* was published in English. Apparently in the book Mancia and Katjus claimed that the AK girls at the Oberlangen camp had treated them badly and repeatedly threatened to expose their Jewish identity to the Germans. Zieman also claimed that Belgian POWs in a nearby camp had had to get involved and threatened reprisals if the girls were betrayed.

This came as a complete shock to me. I had been aware that Mancia and Kajtusz also ended up at Oberlangen although I do not recall seeing them there. From my experience and from what I heard I simply could not believe this account was true. I recalled liking Mancia even though I only knew her briefly. During those few days we spent together in the cattle wagon heading into Germany I know that everybody on the train treated Mancia and Kajtus very well and there was never the slightest suggestion that anyone even considered betraying them. The sisters spent six months in captivity in Germany and as they looked so obviously Jewish they must have been protected by the other AK girls. That period in Oberlangen was one of complete despair and fatigue for everybody. Of course there may have been the odd individual who harboured ill feeling towards the girls for whatever reason, but as everybody was so united in distress it is difficult to conceive that people might have taken their frustrations out on the sisters. Furthermore the notion that POWs from another camp had to become involved is incomprehensible; we had no idea whether there were any other camps near ours, and any contact would have been impossible. Kajtus was only a little girl at the time and although Mancia was older I found it hard to believe that she would make such claims. I can only conclude that she was encouraged to do so by people who wanted to portray Poles as anti-semitic for political reasons.

A number of girls from Oberlangen who read the book were similarly incredulous. I couldn't ignore this misrepresentation of events and in anger I wrote some letters seeking redress, including to the Polish Daily newspaper in England and to Zieman's publisher. I stated my belief that the account attributed to Mancia and Kajtus was inaccurate and I questioned the morality of attacking others who had also suffered. I argued that at the

time in question Poles were also being persecuted and killed, yet, despite
the great risks, had been particularly willing to shield Jews in Poland during
the years of occupation. I invited a response but nothing came back.

I was saddened by such blatant anti-Polish sentiment. I have always
been a patriot but one consequence of *The Cigarette Sellers of Three Crosses
Square* was to make me even more sensitive to unfounded, exaggerated
and generalised criticism of Poland and Polish actions during World War
II. Often, it seems books, films or articles appear which contain subtle
or even blatant slights against the conduct of Poles during the War, with
the frequent implication that many Poles had been actively anti-semitic.
I am convinced that this post-war anti-Polish bias which purports to be
straightforward historical account has politics at its root and has spread
through a combination of ignorance, pride and prejudice. These authors
insult the memory of so many Poles who risked their lives and those of
their entire families to help Jews during the German occupation. They
feed prejudice and antagonise relations between communities. These days
the older Polish generation is dying out while, for diplomatic reasons,
the current Polish government has opted to say little or nothing in reply
to these slurs. I have always believed that if something is false then you
have to speak out about it, challenging ignorance and disinformation. If
you say nothing in your defence, others will conclude that what is being
proclaimed must be true.

I have subsequently corresponded with Eugenia Cegielska, President of
the Oberlangen POW Association in Warsaw, who was commandant of the
number three barracks in Oberlangen at the time. Although she cannot
recall the exact barracks that Mancia and Kajtus were in, as a commandant she was aware of the sisters' particular situation. Eugenia attests that
Mancia and Kajtus were given a greater share of the meagre food rations
because of their weak physical appearance. Eugenia had first heard that the
sisters were speaking ill of their fellow prisoners back in the 1950s from
correspondence with AK girls who, like the sisters, had emigrated to the
USA. Like myself and others, Eugenia also wrote letters of complaint about
the book and received no responses.

Chapter 13

VOLUNTEER

Once I had retired I was able to indulge once again in writing letters to various newspapers. These mostly but not exclusively expressed my views about issues relating to Poland. One such letter trail from 1990 began with an article I read reporting that the Conservative-controlled Ealing Council had opposed twinning Ealing with a Polish town and chosen to partner with a French town instead. I was provoked into writing to my local Conservative ward and to the newspaper. Within the letter I argued:

> "There was so much talk that Britain would be helping these countries which freed themselves from Communism, a system they were pushed into when the Western Allies signed the Yalta agreement after World War Two. Polish people fought alongside the British on all fronts in large numbers but never received recognition for their contribution in the fight for democracy. The Conservative Party always seeks the support of Poles in local elections and Poles give that support. But when the situation arose where we could expect some show of appreciation and help such as the twinning plan the Poles got the cold shoulder. It seems there is no sincerity in our relations."

I first got involved to a small extent with the Polish Underground Movement Study Trust after Janusz died. The Trust had been founded in 1947 as a research and academic institution and contains historical material relating to the Polish Underground State during World War II. The Trust needed volunteers and I needed a sense of belonging. We started building an official list of former AK members and I agreed to help with typing verifications for the registration of eligible members.

Now, with more time on my hands, I became actively involved with other Polish organisations including the Polish Home Army Ex-Servicemen's Association London Branch. The Association had been formed in 1946 with the main aims of promoting Poland's independence, nurturing the Polish identity and providing support for war veterans. By now our main role was welfare-related. We provided a point of contact, information and mutual assistance to the ageing AK membership in London and the South. For a period of about five years from the mid-1990s, I was consecutively Vice President, Treasurer and Secretary of the Association. I also produced a news booklet twice a year for our 240 or so remaining members.

Fund-raising was a big part of our activities. One cause we supported was the AK Invalid Fund for the disabled AK veterans and their families, most of whom were in Poland. Before the fall of communism in Poland my colleagues had been distributing these funds secretly through a network of priests. Gradually it became possible to dispense them openly. We also raised money for the maintainance of Polish memorials and the graves of Poles who had participated in the January Uprising of 1863 against the Russian Empire. Some of these Poles were buried at Highgate Cemetery in London, which is also the resting place of Karl Marx.

In addition we raised funds to help AK Poles who had stayed in the former Polish territories in the Kresy, now in Lithuania. The issue of Polish ethnicity in Lithuanian territory was a touchy subject for the authorities and caused some suppression of Polish identity. I made contact with the president of the AK organisation in Lithuania and a number of us made private arrangements to provide funds. Some of our donations went towards schools, books and Polish publications. Eventually, as the post-communist transition continued, the Polish government started applying diplomatic pressure to secure greater freedoms for Poles in Lithuania and even started paying for young people of Polish descent from Lithuania to visit Poland on cultural trips.

Over time I became involved with the AK Foundation. The Foundation's primary aim is to protect the memory and promote awareness of the AK and the Polish Underground State among future generations. It also seeks to raise funds for the upkeep of the AK archives and to encourage their use for historical purposes. I was active on the board of the Foundation for a decade or so until recently.

Another organisation I supported was the Foundation in Support of Polish Deportees set up in Poland by Halina Borek. This was to help the large numbers of Poles deported and left behind by the Soviets during and immediately after the war, in Kazakhstan and Siberia in particular. These deportees had been deprived of their identity and treated badly solely because they were Polish nationals. The ultimate aim was to enable these long-suffering deportees to eventually return to Poland.

I also became involved with Medical Aid for Poland, which was still going strong ten years after its inception. With the removal of communism, Poland's aid needs began to change. Supplies of medicine and clothes were no longer as essential and money became the main requirement. In 1998 MAFP opened a charity shop in South Ealing; I volunteered happily to help in the shop and have continued to do so ever since. Sixteen years on I am one of the longest-serving volunteers left.

There have also been many other organisations over the years that have helped Poles and Poland which I have tried to support as part of the AK or individually. One such was the Bouverie Foundation, which was established in 2000 by Sue Ryder, the Baroness Ryder of Warsaw.

LIFE AND DEATH

My sons had both married in the early 1990s. First my eldest son Andrew married Edyta from Nowy Sącz in Poland in 1992. George arrived from India for their wedding with his girlfriend Jacqui on the last leg of their round-the-world travels. The following year George married Jacqui in Guernsey.

I was almost 70 years old and I remember so clearly that wonderful moment when my daughter-in-law Jacqui announced that she was pregnant. It was a moment of pure joy. Emma Millicent, my first grandchild, was born in February 1999, two months premature. She was jaundiced and reminded me of my Andrew and his difficult start in life. Holding Emma for the first time was a precious feeling. I was surprised by how much love I felt for that little girl; I had never expected that I could love a grandchild as much as my own baby. My first grandson Oskar came next in December 1999, followed by Edward in May 2000. After waiting so long for grandchildren this was a wonderful period on the family front. Alice would follow a few years later in January 2004.

My happiness at becoming a grandmother was contrasted with the great sadness of another loss. Frank and I were looking forward to our holiday in Cyprus in the spring of 2000 when he fell ill and declined rapidly, losing a lot of weight. He was quite a slim man who barely drank alcohol but after the death of his wife 20 years earlier he had developed diabetes. We had managed to control the disease quite well. On 26th February 2000 I went over to his house in Iver with my dog at the time, a King Charles spaniel called Piper. Frank had no appetite: all he wanted to eat was custard and milk, which I prepared for him. He asked me to stay the night but regrettably I declined. As I left he waved me goodbye; he looked so sad and I sensed something was wrong. At 2am that morning I received a call from Frank's son, who told me that he had passed away. I was in a state of shock. I couldn't take it in. I had only left him a few hours earlier. His son explained that later that night Frank had started feeling unwell and after calling the doctor had been taken to hospital, where he suffered a fatal heart attack.

It was so cruel that Frank was taken away from me so suddenly and his death left a huge hole in my life. He had been my rock, an unerring companion and dear friend, for almost 20 years. He had brought great stability to my life when I most needed it; he had been very understanding, sensitive to my feelings and so tolerant – particularly as we came from different backgrounds with ways of thinking. Frank had always been the finest of Englishmen.

I took his death badly; it was one of the three major losses in my life, following that of my mother and sister in 1944 and Janusz in 1975. That summer I went to Poland to recuperate at a spa in a small town called Busko-Zdrój which my mother had frequented before the war. When I returned to England my whole body was hurting. The doctor diagnosed polymyalgia, which he put down to the suddenness and shock of Frank's death. As a result I have been on harmful steroids ever since.

Chapter 14

REMEMBERING THE WARSAW UPRISING

An important consequence of the fall of communism in Poland was the freedom for Poles to start looking at their history impartially. For almost 50 years the Warsaw Uprising had been portrayed domestically as the ill-judged exploitation of the civilian masses by incompetent leaders of the AK for political reasons. Now a more open and balanced debate became possible. Finally the sacrifices of the Warsaw Uprising began to be seen as a source of pride for an increasing number of Poles.

In 2002 Lech Kaczyński became Mayor of Warsaw. Kaczyński had been a leading figure in the anti-communist movement in the 1970s and an advisor to the Solidarity movement. Both his parents had participated in the AK and his father had fought in the Warsaw Uprising. He was therefore a great friend of those who had resisted the Germans during the occupation, and he determined to remind the world of the AK and why it had fought for a free and independent Poland. In August 2004 Kaczyński was the driving force behind the first global gathering of veterans of the Uprising who celebrated its 60th anniversary in Warsaw.

The opening event of the anniversary celebrations was a poignant evening concert in Napoleon Square, where my personal Uprising had begun. The square had since been renamed Plac Powstańców (Upriser's Square). I sat in the VIP section in the front rows along with many former AK colleagues, with my son next to me. We listened to moving speeches from Lech Kaczyński, US Secretary of State Colin Powell, German Chancellor Gerhard Schröder and other dignitaries, as well as a rather more frivolous and slightly inappropriate speech by the British Deputy Prime Minister John Prescott. There was no official representation from Russia. Crowds of people stood behind us in front of the rebuilt Prudential building that had been my base during much of the Uprising. The building now stood illuminated with symbolic flames against the night sky and presented an incredibly moving scene.

The following day I attended the grand opening of the Warsaw Uprising Museum, which was established on Lech Kaczyński's initiative. Appropriately the museum is located in Wola, the district where some of the most vicious slaughters of civilians took place. The event began with an outdoor Mass attended by a huge audience of elderly veterans and their families. There was a steady stream of stretchers carrying out veterans as they fainted from the scorching heat; they had survived the Uprising but the midday sun of the summer of 2004 almost finished them off. After Mass and numerous speeches, the doors to the museum were finally opened and I walked to the front of the huge queue. With my combatant's armband and honorary membership I was welcomed straight inside – a small but much-appreciated benefit of being a veteran of the Uprising. In due course I donated my AK Uprising pass card, which I had somehow managed to retain from the war, to the museum archives, along with my German POW camp identification tag. These days the museum attracts huge numbers of people eager to learn about this important moment in Polish history.

During the anniversary commemorations, events were held at a variety of sites around Warsaw, including at the Monument to the Warsaw Uprising. A major celebration took place at the AK Powązki military cemetery, where many of those who perished fighting in the Uprising had been laid to rest.

The next evening we had been invited to speak to a group of scouts about our experiences during the Uprising. This was followed by a general audience in the crypt of my childhood church, the Church of the Holy Cross. The large audience of mainly young people stood in silence as we spoke; my friend Grażka seemed to do most of the talking. When we were finished the audience honoured us with their extended applause, clapping in unison for what seemed a very long time, the sound echoing atmospherically in the dimly lit crypt.

THE KNIGHT'S CROSS

Lech Kaczyński became President of the Republic of Poland in December 2005. Earlier that year the Polish Office for War Veterans and Victims of Oppression established the Pro Memoria medal which is a civil state decoration to be awarded for 'outstanding contributions in perpetuating the memory of the people and deeds in the struggle for Polish independence during and after World War II'. The following year I was informed that I was to be awarded the Pro Memoria medal at a ceremony to be held in the grounds of Łazienki, my childhood park in Warsaw. Sadly I felt unwell and was not able to attend the ceremony, so I asked that it be sent by post instead. I was also nominated for the Pro Patria medal, which I would finally receive many years later. The Pro Patria is similar to the Pro Memoria but relates only to the period of the war.

In August 2009 I was informed that I was to receive the Krzyż Kawalerski Orderu Odrodzenia Polski (Knight's Cross of the Order of Polonia Restituta), which is the second-highest civilian order of merit awarded by Poland. This decision meant a great deal to me, particularly as the nomination had been made by the President of the AK organisation in Poland and approved by the office of the Polish President Lech Kaczyński. The following month I was invited to an official presentation of the merit award at the famous Wawel castle in Warsaw's Old Town. The award was to be presented by President Kaczyński himself. I had only just returned from a visit to Warsaw and, having just turned 80, I didn't have the strength to travel again so soon and so chose the option of receiving the award in London. This decision remains a great source of regret for me in the light of what was to follow.

In April 2010 Lech Kaczyński was travelling with a high-level public and military delegation from Warsaw to Russia to commemorate the Katyn massacre. Among the many other important people on the plane was the last president of our Polish government-in-exile, Ryszard Kaczorowski. While attempting to land at Smolensk Air Base in Russia the plane crashed. There were no survivors. Once again Katyn was linked with tragedy for the Polish nation. Lech Kaczyński had many enemies both domestically and internationally. On the homefront he had stood against corruption and those who had been responsible for communist crimes. He had also sought to strengthen relations with the USA and the European Union as well as pushing for greater cooperation with the Baltic States to further reduce Russian influence.

The investigation into the disaster has been criticised due to concerns about procedure, access and transparency. Recently the District Military Prosecutor's Office in Warsaw ruled that the plane crash was due to bad weather and human error. This conclusion, however, continues to be challenged by other experts, not least because of the significant number of positive readings of explosive traces at the site. They believe this evidence was too easily dismissed by the Prosecutor's Office. My impression is that the Polish government is appeasing Russia in order to avoid damaging relations, but there is no evidence that those relations have improved. The likelihood is that now we will never know the truth about this plane crash. After everything I and my compatriots have been through it is hard for me to accept that the Smolensk tragedy was just an unfortunate accident.

In November 2010 Andrew and George accompanied me to the Polish embassy in London to finally receive the Knight's Cross from Barbara Tuge-Erecińska, the Polish ambassador to the UK. The accompanying certificate stated that the award was for my ongoing participation in the Polish Underground Army Organisation as Vice President, Treasurer, Secretary and Newsletter writer, and for my involvement with the Polish Underground Movement Study Trust and the charity Medical Aid for Poland. It was a very proud moment for me and I shed a small tear as I was presented with the medal.

In recent years I have also received a number of honorary military promotions from the Polish Ministry of Defence; I am sure that Grażka has been putting my name forward for these. Initially I was promoted to Second Lieutenant, then to Lieutenant and finally to my current rank of Captain in Reserve. Amusingly, I am technically now higher-ranking than Janusz. Of course I wouldn't dream of comparing my military role as a young girl with that of a battle-hardened soldier who spent six years fighting in major campaigns and commanded a good number of soldiers.

For that reason I regard my military rank purely as an honour and certainly of less significance than the Knight's Cross. These military promotions were awarded at the Polish embassy in London, although for the last promotion to Captain I wasn't feeling well again and was unable to attend. As an alternative it was suggested that I receive an official visit at home to be handed the promotion document. I didn't want to seem ungrateful but it would have taken quite a lot of effort to prepare the house for such a visit – at the very least I would have had to put on a small reception, which I didn't feel up to – so I requested that the documents be sent by post. Grateful as I am, I have asked Grażka not to nominate me for any more honorary promotions. However, Eugenia Cegielska, President of the Oberlangen POW Association in Warsaw, has now nominated me for the rank of Major...

Like many other London-based Poles earlier awarded AK and Uprising medals before the end of communist rule in Poland, I refused back then to attend the embassy. Since Polish independence my non-attendance has been entirely on health grounds.

The Polish administration's whole process for assessing the granting of my awards and promotions threw up one little surprise: it seems that my birth certificate somehow survived the war and shows my actual recorded date of birth as 17th July 1929, making me a day younger than I thought.

Chapter 15

REFLECTIONS

THE UPRISING

The Warsaw Uprising has been with me every day of my adult life. So much faith and hope were buried in those ruins of my home city. With the perspective of 70 years my view has not changed significantly. I know that the Uprising was necessary. I had hoped that, once the fog of communism lifted, we would be recognised as patriots who were prepared to pay the ultimate price for Poland's freedom and respected in a similar way to those who fought in the January Uprising of 1863.

However, for the 50 years following the war the communists portrayed the Uprising as a political misadventure by the AK, and this teaching influenced generations of Polish school children. This ideological misrepresentation was further fostered by the lack of awareness and understanding of the Uprising in the West. The role of our Western Allies in appeasing Stalin during the war ensured that the Warsaw Uprising became an uncomfortable topic. As former members of the AK living abroad, we, at least, could speak our minds – but nobody wanted to listen. As a result most people in the west associated Warsaw with only one uprising, that of the Jewish Ghetto in 1943.

After the collapse of communism Poles were able to assess their history more freely, although this process was gradual. In 2004, before the opening event of the sixtieth anniversary of the Uprising, I realised that we still had a long struggle ahead. I was wearing my uniform when a young lady walked past with friends. On seeing my red-and-white AK armband, the girl had a little laugh at my expense. Although I was not offended, the incident suggested that she and many her age were ignorant of their heritage.

Those sixtieth-anniversary celebrations, which coincided with the opening of the Warsaw Uprising Museum, marked the beginning of a national quest for knowledge about the Uprising. Authoritative books were published, including *Rising '44* by Norman Davies, which was printed in English and Polish and covered the Uprising in depth. Poles began to view the Uprising with great pride.

More recently, however, books critical of the Uprising have been written. The critics do not question the heroism and suffering of the Uprising but they argue that it should not have been started as it had no hope of success: with our lack of weapons and ammunition, with the strength of the German forces ranked against us and without a guarantee of outside help, it was doomed from the start. The argument follows, therefore, that the Uprising needlessly resulted in the deaths of countless civilians and the destruction of the city. As a result I sense that sentiment towards the Uprising in Poland is again moving towards being more equivocal.

I believed at the time that the Uprising had to happen as there was no other way – and I still firmly believe this now. It seemed that by doing nothing we faced certain destruction. We couldn't just wait for the Germans to finish us all off; and Warsaw's civilian population was with us. I believe that the outcome could not have been predicted.

Our desire to fight was irresistible. Only those who lived through the occupation can understand just how much we wanted to act. For years we had lived with torture, executions, łapanki, the destruction of the ghetto and the mass murder of the Jews. So many of our people were already in concentration camps, in forced labour or dead. The extreme level of violence that had already been inflicted on us had created a hunger for revenge. The atmosphere in Warsaw was such that the city was bound to explode. When the opportunity finally presented itself, in despair we decided to risk everything. It can be argued that discipline within the AK was strong and that, if the leadership had ordered us not to fight, the order would have been obeyed in general; but the decision would have been utterly demoralising, and I have no doubt that there would have been uncoordinated outbreaks of fighting leading to severe reprisals. This general mood put the AK leadership under great pressure to order the Uprising.

Hitler had designated Warsaw a 'fortress city', meaning it was to be defended to the last. Nobody believed that the Germans would simply leave Warsaw ahead of the inevitable Soviet offensive. It is inconceivable to me that, in the event of a Soviet assault, we would have remained passive. We had been preparing and longing for an uprising for years; how could we, as the Polish army on home soil and in the capital city of our country, not join in the fight? It was also our duty and a matter of honour. Poland had never surrendered, our army was continuing the fight against the Germans alongside our allies overseas and it was our role to fight them at home. The Germans would eventually have been defeated in Warsaw but all the evidence suggested that they would have acted with malice, murdering large numbers of Warsaw's population and destroying the city.

We had the support of the civilians of Warsaw. The Uprising was not only the action of the AK, it was the majority response of the population of Warsaw. Everybody knew about the resistance and tacitly or openly supported resistance activities throughout the occupation. Most people in Warsaw knew somebody who had been killed, arrested or taken into either captivity or forced labour, and knew their lives were not safe until the Germans were gone. As a result almost everybody was involved in the Uprising or knew a young friend or relative who was. Only after events moved against us did criticism of the decision to fight grow among the civilians.

As a 15-year-old girl, I had little knowledge of politics at the time of the Uprising. The main criticism of the Uprising is directed against the Polish government-in-exile and against the AK leadership in Warsaw. The government is accused of being divided and ineffectual, particularly after the death in suspicious circumstances of its Prime Minister, General Sikorski. This may be the case although I can imagine the difficulties involved in forming an effective coalition government overseas to preside over an occupied homeland. With subsequently acquired knowledge I can see that these difficulties were magnified by the lack of clear communication from our Western Allies: the Tehran Conference had been conducted largely behind Poland's back. The AK leadership in Warsaw has also been criticised for poor planning and timing. Once again, I can only imagine the difficulties involved in gathering accurate information from within an occupied city. I am, however clear on two key points. First, our leadership should not have counted on independent help from the Russians; secondly, we had every right and reason to expect greater support from our Western Allies.

Regarding the Russians, there is no doubt that they had encouraged us to rise up and fight the "common enemy". It also seemed strategically sensible for the Russians to take Warsaw at the earliest possible date, and with the help of our fighting force within the city, rather than waiting another four months. However there were no diplomatic relations in place between Poland and the Soviet Union as Stalin had severed these relations in 1943 following the Polish request for investigation into the Katyn massacres. This added to our belief that the Russians had been responsible for those massacres. It was well known that the Russians had deported vast numbers of Poles to gulags in Siberia. We also knew that the Soviets were arresting AK fighters in Eastern Poland. As the Red Army advanced into Eastern Poland, the AK joined the fight against the retreating Germans. Having encouraged them to do this, the Soviets initially praised the AK. Once the fighting was over, however, the AK units were disarmed by the Soviets and their leaders arrested or killed. Stalin's malice towards Poland was clear to see. It seemed one occupier would simply be replaced by another with the intention of eradicating the Polish nation. Given all this, how could anybody believe that the Soviets would help us without pressure from our Western Allies?

General Anders himself was critical of the decision to fight in Warsaw at the time due to his deep distrust of the Russians following his incarceration in the Lubyanka prison in Moscow. However even General Anders was fallible and took risks, such as pushing his men to the battlefront ahead of other nationalities. At Monte Cassino he volunteered his troops for the virtually suicidal attack on the monastery slopes and withdrew their right to retreat. Anders wanted the Polish army to show the world that it was fighting the Germans and therefore that Poland deserved to retain her independence. But with hindsight it is clear that this had no impact on the approach of our allies towards Poland. How many more Polish soldiers died because of this strategy, and for what?

I can, however, see why the Russian ill intent towards Poland was a factor in the decision to start the Uprising. After disarming and arresting AK fighters in the east, Soviet propaganda then either denied the AK's assistance in fighting the Germans or portrayed the AK as a marginal political group that was unrepresentative of our nation. Our Western Allies were therefore getting contrasting reports about what was happening in Poland. A general uprising in Warsaw would send a clear message to our allies that the AK and Poland were united and fighting and therefore deserved their support. I can also see why taking Warsaw before the Russians arrived would have strengthened our political hand in negotiating post-war territory and sovereignty.

The key to the failure of the Warsaw Uprising is that our Western Allies let us down, both militarily and politically. It is too easy to assert that our government-in-exile should have known that the level of support would be negligible. The messages being received from our allies regarding their stance towards a Polish uprising were ambiguous. Our forces were fighting with the Allies on all fronts, not to mention the important role played by our pilots in the Battle of Britain. We had a right to expect more support. This could have altered the outcome of the Warsaw Uprising. The Polish Parachute Brigade in Britain could have been deployed for its original purpose, which was to support a Polish uprising, instead of being diverted to the Western Front. Most importantly, even though the Allies still had some influence over the Russians at the time, no serious attempt to apply pressure on the Russians was made. Even without direct Russian help for the Uprising, permission for more Allied plane landings would have enabled a significant increase in arms to Warsaw, which could have tipped the balance significantly. Instead Stalin was left with the impression that he had a free hand. As one of our leaders later reflected:

> "It seemed inconceivable that Churchill and Roosevelt would
> not help broker a deal with the Soviets over Warsaw. That no
> serious attempt was made to achieve this, and that we were
> thrown to the wolves, will always be regarded by the Poles as
> a great act of betrayal."

In my opinion, given Churchill's subordinate position by this time, the greater part of the blame for this appeasement of Stalin lies with Roosevelt.

Up to 200,000 civilians died during the Uprising. I am fully aware of this human cost through personal experience. However up to six million Polish citizens died, mostly murdered, throughout the war. Almost two million Polish citizens were deported to Germany for forced labour. About one-and-a-half million Polish citizens were deported by the Soviets to prison camps, mainly in Siberia and Kazakhstan. The history of the whole of Poland during the war was tragic, not just that of Warsaw.

Despite the terrible cost, I believe that some small good came out of the Warsaw Uprising: it showed the world the truth behind Stalin's posturing and, I believe, helped prevent Poland from becoming yet another state of the Soviet Union. Poland's status as a satellite country was undoubtedly preferable. I also like to think that the Uprising was an inspiration for the peaceful Solidarity movement, which was a catalyst for the removal of the communist regime in Poland.

In conclusion, I will never regret standing up and fighting for my country in the face of such hatred towards us. It was our right to fight for our freedom and independence. It was also our right to expect more assistance from our allies. I was prepared to give my life for my people and my country but I do not regard myself as a martyr, rather as a rational human being. I hope the memory of the Uprising will imbue future generations of Poles with pride, dignity, honour and the courage to stand up for what is right.

CLOSURE

I never thought I would make it to the 70th anniversary of the Uprising; the years since the 60th anniversary have flown by. The Warsaw Uprising Museum invited former AK members from around the world and offered to pay for our transport and accommodation. My family joined me in Warsaw and we attended many events and commemorations arranged by the Museum. The events were well organised and we were treated most warmly. There was also a lunch for us girls from the Oberlangen POW camp and our families. It was a great pleasure for me that my grandchildren were there to see me receive a number of awards from Jan Ciechanowski, the government Minister for the Office for War Veterans and Victims of Oppression. I was particularly proud to receive the Veteran's medal, which bestows certain privileges and an honorary diploma expressing the nation's gratitude to those who fought for Poland's freedom and her honour. I also finally received the Pro Patria medal for which I had been nominated many years earlier.

During the visit I realised a great wish, which was for me and my grandchildren to visit my mother's and sister's grave in Bródno cemetery together.

This time, being in Warsaw felt at first like I was home again, but I soon started feeling that something was missing. Although the event was very well attended, so many of my former friends and colleagues were no longer there. Many have departed from us in the last decade and others were too ill to travel. Even among the girls I knew now living in Warsaw, only Grażka was able to participate in the events with me. I missed them all so badly.

This visit gave me a great sense of culmination as I cannot envisage another anniversary, even the 75th, when there would still be many of us survivors left. Warsaw is now a different city; the places and people I once knew are almost gone. It is a different world, to which I do not fully belong. Going back to Poland had always filled me with joy but something has now changed and I regard this as another significant turning-point in my life. I don't exactly know why but I feel that my physical connection with Poland is now over and I no longer yearn to go back again. It was with this sense of finality and closure that I returned home to London.

MY LIFE

My life has not been the one I imagined and those 86 years have felt long. The happiest and most tranquil days of my life were up to the age of ten and I keep being drawn back to them in my thoughts. Christmas in particular evokes happy memories. I picture us as children in Warsaw scurrying between the local churches and comparing the nativity scenes with my friends. I still hear the carol singers with their illuminated stars; I recall our excited talk about the birth of baby Jesus and the magical atmosphere of Christmas at home.

The next stage in my life was turbulent and shaped my entire future. It was dominated by war and the German occupation of my city, culminating in the tragic Warsaw Uprising and the death of the people closest to me. But it also entailed the formation of deep friendships, some of which have lasted to the present day. How we worked together, helped one another and shared our lives is a source of great satisfaction to me. I still feel pride in the Warsaw Uprising even though it led to my great personal loss and the destruction of my dreams.

My life as an emigrant to Britain, which became my permanent home, was very hard in the beginning. When I finally established a family and a close society around me, life began to smile at me afresh and there were moments of happiness and hope for a better tomorrow. But again this did not last. My husband died and the days of depression and unease returned. How much longer could I maintain the mental strength to keep struggling and fighting for a 'normal' life that seemed unattainable? It is difficult to maintain an appetite for life without something realistic to aim for, especially without the help and support of family. I was fortunate to have so many warm-hearted people around me to keep me going.

I found a man who gave me the support I needed to carry on and with him I was able to enjoy life again for the next 20 years. During this time my boys grew into men. I hope I was successful in raising them to be kind and sensible people. They received a good education and achieved careers which enable them to live secure and comfortable lives.

My sons built their own families and I have four grandchildren whom I love very much. We live close to each other and I derive my greatest pleasure from time spent with them. Emma, whom I call Emulka, is the oldest and is growing into a beautiful young lady. I cherish our little private chats. Her 15th birthday last year was very moving for me, as it reminded me that I was only her age when 70 years ago I ran away to join the Uprising. She looks remarkably similar to me when I was her age. Oskar, my second grandchild, is very similar to his father Andrew with his curly hair. Eddie, whom I call Edus, is six months younger than Oskar and has already exceeded his father George in height by several centimetres, despite only recently turning 15. Alice is the youngest at 11 and I call her Alineczka; a very sweet-sounding name in Polish. I am happy that she seems to have a lot of luck in every aspect of life.

As the years have passed, fewer of my friends are left. 2012 was a particularly sad year as I unexpectedly lost two people very dear to me, first Stefa, and then Hania just before Christmas. I had known them both for almost 70 years and it was hard to bear. In all those years I never once fell out with Hania; the only disagreement we ever had was over her refusal to give up smoking towards the end, when it was clear that she was ill. Of my original Stowell Park group only Celina remains. Some of my former friends' children are in frequent contact with me and look out for me. I remember their childhoods and their coming of age and I guess they see me as a remaining link to their parents who are no longer with us. In Poland I remain in particularly close contact with Janusz's niece Ola.

There have been some good years in my life and had I not made some bad decisions along the way those years could have been even better. But there has also been too much misfortune, sadness and regret which now prevents me looking back at my life fondly. I am troubled by an enduring sense of bitterness and regret for my lost childhood and family. My mother had been so keen for me to have a good education and I regret that this was never possible. Our men all died so early, weakened by the stresses of war, by losing their families and country, and from the strain of having to rebuild lives in foreign lands from nothing. I was lucky enough to have two boys, unlike so many of the other girls, who lost their fertility due to physical hardships they had suffered. Although our community was close by necessity, almost like a family, deep down I have always carried a sense of loneliness, lacking someone truly close, a real sibling of my own to talk to. I have always felt that if I could only have had my sister Henia, then I wouldn't have felt so alone in my life. Nothing can make up for losing her so early. Perhaps having a daughter of my own would have helped to fill this hole in my life.

Despite all the sadness in my life I have always had an aim. I feel content that I have served my country well in the fight for independence, freedom and justice. I also take pride in the fact that I raised my two sons to be good and enquiring individuals. My life has had a meaning.

Certain thoughts, however, will never leave me. Even now, I see my poor mother in my head all the time, lying there, with no one to help her. Some wounds will never heal.

My oak tree still grows by the church. It stands alone, reaching out in every direction as if searching for something it can never find.

EPILOGUE

Writing my mother's memoirs has been a deeply emotional experience for me and an honour beyond words. During the last three years I have spent countless hours in discussions with my mother as she has recalled her life, sometimes with steely determination, other times in tears. This time has brought us much closer together, which I will always cherish. I feel a sense of shame that I have taken so long to show an adequate interest in my mother's past and that I previously knew relatively little of the patriotism, selflessness and bravery of an entire generation of Poles who lived through such difficult times. The choices they made to resist the occupying forces were far from easy; a recent visit to the Gestapo museum on Szucha Street showed me only too vividly the risks these young people took during the resistance movement. Despite the pain and suffering of the Uprising, the people of Warsaw stood firm far beyond all hope. The price was terrible but their sacrifices will be remembered forever.

I am thankful that I have had this opportunity to reflect with my mother upon her life and sad that I was not able to learn more from my father about his experiences. He left behind his medals but nothing written down about his life for my brother and me to read when we were older. I am at least grateful that I was able to obtain his British service record from the Ministry of Defence Polish Section, which is very informative.

My childhood was as happy and as loving as anybody could wish for. It is a great source of wonderment to me that despite what my parents suffered, particularly my mother in losing her entire family while still so young, our upbringing was so perfectly 'normal'. Her love for us has been immense and unconditional since the day we were born. It must have taken incredible mental strength to overcome such adversity and avoid burdening her children with the sadness of her past. It is also a testament to the family spirit within the post-war Polish community in London that for a long time I didn't even realise that I had no grandparents, aunts or uncles. I had plenty of loving, surrogate family members around me. My brother and I had a good education which has enabled us to progress in life and it touches my heart to see my mother crying about her unfulfilled potential.

I have been left with a strong feeling of pride in my parents and also with a sense of sadness. I can now see how difficult life was for my ancestors, and indeed for all those who experienced the war. I sometimes imagine how happier life could have been for them under different circumstances. Most importantly I have been struck by a realisation that our lives can dramatically change so quickly and that nothing can be taken for granted.

In 2014 I returned from Warsaw with my family and my mother, having joined in the commemorations for the 70th anniversary of the Warsaw Uprising. Our meetings with other combatants and visits to the Warsaw Uprising Museum brought home the courage required from the participants during this incredible episode. One short discussion with an elderly combatant remains with me. I asked this gentleman which AK unit he had belonged to and he replied the Kiliński Battalion. I told him that my mother must have seen him in the first days of the Uprising attacking the main Post Office in Napoleon Square. The old soldier replied that what my mother probably didn't realise was that as he attacked the well-defended building his rifle had no bullets in it.

The warmth with which my mother was received by the younger Polish generation touched me. I believe that, in the fullness of time, the Warsaw Uprising will be remembered with pride by all Poles and viewed as a struggle that helped Poland regain her confidence and freedom.

I hope that when our children read this book it will make them proud and they will realise how brave their ancestors were. I would be content if I had even a fraction of the courage of those who fought and died for Poland during World War II. May they live on in our memories.

George Szlachetko

ACKNOWLEDGEMENTS

Many people have contributed selflessly to this book and have made my experience rewarding for which I shall be forever in their debt. I could never have achieved this without the unstinting support of my loving wife Jacqui. Whenever I reached a block she was there to talk things through. Her help with everything to do with this book was immense, not least the moral support I needed on numerous occasions.

My brother, Andrew has been invaluable in numerous ways, not least regarding production issues and constant support. This is his history too.

I would like to express my gratitude to my mother's former colleagues from the Grey Ranks and the AK. Ania ('Grażka'), now aged 90, displayed incredible energy and drive to make sure that I had all the answers to my questions. She accompanied us throughout our commemoration visits to Warsaw and helped liaise with various people and organisations in Poland. As President of the Oberlangen Association, Eugenia helped greatly regarding that part of their lives. Marzena, 'Iga' and Andrzej all contributed precious information about their experiences which added greater context to my mother's story.

I am grateful to my family members from my father's side for their contributions relating to his history and that of his family from the Kresy. Particular thanks goes to Ola, Beata and Piotr. Beata's family tree is extensive: I only wish my mother's branch looked as leafy.

Mark was my committed editor, throwing himself into my mother's history and helping move the book from the rudimentary to the finished article. I can only apologise to Mark's family for keeping him from them all those weeks. I received great structural advice from Angela, for which I am truly grateful. I am also grateful to Nel who was my excellent proof reader. Jean, Roger and Joyce, your input as critics, additional proof readers and supporters was extremely valuable.

I would like to thank Richard my illustrator, Isabel my image designer and Trevor for his technical support in the production of this book. Also many thanks go to Bogusia for the records of her early interviews with my mother and for inspiring me to write this book.

Publishing the book has been a family project and I would like to thank my daughter Emma for her dramatic cover design with encouragement from Nicola. Thanks also to my other children, Eddie and young Alice, for their interest and input.

I am grateful for the historical information received from the Warsaw Uprising Museum, including copies of my mother's wartime documents, images and copyrights. Many members of the museum's staff helped me and I am particularly grateful for access to the Sylwester Braun photographs with the blessing of Museum Director Jan Ołdakowski and support from Alexandra Duralska.

I would also like to thank the Polish Underground Movement Study Trust (PUMST) and the Sikorski Institute in London for access to their archives and overall knowledge and experience. Special thanks goes to Chris and Krystyna for their support beyond the call of duty.

My gratitude for images and copyright also goes to the Bundesarchiv and FotoKarta.

So many other people contributed in some way to the final outcome. In particular I would like to thank Stefan Mucha for sending me a copy of *The Auschwitz Volunteer: Beyond Bravery*, published by Aquila Polonica, as a basis for layout and historical guidance; Lisa for some proofreading and advice; Gillian for her input during the entire process; and Duncan for his counsel. Also Erwin, who sadly passed away recently, for information about his father and my godfather. I apologise if I cannot mention everybody else who contributed in some way but I thank you all.

Above all, I would like to thank my mother who lived this incredible, courageous, selfless, sad yet rich life. Her patience during my insatiable questioning was extraordinary and I apologise for making her live it all over again. Her love for her family has been immense and unconditional. I hope that I have left a true, accurate and worthy record of her long, twisting yet proud story so far.

ADDITIONAL READING

Anders, Władysław, *An Army in Exile*, The Battery Press, 2004

Bankowska, Felicja & Kabzinska, Krystyna, *Dziewczęta ze Stalagu VI C Oberlangen* (*Women of Stalag VI C Oberlangen*), Bellona, 1998

Cygan, Wiktor Krzysztof & Skalski, Jacek, *Poland: In the defence of freedom 1939–1945*, Barwa i Broń and The Memory of the Diaspora Association, 2005

Davies, Norman, *Rising '44: The Battle for Warsaw*, Macmillan, 2003

Dawidowicz, Lucy, *The War Against the Jews*, Bantam, 1975

Edelman, Marek, *The Warsaw Ghetto Uprising*, Interpress 1990

Forczyk, Robert, *Warsaw 1944: Poland's bid for freedom*, Osprey Publishing, 2009

Garlinski, Jarosław, *The Auschwitz Volunteer: Beyond Bravery – Captain Witold Pilecki, Auschwitz Prisoner No. 4859*, Aquila Polonica, 2012

Garlinski, Jozef, *Poland in the Second World War*, Macmillan, 1985

The Institute of National Remembrance, *Polska 1939–1945: Straty Osobowe I Ofiary Represji pod Dwiema Okupacjami* (Poland 1939–1945: Human Losses and Oppression under Two Occupations), City of Warsaw, 2009

Jeffery, Ron, *Red Runs the Vistula*, Nevron Associates, 1989

Kershaw, Ian, *The End*, Penguin Books, 2012

Komanski, Henryk & Siekierka, Szczepan, account by Marian Nehrebecki, *Ludobójstwo dokonane przez nacjonalistów ukraińskich na Polakach w województwie Tarnopolskim 1939–46* (Genocide of Poles by Ukrainian nationalists in the voivodeship of Tarnopol 1939–46, Nortom, 2006

Komorowski, Tadeusz 'Bór', *The Secret Army: The Memoirs of General Bór-Komorowski*, Frontline Books, 2011 edition.

Leski, Kazimierz, *Zycie Niewlasciwie Urozmaicone: Wspomnienia oficera wywiadu I kontrwywiadu AK* (Life wrongly altered: Recollections of an AK intelligence and counter-intelligence officer), Finna, 1989

London Branch of the Polish Home Army Ex-Servicemen Association Essays /Articles, 'AK: Polish resistance in World War II'

Ney-Krwawicz, Marek, *The Polish Home Army 1939–1945*, Polish Underground Movement Study Trust, 2001

Nowak, Jan, *Courier from Warsaw*, Wayne State University Press, 1983

Olson, Lynne & Cloud, Stanley, *For Your Freedom and Ours: The Kościuszko Squadron*, Arrow Books, 2004

Orr, Aileen, *Wojtek the Bear: Polish war hero*, Birlinn, 2010

Piotrowski, Tadeusz, *Genocide and Rescue in Wolyn: Recollections of the Ukrainian Nationalist Ethnic Cleansing Campaign against the Poles during World War II*, McFarland, 2008

Polish Academy of Sciences, Dialogue and Universalism, *Warsaw Uprising 1944 Part One*, Warsaw University, 2004

Polish Ex-Combatants' Association of Great Britain, *First to Fight: Poland's contribution to the Allied victory in WWII*, 2009

Polish Parish in Ealing, *Polish Roman Catholic Community in Ealing 1950–2000*, 50th Anniversary Commemoration Committee, 2001

Richie, Alexandra, *Warsaw 1944: The fateful uprising*, William Collins, 2013

Snyder, Timothy, *Bloodlands: Europe between Hitler and Stalin*, Vintage, 2011

US Commission, *Morgenthau Report*, 1919

Warsaw Uprising Museum, *Almanach Powstańczy 1944* (Uprising 1944 Almanac), City of Warsaw, 2004

Wasserstein, Bernard, *On the Eve: The Jews of Europe before the Second World War*, Profile Books, 2012

Williamson, David G, *Poland Betrayed: The Nazi-Soviet Invasions of 1939*, Pen & Sword, 2009

Wojciechowska, Bogusia, *Waiting to be Heard*, AuthorHouse, 2009

Ziemian, Joseph, *The Cigarette Sellers of Three Crosses Square*, Vallentine Mitchell, 1970